OUT OF THE BLUE

OUT
OF THE
BLUE

THE STORY OF
SEPTEMBER 11, 2001,
FROM JIHAD TO GROUND ZERO

RICHARD BERNSTEIN

AND THE STAFF OF
The New York Times

TIMES BOOKS
Henry Holt and Company
NEW YORK

TIMES BOOKS
HENRY HOLT AND COMPANY, LLC
Publishers since 1866
115 WEST 18TH STREET
NEW YORK, NEW YORK 10011

Library of Congress Cataloging-in-Publication Data
Bernstein, Richard, 1944–
  Out of the blue : the story of September 11, 2001, from jihad to ground zero /
Richard Bernstein and the staff of the New York Times.— 1st ed.
     p.   cm.
  Includes index.
  ISBN 0-8050-7240-3 (hardbound)
    1. September 11 Terrorist Attacks, 2001. 2. Terrorism—United States. 3. Victims of
terrorism—New York (State)—New York. I. New York times II. Title.
HV6432 .B47 2002
973.931—dc21   2002020396

Henry Holt books are available for special promotions and premiums.
For details contact: Director, Special Markets.

FIRST EDITION 2002

Designed by Cathryn S. Aison

Printed in the United States of America

3   5   7   9   10   8   6   4

CONTENTS

FOREWORD

Howell Raines

The title of *Out of the Blue* captures exactly the stark, heartbreaking nature of what happened in the home city of the *New York Times* on the morning of September 11, 2001. "Out of the blue" also expresses the suddenness with which the American people were confronted with a new kind of war. Not since Pearl Harbor had United States territory and the American psyche been so abruptly assaulted. It seems to me that every New Yorker, every American, and people around the world will make some personal connections with these four words. I think, for example, of the photograph published on the front page of the *Times* on September 12 showing the second airplane approaching the south tower of the World Trade Center. The first time the editors saw that photograph, we knew that we were seeing a freeze-frame of a world-altering moment. Richard Bernstein, for his part, opens this book with a meditation upon another stark picture—that of a man, upside down, falling to his death from one of the towers on "a glorious fall day." It is an image that sums up the transience of life, the finality of death, the timelessness of the universal sky, and perhaps most of all the fragility of peace.

Some journalism critics and a few readers complained about our decision to print that picture. It was a decision debated in an editors' meeting on September 11, and we considered whether friends or loved ones might be able to recognize the falling man. Bernstein's eloquent description of the picture convinces me that its use was the correct journalistic response. Sometimes tragedy must be confronted directly, for it is an indelible part of the human experience. How terrible, for instance, are the pictures of the emaciated survivors of the Nazi death camps, how heartrending Robert Capa's photograph of an infantryman being shot in the Spanish Civil War. And how much less would we understand our world if we did not have those images to instruct us about the agony of war and the killing power of hatred in our world.

As daily journalists, of course, we do not set about our work with the idea of being teachers or moral historians. We are engaged in an intellectual enterprise built around bringing quality information to an engaged and demanding readership. Sometimes that means writing what some have called the first rough draft of history. Sometimes it also means constructing a memorial to those whose courage and sacrifice we have recorded or—to speak more precisely—erecting a foundation of information upon which our readers can construct their own historical overviews, their own memorials to those who are lost and to the struggle to preserve democratic values.

I offer these observations on journalistic process because as executive editor of the *Times,* I have a responsibility to the 1,100 men and women of our news department to recognize an extraordinary performance that produced six Pulitzer Prizes, two George Polk Awards, and honors from the Overseas Press Club and the American Society of Newspaper Editors. The work of this generation of *Times* journalists can stand alongside the best work of our 151 years of newsgathering—in the Civil War, at the dawn of the nuclear age, on the frontiers of space. But you will not find our journalists as actors in the pages that follow, for every writer, photographer, editor, graphic designer, researcher, and support staff member in our newsroom and our bureaus around the world understands that we are not the story. The story of how we got the story has its moments of drama and danger, but even that professional epic is not central to the pages that follow.

What Richard Bernstein, a gifted correspondent, author, and critic, has constructed from his original reporting and the work of his *Times* colleagues is a record of the things we observed in our roles as witnesses, recorders, and analysts. Bernstein has also drawn on the fine work of our colleagues at other news organizations, and we are proud to credit their contributions. The result is a masterly mosaic that when viewed in its totality gives us a comprehensive picture of the events of September 11, the forces and players that led to them, and the consequences that produced those events. We see the connections between an impressionable young Saudi millionaire and a radical Islamic preacher now serving a life sentence for the first attack on the World Trade Center back in 1993. We see links between a terrorist cell in Hamburg and a flight school in Florida. We glimpse as fully as we ever shall the heroism of passengers on United flight 93, which might have crashed into the White House rather than a field in Pennsylvania.

How fitting that this sweeping international narrative ends quietly with a chapter reminding us of the largest global constituency, those joined by the "democratic tombs" produced when thunderous events seem to roll out of the blue. In the final chapter, we meet Tsugio Ito, a man who lost a brother at Hiroshima and a son at Ground Zero. The first loss arose from dictatorial passions run amok in his own land, the second by a religious hatred that, one fears, has yet to run its course.

Here, then, is the story up to now, as produced by a news staff whose ability, endurance, and sacrifice awed all of us who were privileged to be part of their enterprise.

AUTHOR'S NOTE

There is no universally recognized method of transcribing Arabic into English, and that explains why this book, and other books on related topics, contain inconsistencies in their transcriptions of Arabic words and names. Family preferences and historical usages have meant that the same letters in Arabic can come out in two or even three different ways in English. In this book, I have followed the spellings most commonly used in the New York Times. Thus, for example, Marwan al-Shehhi, not Alshehhi, and Nawaf Alhamzi, not al-Hamzi.

OUT OF THE BLUE

ONE

"We Saw People Jumping"

T he forms, sometimes not much more than specks against the gleam of the skyscraper, tumbled downward almost indistinguishable from the chunks of debris, the airplane parts, the vapors of flaming aviation fuel that filled the air like fireworks. They fell at the rate of all falling bodies, thirty-two feet per second squared, slowed a certain amount by the friction of the air, so they fell for eight or nine seconds and they were going at least 125 miles an hour when they hit the pavement or crashed into the roof of the Marriott Hotel at the bottom of the World Trade Center. It took a few instants for the witnesses to understand what they were seeing: that the forms silhouetted against the sky or against the flaming buildings themselves were bodies; they were men and women who had chosen to leap to their deaths from a 110-story building rather than endure the conflagration that had engulfed them inside.

Those eight or nine seconds made up the dreadful interval remaining to these victims, an interval spent hurtling past the vast geometrical precision of windows and pillars downward to death. And then everything, the towers themselves, all 110 ten stories of them, the entire 1,368 feet of the north tower, the 1,362 feet of the south tower with their 400,000 tons of steel and their 10 million square feet of offices, trading spaces, bathrooms, and conference rooms disintegrated in an avalanche of concrete, steel, glass, airplane parts, and thousands more bodies, all compressed into seven stories of rubble below.

The television stations and the newspapers delicately chose not to show too many images of the falling bodies. But there was one photograph published on September 12 in the *New York Times* that captured the horror. It was of a man in a white shirt and dark pants and what looked like large shoes or boots falling headfirst, upside down, frozen for all time against the background of one of the twin towers, which is a ghostly, silvery white in the morning sunlight. September 11, 2001, as many have ruefully noted, was a glorious fall day. It had to have been for the pilots of the hijacked airplanes to see clearly enough to carry out their missions. The autumnal glitter brought the event into sharp focus for those who witnessed it nearby and for the hundreds of millions around the world who watched it unfold, in real time, on television. And so, the camera was able to record the falling man's descent with icy clarity. It is an outlandish, incongruent image, surreal, absurd, a man suspended in a place where no human being should be. It is easy not to realize, stilled by the camera as he is, that his experience of falling and ours seeing the image of his fall are utterly different. Going headfirst like he was, the air resistance would have been minimal, and he would have reached a speed of close to 170 miles per hour before he hit . . . whatever it was that he hit below. It is a gruesome detail, but it is details like that that make up a tragedy; it is their accumulation in the experience of thousands of victims that adds up to the human cost of September 11.

It was a large event, three dimensional, and any one person seeing it on the ground saw only a narrow fragment of it, like George Shea, for example, a public relations executive who was in a car just emerging from the Brooklyn Battery Tunnel and heading north on the West Side Highway when American flight 11 hit the north tower. He saw an immense wheel materialize from above—he assumed it was the wheel of the airliner—strike a blue-gray SUV in front of him and then bounce away into a building. The director of graduate admissions at the Nyack College Alliance Seminary, Carol Webster, saw no airplane parts crashing to the ground; what she saw was people getting hit and burned by aviation fuel, people dropping purses so their money fell out, people dropping their children as they ran and other people behind them stopping to pick them up, and then running too.

But it was the falling bodies, the desperate suicidal leaps caused by the actions of suicide terrorists that made for the grimmest images, the images that would haunt forever those who were there to see them with their own eyes.

They were anonymous. Like the man pictured in the *New York Times* photograph, those who jumped remain unidentified and unenumerated. The tragedy of September 11 was televised; millions around the world saw it in their own homes as it happened in lower Manhattan. And yet these hundreds of millions of spectators watching simultaneously in France and Japan, Brazil and California, could not see the event's human details, which were obscured inside a fog of dust and debris. And therefore, the jumpers died in a paradoxical sort of obscurity, their deaths witnessed but their identities unknown. And it's not just that we don't know who they were; we also don't know how many of them there were among the 2,813 who died when the planes hit and the two towers disintegrated behind the billowing curtain of dust and debris visible to the world that watched. But videotapes scrutinized later show that there were at least sixty people who jumped or fell, almost all from the north tower, the first to be hit.

An emergency medical technician named John Henderson was on Fourteenth Street when he and his partner, Lou Parra, heard the sound of the plane hitting the north tower, and the two of them then raced toward the scene. They could see heavy pieces of debris falling from the gash that the plane, a guided missile with ten thousand gallons of aviation fuel on board and edges like knives, made as it tore into the tower, shattered the aluminum façade, sliced through eighteen-inch-thick exterior steel columns, and erupted in flames. They saw shards of the plane that left streaks of sparks against the tower's vertical lines. Then they saw bodies begin tumbling down, one, two, three, men in business suits and white shirts, then another and another.

"We saw people jumping," Leonore McKean, a paralegal at the brokerage firm Merrill Lynch, said. When the south tower was struck about twenty minutes after the north tower, Ms. McKean was evacuated along with the rest of her office. "We had to walk north. I saw what might have been a piece of the engine from the plane. You could hear people screaming as they saw people jumping."

But nobody heard the jumpers. They fell in what seemed like silence, though very likely they were screaming too, as though echoing the screaming of the people below who saw them. And nobody knows what it felt like to be falling, what it felt like in their stomachs and bowels to leap from so terrifying a height and to drop like stones. Did the jumpers remain aware as they plummeted downward? Could they see the ground rushing up at them, the parked cars, the roofs of lower buildings, the pedestrians who had the luxury of running to safety? Did they see their lives pass before them, or think of their loved ones, whom they had kissed good-bye an hour or two before in what seemed like the start of just another day? Or did they black out as they accelerated, their guts churning, their lungs pressed flat against their diaphragms, their skin scorched from the burns they suffered before they jumped? What was it like to be sitting at a desk one minute, perhaps to be sending an e-mail or drinking a cup of coffee or checking the schedule of the day to come, and the next instant to be pressed so hard by the hot iron of burning aviation fuel against the exterior walls of the office that you tumbled out in your desperation to get away?

We know that at least a few survivors from the stricken towers, people who managed to climb down the stairs to safety, actually saw the planes banking in the morning air just instants before they struck. But what of the victims? Did any of them happen to be looking outside their windows, perhaps admiring the view of the Hudson River as it flows past Manhattan's West Side, and actually see the airplane, its fuselage glinting in the sun, hurtling right at them? Did they dive for cover or did they stand there transfixed by the inconceivable, like a deer caught in headlights? Did they understand for a flickering instant that men from faraway countries whom they had never met and didn't know were bent on the task of murdering them? And those who didn't jump—those, for example, among the 160 or so people who were having breakfast in Windows on the World, the restaurant with the million-dollar view on the 107th floor of the north tower, or the 135 people attending the Risk Waters Financial Technology Congress one floor below? When the buildings collapsed, were they killed instantly, painlessly, or did some of them remain conscious for a few seconds as the once solid, carpeted floor dematerialized beneath them and they fell, at the same speed as their desks and water coolers and file cabinets and computer terminals and boxes of paper clips and framed photographs of their children?

On Park Place, the busy commercial thoroughfare near City Hall, pedestrians heard the whine of the jet and some who looked up saw the plane coming in extremely low. And then they saw people jumping out of the building. One person said he was even able to make out a lady in a green suit and a man in jeans, both jumping out and falling to their deaths. Another witness, a photography student named Jamie Wang who had been taking pictures of people doing tai chi exercises in a nearby park, described the jumpers as figurines. He remembers one woman in particular, the way her dress billowed out in the wind created by her fall. Firemen rushing to the scene reported that they had to dodge bodies being propelled from windows on the upper floors.

"I saw at least ten people jump," one fireman said. "I heard even more than that land and crash through the glass ceiling in the atrium. We could hear them crash. We thought the roof was crashing down, but then we looked up and saw that people were falling through the glass. Some people fell right onto the pavement."

People getting out of the towers, walking down the stairs and out onto the plaza level, saw them too, even though, once they had arrived on the scene and began organizing the evacuation, policemen told them not to look. "There was a head, a whole body, just mangled, two feet with shoes on them," an evacuee from the 82nd floor said. "I saw heads. I saw feet." People watching from their offices in buildings whose chief attribute was the view they offered of the trade center saw a ball of fire erupt from near the top of the north tower and then some of them said they saw as many as twenty people jump, some of them blown by the wind around the corner from where they had started.

A veteran lieutenant in the Fire Department, a member of the elite Rescue 1 squad in midtown Manhattan named Steve Turilli, was searching for a command post near the Customs Building on West Street, which runs between the Trade Center itself and the World Financial Center closer to the Hudson River.

"That's when we started to get hit by all the bodies, or people, jumping out of the towers," he said. "You would get hit by an arm or a leg and it felt like a metal pole was hitting you. It was like a war zone, seeing body parts everywhere. Then we'd be hit by the bodies."

"It wasn't pretty," Lieutenant Turilli said. "The bodies would hit the ground and they would explode and disappear. I saw this black guy impaled on a street sign. He was like hanging on the pole pierced right through him. That sticks in my mind. The pole through his body. From Liberty and West we went to Liberty and Washington. Firemen were yelling at us. One guy told us to get out of the way, away from the buildings, because a fireman was killed when a jumper landed right on top of him."

Even though millions of people saw on live television what witnesses on the ground saw, when the towers crumbled into rushing billows of dust, powder, and smoke, few minds could encompass exactly what had happened. The words most commonly heard were "unbelievable" and "unimaginable"—that so many could die in an enemy attack on American soil; that four airplanes could have been hijacked on a single day, and used as aviation fuel-laden missiles to hit targets that symbolized American might and prosperity; that the president of the United States was, for the better part of a day, kept from the nation's capital out of fear for his safety. Perhaps Joe Disorbo, who escaped to the street from the 72nd floor of the south tower, the second to be hit, best expressed the American loss of innocence. His clothes and skin coated gray, blood drying on his ears and left leg, he stood for a while fumbling with his cell phone trying, unsuccessfully, to call his wife on Long Island to tell her that he was all right. He had been too busy surviving to contemplate the scope of the disaster. Then he happened to look up, and he realized that he was staring into a dusty vacant sky.

"Where is the building?" he asked, not quite believing the evidence of his eyes. "Did it fall down? Where is it?"

What happened on September 11 is the story of terrorist attacks on the World Trade Center and on the Pentagon, but it is not a single story. It is the 3,046 individual stories of the dead and the much higher number, the tens of thousands of people, the children, the wives (many of them pregnant), the husbands, the parents, the friends and colleagues they left behind. There were brothers, like Peter Langone and Thomas Langone, one a fireman and the other a police officer, who both died trying to rescue others. Peter was forty-one and Thomas was thirty-nine. They each had wives, Terri and JoAnn, and four children, Caitlin, twelve, Brian, ten, Nikki, nine, and Karli, five.

"We owe you a great deal," New York mayor Rudolph Giuliani told their family members at a joint funeral service. "It will be paid back."

But it won't be paid back. It can't be paid back.

About 15 percent of the total dead were firefighters, police, and other rescue workers—not people who failed to get out of the buildings on time, but people who rushed into them after the planes had struck.

Whole families, traveling together on the hijacked planes, were obliterated together. Leslie A. Whittington, a professor of public policy at Georgetown University, was on American Airlines flight 77, the one that crashed into the Pentagon, killing the 64 people who were on board, including the five hijackers, and 125 who were in the building. She had gotten a visiting fellowship at the Australian National University for two months, and so she was traveling with her husband, Charles S. Falkenberg, a software developer at the ECOlogic Corp. in Washington, D.C., and their daughters, Zoe, eight, and Dana, three, on the first leg of their journey to their long-anticipated Australian adventure. The last anybody heard from the Whittington-Falkenbergs was when Leslie called her mother from the airport waiting lounge to say good-bye. Later, at the funeral, the Reverend Barbara Wells remembered Whittington as "the irreverent economist with a razor-sharp wit" and Falkenberg as "the bike-riding, mountain-climbing, love-to-be-at-home-with-his-girls kind of dad." Zoe was strawberry blond and had "perfect ballerina feet" and no doubt she had long, serious conversations with her stuffed bears. Dana was, Wells said, "the toddler robusto, who filled the room with her curly-headed smile."[1]

The Hanson family—Peter, his wife, Sue Kim, and two-year-old Christine—were on United flight 175, going to San Francisco to visit Sue's family. Peter Hanson, a software salesman for TimeTrade in Waltham, Massachusetts, was an avid gardener and an ardent Grateful Dead fan. Sue Kim, who had lived with her grandmother in Korea when she was a child, was a doctoral candidate in microbiology at Boston University. Christine was a little girl just getting steady on her feet. When the hijackers took control of the aircraft, Peter called his parents in Easton, Connecticut. "They've gotten control of the cabin, and they've killed a stewardess," he said. "I think we're going down, but don't worry. It's going to be quick."

When Peter signed off, his parents, Eunice and Lee Hanson, turned on the television, and then they watched as the plane their son, daughter-in-law, and granddaughter were on slammed into the south tower of the World Trade Center.[2]

Stephen Adams, fifty-one, the beverage manager at Windows on the

World, and Christopher Carstanjen, thirty-four, a computer expert at the University of Massachusetts, knew each other because of a common interest. Both were passionate about Morris dancing, a kind of ritual dance from the west of England performed with bells and sticks and the waving of white cloths that is the recreational passion of teams of devotees that meet and greet each other around the world. Adams and Carstanjen attended performances together at Marlboro College in Vermont. Carstanjen was a motorcycle enthusiast, and he was on flight 175 to California to bike up the Pacific Coast with some friends. Adams, according to his wife, Jessica Murrow, a musician and another Morris dance enthusiast, had found himself professionally after some years of drift, serving as a beverage manager at Windows and planning to be a wine steward. He was going to San Francisco for a tasting of German wines. The two of them, Adams and Carstanjen, hadn't seen each other for some time, though they ended up almost in the same place when they died. Adams was at work when flight 11 struck the north tower. Carstanjen was on flight 175, which slammed into the south tower.

Edward F. Beyea and Abe Zelmanowitz both died because Zelmanowitz, a computer programmer at Empire Blue Cross/Blue Shield, refused to leave Beyea, also a programmer and a quadriplegic, who got around in a wheelchair. Beyea was an enormously resilient man who never allowed his disability, sustained in a diving accident, to overcome him. He typed with a stick he held in his mouth; he played computer golf at home, listened to music, and didn't spend his days feeling sorry for himself. Zelmanowitz, his loyal friend, his blood brother in life and death, rigged up a special tray for him that allowed him to read in bed. Zelmanowitz, as his brother Jack said, "could never turn his back on another human being," words that might seem florid in another context, but Zelmanowitz proved on September 11 that they were true. Lisa and Samantha Egan, thirty-one and twenty-four, sisters and co-workers at Cantor Fitzgerald, the bond information company that lost 658 of its thousand Trade Center employees, died together. The victims were from many countries. At Windows on the World alone, they came from Bangladesh, Mexico, Ecuador, Colombia, Haiti, Ghana, Senegal, Cuba, India, Pakistan, Yemen, Egypt, El Salvador, Peru, Costa Rica, Uruguay, Jamaica, China, Brazil, Hong Kong, Vietnam, Indonesia, and Ireland.[3] The Trade Center site is a mixed grave where millionaire security traders are entombed with undocumented immigrants. It is a democratic tomb, a grim melting pot, an unwanted emblem of the genius of America life, of the quality that made New York so special.

The events of September 11 are also the story of the nineteen Arab men who hijacked the planes and killed themselves so that Stephen Adams and Christopher Carstanjen, Edward F. Beyea, Abe Zelmanowitz, and the four Whittington-Falkenbergs, and Peter and Thomas Langone, Lisa and Samantha Egan, and the three members of the Hanson family, and three thousand others would die. And, of course, it is also the story of the evil mastermind named Osama bin Laden who was almost without a doubt ultimately behind their actions.

It is worth noting in this regard how bin Laden himself experienced September 11, and, thanks to a videotape discovered by American forces in Afghanistan, we have his testimony on exactly that. A few weeks after the attacks, bin Laden was with some of his close aides and a visitor from Saudi Arabia, and, sitting on a rug, relaxing with their backs leaning against the wall behind them, they expressed joy at the extent of the destruction, and they made jokes—yes, jokes—about the events of September 11.

"The TV broadcast the big event," said Sulaiman Abou-Ghaith, a radical Kuwaiti cleric who served as a close adviser to bin Laden. "The scene was showing an Egyptian family sitting in their living room. They exploded with joy. Do you know when there is a soccer game and your team wins? It was the same expression of joy."

"A plane crashing into a tall building was out of anyone's imagination," the visitor from Saudi Arabia put in. "This was a great job." The identity of this visitor is not certain. Initially, Saudi officials said he was a religious scholar named Ali Sayeed al-Ghamdi, but a different Saudi official later said he was Khaled al-Harbi, a veteran of the wars in Afghanistan, Bosnia, and Chechnya who had lost his legs in combat.

"It was 5:30 P.M. our time," bin Laden said. "Immediately, we heard the news that a plane had hit the World Trade Center. We turned the radio station to the news from Washington. The news continued and there was no mention of the attack until the end. At the end of the newscast, they reported that a plane just hit the World Trade Center."

The visiting sheik interrupted to give a kind of religious sanction to this happy news. "Allah be praised," he intoned. It is worth noting here this religious scholar's, this man of learning's casual conviction that committing mass murder and doing God's work are one and the same.

Bin Laden continued his account of how he experienced September 11.

"After a little while," he said, "they announced that another plane had hit the World Trade Center. The brothers who heard the news were overjoyed by it."

Sasha Tsoy-Ligay is a four year-old girl from the Central Asian Republic of Kazakhstan. She didn't speak English at the time, having only arrived in the United States three weeks before September 11. Sasha—the name on her birth certificate is Alexandra—will always remember the morning when her mother, Zhanetta Tsoy, thirty-two years old, left their house in Jersey City, New Jersey, without eating breakfast, because it was her first day in a new job in the new country called America and she was too excited, in too much of a hurry, to eat. Zhanetta went from Jersey City to lower Manhattan that morning since her job, as an accountant for the firm Marsh & McLennan, was in that amazing building that she could see from New Jersey, rising megalith-like on the far bank of the Hudson River. Probably she took the express elevator in the north tower of the World Trade Center to the 79th-floor Sky Lobby, transferring to the local to go to 93, where she arrived sometime before 8:46. She wasn't actually due at work until 9:00, and her eagerness to arrive early that first day probably cost her her life.

They're telling Sasha that her mother had to go on a long trip, and that's why she hasn't seen her since that morning she went to work. Sasha has Barbie dolls and stuffed toys to play with, donated by kind, sad neighbors. Her father, Vyacheslav Ligay, takes her to a nearby pet store so she can stroke the animals. Someday when she is older she will understand what happened to her mother on September 11, and she'll probably wonder what kind of people those faraway and unknown "brothers" were to be laughing about it.

T W O

Peshawar: The Office of Services

I f you take the long view, you could say that the attacks of September 11 had their origin in the very distant past, perhaps in the fourteenth century when a militant Islamic purism and the concept of jihad were born out of the Mongol invasion of the Middle East. Or perhaps the origin of September 11 lies even further back, in the seventh-century Muslim sect known as the Kharajites, who believed that it was God's work to slay non-believers—and nonbelievers in this view included Muslims who did not practice a strict interpretation of Islamic law. As scholars have pointed out since the attacks on the World Trade Center in New York and the Pentagon in Washington, there has always been a powerful strain in Islam, one of the great monotheistic religions of the world, of a cult of death and sacrifice, a conviction that the highest calling, the quickest path to worldly prestige and heavenly reward, is through the slaughter of infidels and the enemies of Islam.

In fact, as some of these same scholars have written, the vengeful, fanatical, intolerant Islam that lay behind the September 11 attacks has always been a minority strand in a religion with many historical attributes, including tolerance and pluralism, pacific mysticism and gentleness.[1] If you, for example, were a Jew in the fifteenth century, you would have been far better off in Muslim Baghdad or Alexandria than in Christian Paris or Madrid—indeed you might have taken refuge in one of the Muslim places after being expelled, in the name of religion, from the Christian ones. "There must be no coercion in matters of religion" is a line that comes straight from the Koran.[2] But it is a line that, quite obviously, is ignored by many Muslims today, who embrace, not the pluralist concept of their faith, but a narrow, anti-modern, vengeful, and fanatical version of it.

In many ways, the story of September 11 is a story of a battle within Islam itself—between the Islam that is not spread by the sword and the Islam that is spread not only by the sword, but by a fetish of martyrdom and murder. In recent years, this second Islam has been sanctioned by the rulings of a contingent of fanatical religious scholars for whom Islam is locked in a duel to death with the rest of the world and with the impure elements of the Muslim world itself. The theological basis for this point of view also goes back many hundreds of years, to the concept that the *umma*, the Muslim community, sometimes becomes internally corrupted and humiliated by foreign conquest, and that, under those circumstances, Muslims should be summoned to wage Holy War. In this view, Islam itself needed to be purified, brought back to its fundamentals, and the foreigners thrown out. One very influential figure who espoused that doctrine was the Ayatollah Ruhollah Khomeini of Iran who, upon taking power in 1979, popularized the slogan "Death to America!"

But there have been other such figures, less known in the West but immensely prestigious and famous in the Middle East, and in many ways the more recent origins of September 11 lie with one of them, an intense, charismatic Palestinian religious scholar named Abdullah Azzam. Indeed, in this sense, the origins of what happened on September 11 in New York and Washington can actually be traced to a specific place and time— the dusty, frontier city of Peshawar in the Northwest Territories of Pakistan in 1979. It was there and then that Azzam set up a modest storefront office aimed at recruiting volunteers for an Islamic army that would win historic renewal and glory for Islam. Out of Azzam's call to Muslims everywhere to join him in a new jihad, or holy war, grew the force that would eventually carry out the worst foreign attack on American soil since the War of 1812.

Even now in the wake of September 11 and other terrorist attacks on the United States, carried out by men proclaiming Islam as their guide and inspiration, few Americans have heard of Abdullah Azzam and far fewer knew of him in 1979 and the early 1980s. And yet, perhaps more than any other single person in recent history, Azzam galvanized Muslims around the world to fight against what they deemed to be the enemies of Islam. He was a fierce and forceful man of about thirty-nine years of age when he arrived in Peshawar, with his full beard and his knack both for international organization and for the florid rhetoric of Islamic militancy. In his own autobiographical writings, he talked of his "untold love to fight in the Path of Allah." He repudiated the very concept of compromise: "Jihad and the rifle alone" is one of his most quoted pronouncements. "No negotiations, no conferences and no dialogues."

Azzam was born in the West Bank town of Jenin in 1941, though he left for Jordan after Israel occupied the West Bank in the Six Day War of 1967. In Jordan, he worked as a village schoolteacher, but he was also a political activist—or, as this is put in the glowing articles written about him in publications devoted to jihad, he "joined the jihad against the Israeli occupation of Palestine." According to some accounts, Azzam was a founder of Hamas, which was later to turn to suicide bombings as its chief weapon against the hated Israeli enemy. If Azzam did turn to Hamas, it would have been out of a disillusionment with the mainstream Palestinian movement, a disillusionment that he often expressed, and in this sense illustrated an important element in the larger Arab contention with Israel and with the West. You can say that modern Arab political movements are of two kinds. One is secular and nationalist, and its heroes are figures like Gamel Abdel Nassar of Egypt and Algerian independence leaders like Ahmed Ben Bella, who were inspired by socialist or Marxist ideas that came from Europe. These men who came to power in coups or independence struggles in the 1950s and 1960s were Third World revolutionaries and they had more in common with Vietnam's Ho Chi Minh or Ghana's Kwame Nkrumah than they did with the Prophet Mohammed or his modern-day followers.

The other movement, smaller and less powerful during the early years of Azzam's life, is religious. Its members believed that a revitalized and usually very strict Islam would provide the true path to restored greatness for both the Arab and the Islamic worlds, since Islam was the great invention of the Arabs and without it, in this view, the Arab states would be mere copies of the decadent and spiritless West. These two visions, one secular, the other religious, have often come into conflict in the Arab world, most conspicuously in the Egypt of today where the secular government is bitterly opposed by Islamic parties, many of whose leaders have been, or are, in prison. The religious movement was also consciously and fiercely anti-modern and anti-Western; its adherents believe in sharia, or rule by Islamic law with its strict punishments for all offenses and its subordination of women, and they cultivate the notions of jihad and the glories of martyrdom, of dying for Allah.

Azzam belonged to this second tendency; he believed in jihad, in sharia, in martyrdom, and that is what led him to break with the mainstream Palestinian movement, which, under the overall leadership of Yassir Arafat and the Palestinian National Council, has always been secular, not religious. Azzam used to tell, with disapproval in his voice, stories of how Palestinian fighters spent their nights listening to music and playing cards. In one camp of thousands of people, he said, only a handful went to daily prayers in the mosques.

In 1970 or thereabouts Azzam went to Egypt where he got a degree in sharia from Al-Azhar University, the world's oldest and most prestigious institution for Islamic scholarship. For a time, he taught at King Abdul-Aziz University in Jeddah, Saudi Arabia, a place where the Islamic movement was favored over the secular nationalist one. Then, in 1979, when the Soviet Union invaded Muslim Afghanistan, Azzam saw the opportunity he believed he was born for. He went to Peshawar, the city in northwest Pakistan just thirty miles from the fabled Khyber Pass, the gateway to Afghanistan. He traveled extensively in Afghanistan itself, and though it is not clear whether he took part in actual fighting, it is certain that he was deeply moved and inspired by the spectacle of Muslims fighting against a great, infidel power. Returning to Peshawar, he founded the Office of Services for the mujahedeen (*mujahedeen* meaning "holy warriors"), which was soon to become a global network recruiting Muslims to do jihad against the Soviet Union.

At the time, Peshawar, which had been a military outpost in the years of the British empire, was the global epicenter for the anti-Soviet fight, the place where an international assortment of spies, mullahs, mujahedeen, journalists, relief agency officials, arms dealers, and men with money from the American Central Intelligence Agency could be found in the city's seedy hotels and large masonry houses. The United States was in the process of funneling what would become some $3 billion to Afghan freedom fighters in their successful guerrilla struggle against the Russians. It was a time, in other words, when the United States was favorably disposed to the growing band of foreign Muslims, from places like Algeria, Egypt, Jordan, and Saudi Arabia who were inspired to fight against the Soviet infidel. In fact, accounts differ as to the military importance of the Arabs in Afghanistan itself. They themselves developed an entire inspirational literature about their bravery under fire, their importance in the Afghan struggle. But other accounts depict them as minor players in the anti-Soviet war who built large legends out of a couple of small engagements. But there is no question that in summoning thousands of Arabs to Peshawar, Azzam created what was to become an important new force in the world, a kind of Muslim international, a corps consisting of many thousands of young men—and a smaller group of radical religious teachers—who were deeply dissatisfied with conditions in their home countries and ever more eager to bring about radical changes there; or they had been branded criminals in those countries and were unable to return home. Before the Soviet war in Afghanistan, Peshawar and its surrounding region was an isolated, picturesque, Kiplingesque backwater with very little importance for the outside world. After that war began, it became full of people fired with messianic Islamic zeal, the sense that, if they could defeat the Soviet superpower in Afghanistan, they could do anything.

Azzam and his Office of Services were thus at the center of the spirit of a newly armed Islam. Like such other Islamic figures of the time, most notably the Ayatollah Khomeini of Iran, he communicated to his followers and to potential recruits to the cause by making audiotapes of his lectures and sermons. "Jihad must not be abandoned until Allah alone is worshipped" was typical of the sort of statements that he made, and that would be heard in mosques from Tucson, Arizona, to Jeddah, Saudi Arabia. "Jihad continues until Allah's Word is raised high . . . Jihad is the way of everlasting glory."[3] His Office of Services moved from its original storefront location to a large house in a quiet, affluent area of Peshawar called University Town, because of its proximity to Peshawar University. The American consulate and cultural center are nearby. When a young Arab fighter or a not-so-young Muslim cleric would arrive in Peshawar, Abdullah Azzam's house would often be the first place he would go. There he would get oriented, assigned for military training, and eventually he would be put into a group that would cross over the border into Afghanistan itself.

Azzam's main activity was recruitment, and for that purpose he rapidly expanded the Office of Services into a truly global organization. There were branches in most of the Arab countries as well as in Britain, France, Germany, Sweden, and Norway, all of which had large numbers of Muslim students and immigrants. Azzam dispatched a close follower, one Mustafa Shalabi, to Brooklyn, New York, where a branch of his office was flourishing by the mid-1980s, a part of another organization called Al-Kifah, which had centers in Atlanta, Boston, Chicago, Brooklyn, Jersey City, Pittsburgh, and Tucson, and minor branches in some thirty other American cities.[4] Mosques and Islamic centers around the world reverberated to Azzam's call to do jihad in Afghanistan, and tens of thousands of volunteers for jihad, a large number of them Arabs, heeded that call.

What is extraordinary is the large number of figures who came to Peshawar during the Soviet war, or shortly after it, and who later participated in terrorist attacks against the United States. Two of the men implicated in the Sadat assassination later turned up in Peshawar where they became part of the Azzam circle. One of them was Omar Abdel Rahman, a blind preacher from the city of Fayoum in southern Egypt who had provided a religious sanction, known as a fatwa, for the assassination of Egypt's president Anwar Sadat. Another was Ayman Zawahiri, a Cairo medical doctor who was arrested after the Sadat assassination and spent three years in prison. Zawahiri, another of the charismatic figures who emerged in this period, was the leader of Egyptian Jihad, one of several radical Islamic groups. Among the others who passed through Peshawar, getting their first taste of jihad, was el-Sayyid Nosair, who would later assassinate the Jewish extremist Meier Kahane in New York and would be a primary instigator of the terror bombing of the World Trade Center in New York in 1993. There was Mahmud Abuhalima, an Egyptian who was later convicted in the 1993 bombing. There was a mysterious Egyptian army officer and secret jihadist named Ali A. Mohammed, who would later become at the same time an informant for the FBI and, unknown to the

FBI, a trainer of terrorists in the United States. There were the members of the terrorist teams that blew up the American embassies in Nairobi, Kenya, and Dar es Salaam, Tanzania, on the same day in 1998. In other words, many of the men who would later figure in the story of terrorism against the United States were first received into the jihad movement in Peshawar by Abdullah Azzam or by one of his successors (since, as we will see, Azzam himself was assassinated in 1989).

But none of these figures would turn out to be more important than a young Saudi who, as best as can be determined, came first to Peshawar in about 1980, in the early stages of the anti-Soviet struggle, and became a key Azzam supporter. He was about twenty-three years old at the time, an extremely tall, self-possessed, and sad-eyed young man from a very rich, well-connected family, the kind of man, Azzam understood, whose wealth and connections, allied to his own religious and political creden- tials, could help to make for a powerful combination.

Arriving in Peshawar, he was distinctive in his carefully tailored shal- war kameez, the long, flowing tunic and trousers favored by the Pashtuns of Pakistan and Afghanistan, and his English handmade leather boots. But he was a young man who wanted to do something more meaningful with his life than spend lavish sums on his own pleasures, which is what he had done until then. It is said that while still in Saudi Arabia he had listened to taped sermons by Azzam calling on Muslims everywhere to do jihad and that they had had a profound impact on him. They gave him the cause that would occupy him for the rest of his life. His name: Osama bin Laden.

THREE

"We're Due for Something"

Rick Rescorla got up at 4:30 on the morning of September 11, 2001, as he always did, and his wife, Susan, remembers that he was unusually playful that morning, singing and dancing and making jokes as he came out of the bathroom. Rick and Susan were planning a trip to Italy for the wedding of one of Mrs. Rescorla's daughters by another marriage, and Rick would have preferred sleeping a little later and then taking a day or so to help Susan pack their bags. But he was vice president in charge of security for the giant investment banking and stock brokerage firm Morgan Stanley, and a man he had recently hired was himself out of the country, so Rescorla planned to go into work every day that week.

As usual, he took the 6:10 train at Convent Station near his home in Morristown, New Jersey, to Hoboken where he switched to the PATH train to lower Manhattan, and he would have been in his office in the south tower of the Trade Center shortly after 7:00. We don't know exactly what he had in store for that day, what meetings with his staff he meant to hold to discuss what plans for the security drills he routinely imposed on Morgan Stanley's always busy employees, and which he did not allow them to ignore. We do know that it was the Rescorlas' custom to talk on the phone around 8:00 every morning and when they did on September 11, Susan told Rick that he had been incredibly funny, more than usually good-humored that morning, and that was in its way a sign for both of them of how good their lives were turning out. Rick and Susan had only met in 1988 and both of them had failed marriages behind them—Rick one and Susan two—but with each other they felt that they had finally found a kind of stable and untarnished happiness. Less than an hour after their regular morning call—at forty-six minutes and a few seconds after 8 A.M.—the north tower of the World Trade Center was struck by the hijacked American Airlines flight 11, and Rick began doing for real what he had practiced doing many times in the past several years, evacuating Morgan Stanley's twenty-six hundred south tower employees to safety.

It is a safe bet that Rescorla, though a man of the world and professionally interested in terrorism, was among the many millions of Americans who, whether in 1979 or 2001, had never heard of Abdullah Azzam or any of the members of his circle—and that is in its way an emblem of how unsuspecting Americans were about the plots being hatched against them. Certainly, it can be said without any doubt at all that Rescorla, like 250 million of his fellow American citizens, including the local police and every special agent in the intelligence and terrorism divisions of the FBI, was unaware of a young man named Mohammed Atta, thirty-three years old on September 11, and just twelve in 1979, when he was getting adjusted to the routines of the big city of Cairo after a childhood in an agricultural village.

Eventually the grown-up Atta would lead the attack in which Rescorla would be murdered. But that is the way with modern warfare and especially terrorism. It involves groups of people that not only do not know each other, but that, in a more humanely logical world, would have nothing at all to do with each other's lives or misfortunes. Whatever it is that drove Mohammed Atta to become a suicide terrorist, Rick Rescorla had nothing to do with it. He was free of any responsibility, even the most indirect responsibility, for Mohammed Atta's frustrations and anger. But history would decree that they would meet and that they would die, together as it were.

To know the lives of these two men, beginning in the 1980s when the underlying protagonists of this story begin to act, is to see the crazy, senseless, and tragic coming together of two worlds that, by every tenet of reasonableness, should never have met.

Around the time that Abdullah Azzam was creating the Office of Services, Rick Rescorla had seen more military action than practically all of the members of the Islamic jihad combined. The most conspicuous emblem of Rescorla's career is the photograph on the dust jacket of the book *We Were Soldiers Once . . . And Young*, the best-selling account by Harold G. Moore and Joe Galloway of the battle of the Ia Drang Valley in 1965, in which 3,561 Vietnamese and 305 Americans were killed. Rescorla is the soldier depicted on the dust jacket of that book. He is shown in full combat gear, helmet on his head, M-16 rifle with bayonet fixed, looking warily but unflinchingly around him. He explained, in an interview he did in 1998 for a documentary filmmaker, Robert Edwards, that he and his Bravo Company had just finished a harrowing all-night battle with North Vietnamese regulars, and they had gone out for a final sweep of the field—just as he was later to make a final sweep of the south tower of the World Trade Center to make sure nobody had been left behind in his evacuation of Morgan Stanley's nineteen floors of offices. A few minutes later, an enemy soldier lying in the grass and apparently playing dead began firing at Rescorla with a machine gun.

"I don't know how he didn't hit me," Rescorla says in the interview. "He was only about seven yards away." Rescorla fell to his right and turned to his radioman, Sam Fantino, who threw him a grenade. Rescorla pulled the pin and threw it over the elephant grass, and, he believes, killed the machine gunner.

Rescorla fought bravely at Ia Drang and in other battles of the Vietnam War, where he developed a reputation for extreme coolness under fire. Thirty-six years later in the south tower of the World Trade Center, he was again professionally cool as the world was literally tumbling down around him. But while Rescorla in 1965 survived the battle of Ia Drang, a conspicuously dangerous place, he was killed in supposedly safe lower Manhattan in 2001.

He was born Cyril Richard Rescorla in 1939 in a town called Hayle on the north coast of Cornwall, England. He grew up in his grandparents' home, since his mother had had him out of wedlock. In fact, as he was growing up, he was told that his grandparents were his parents and that his mother was his older sister.[1] Rescorla never knew his father, or even who he was. The name Rescorla was his mother's and his grandfather's.

Perhaps it was the awkwardness of coming from unconventional circumstances that pushed Rescorla when still very young to an especially
risk-filled life, perhaps it was something else. But whatever the deep psychological reasons, by the time he was twenty-four, he had had several
postings in several widely scattered locations. He was a paratrooper in the
British army and an intelligence officer in Cyprus, where his job was to
coordinate with regular Cypriote forces in their efforts to suppress the
terrorist group EOKA, which was seeking to make the island a part
of Greece. He was then a colonial policeman in British-run Northern
Rhodesia—now the country of Zambia—and after that, he even served a
stint as a detective with Scotland Yard, but he was bored by the routines of
law enforcement, especially the requirement that he spend most of his
time sitting at a desk. And so, in 1963, as his closest army friend, Daniel J.
Hill, put it, "He decided he needed another adventure." He went to the
United States, because he was a paratrooper and he felt the Americans
were the best paratroopers in the world. He joined the army. By 1965 he
had finished Officers Candidate School at Fort Dix in New Jersey, and in
the fall of that year he was off to Vietnam.

"Rescorla was a rifle platoon leader sent in to reinforce me during the
battle of Ia Drang," General Moore, the main author of *We Were Soldiers
Once . . . And Young,* recalled. "I remember on the night of November 15,
Rescorla, myself, a medical aide named Thomas Burlaw, and others were
trapped in a foxhole as machine gun fire was piercing through my command post. We lost a lot of men during this battle, and unfortunately, my
radio guy was shot in the head right next to me, and then Burlaw also fell.
I remember Rescorla holding Burlaw in his arm, trying to comfort him
during one hell of a time. He was superbly cool and inspiring on the battlefield.

"Later that night, it was around 1:30 A.M., we were still heavily
attacked. And you know what Rescorla did?" Moore continued. "He sang
to all the men. I was about a hundred yards away and I hear in the distance, someone singing. I remember asking myself, 'What the hell is
that?' He seems to sing when people are in need of a calm leader."

Rescorla was indeed famous for breaking out in Cornish ballads
during moments of stress—and, according to some reports, he did
so again on September 11 inside the stairwells of the south tower. But

singing was not all he did. There is another Vietnam-era story about him. He was sharpening his Bowie knife when an argument between two American soldiers erupted nearby and suddenly one of them was brandishing a .45 pistol. Rescorla walked between the two men. "Put. Down. The. Gun," he said, and, when the angry soldier did so, Rescorla returned to sharpening his knife.[2]

During the battle of Ia Drang, which was fought in the Central Highlands of South Vietnam near the border with Laos, American troops under General (then Lieutenant Colonel) Moore were attacked by North Vietnamese regulars at a point called X-ray, where the American helicopters had landed. On that first night, the Americans took heavy losses with one company almost entirely knocked out, and Rescorla led a replacement platoon on the American periphery with the job of holding the ground against further assaults. The next morning, his Bravo Company beat back four attacks, killing some two hundred Vietnamese troops with minimum losses on the American side.

"He pushed you, pushed you, pushed you," said Fantino, who remained a friend in the years since the war. "He made you go that extra mile, like at night. He would get us to clean our weapons with blindfolds on. He knew the physical and mental training was very important out there. And some of us used to joke that we were more scared of Rick than the enemy.

"But there was this other side to Rick," Fantino said, "and you saw this side during the war, when he used to sing to us in the foxholes when all you're worried about is how to find a rock big enough to crawl under. And the letters he used to send to the families that lost their sons. He was a literary man, and he was sensitive."

Maybe it was the training in alertness that you get as an infantry lieutenant; maybe it was just a character trait, for the necessities of his later career as a corporate security officer for several large financial institutions, but all during the 1990s, Rescorla saw something terrible coming. His friends still feel their neck hairs standing on end as they remember one instance in particular. During a reunion of veterans of the battle of Ia Drang, Rescorla predicted that the next national security threat would be of a massive plane strike at an American national monument or tall building. And in his interview with Robert Edwards, videotaped in 1998, he predicts that terrorism rather than conventional war will be the great challenge facing the United States in the years ahead.

"Hunting down terrorists—this will be the nature of war in the future, not great battlefields, not great tanks rolling," he says.

But that came later. In the 1980s, after his decade or so of dangerous living as a soldier in both the British and American armies, Rescorla was settling into family life, a career, sedentariness, pursuing literary and musical interests, writing a screenplay, furthering his education. He married Elizabeth Nathan, a special-needs teacher who was born in Texas but raised in Mexico, in 1972. His son, Trevor, was born in 1976 and his daughter, Kimberly, two years later. He stayed for several years in the Oklahoma National Guard where, among other things, he was an instructor in hand-to-hand combat. But he was not one of those guys who are unable to let the war go and to forge another life. Elizabeth remembers that he kept his Vietnam War medals—a silver star, a purple heart, and a bronze star—in a tin can in the attic.

"The war was part of my life," he used to say. "It's not my life."[3]

Rescorla went to college in Oklahoma on the GI bill and then completed law school, also in Oklahoma. He had a brief career teaching criminal justice at the University of South Carolina law school, and then he went into corporate security, a more lucrative field for which his military experience eminently qualified him. He worked in Chicago at Continental Bank and then, in 1984, he moved to New York to begin working for Dean Witter, with an office in the World Trade Center. And it was there that he saw something coming, right there in the twin towers, where it not only happened but happened in the way he predicted. In 1990, he and his friend Daniel Hill toured the Trade Center together.

"When we went into the basement, we both agreed that was the weakest spot," Hill recalled. "We even figured out where to put any vehicles that could carry in bombs. And the place where we figured was the most vulnerable. It ended up being only fifty feet away from where the truck was parked in the 1993 bombing."

Rescorla presented an analysis to Dean Witter in which he stressed the Trade Center's vulnerabilities and called for tightened security, but, according to Hill, these recommendations were ignored. Later Rescorla's analysis became an element in a lawsuit filed by Dean Witter against the

Port Authority of New York and New Jersey, accusing it of negligence and holding it responsible for damages suffered in the 1993 terror attack. The suit is still pending, but Rescorla is one of the people for whom the 1993 attack was a lesson. If he was famous in Vietnam for singing to scared, weary troops in foxholes, he became famous at Morgan Stanley for not allowing anybody to sit at their desks during the evacuation drills he ran. Once, during a drill, frustrated by what he saw as the complacency of many employees to those drills, he jumped on a table and shouted: "What do you want me to do to get your attention, drop my pants?"

"He's a big guy," recalls Ihab Dana, a security director at Morgan Stanley who was Rescorla's chief assistant, "but he was a teddy bear. He may be physically intimidating, but when you sat down to talk to him he was very charming."

"We did a risk assessment every day," Dana continued. "And Rick would often say, 'We're due for something.'" He believed that the dozen or so men who were convicted in the 1993 Trade Center attack were what he would call "tools" and that the more powerful figures who commanded them had never been found.

And yet, while he was attuned to danger, Rescorla, according to his friends, spent the years when Osama bin Laden was gearing up for war, dealing with family problems, honing his skills as a writer, doing nothing more physically dangerous than coaching a kids' soccer team or boxing with Trevor in the basement of their suburban New Jersey house. The bad thing in his life was his marriage to Elizabeth, which went sour. Friends say that the two just grew apart; they don't provide details. In any case, Elizabeth and Rick were separated in the mid-1980s and divorced. His friends say that that was a very hard and lonely time for Rick, at least until a few years later when, jogging near his home, he met a divorced mother of three named Susan Greer, and the two were married in February 1999.

By all accounts, Rescorla always remained an active man, almost compulsively so. He once wrote a screenplay about the World War II infantry hero Audie Murphy. He read a great deal and loved to quote poetry. He carved wooden ducks. He did yoga. He was the kind of man who shoveled his neighbor's driveway after it snowed. He sang songs and danced jigs for the amusement of Susan, his new wife, when they got up before 5:00 every morning. He who went out for ice cream for his staff on hot summer days. But in 1994, when he was fifty-five, he learned that he had prostate cancer, and, while it went into remission after treatment, it worried him. He dwelled on it, seeing it as a kind of proof of the fragility of things, even for a strapping survivor like himself. As he approached his sixtieth birthday in 1999 and then passed it, he had the thoughts of mortality that afflict most people of a certain age, and he talked about them in the way of an ex-soldier.

"I last saw Rick in April," Hill said, meaning April 2001. "We talked about how old we were getting, and our illnesses—Rick with prostate cancer and me with two heart attacks. He said, 'Will you look at us. We're all buggered up and are now old men. Guys like us need to die in battle. That's the way we're supposed to go.'"

The obvious question about Mohammed Atta is what led him to kill himself so that others would also die. Or, to put this another way, what made him so furious? Where did he acquire the conviction that to become a martyr while in the act of mass murder would be doing God's work, would bring him eternal glory?

Many answers to those questions have been offered up. The strictness of Atta's father has been cited; so has the paucity of economic opportunities for the well-educated sons of such fathers and the absence of legal, legitimate avenues of protest and anger at the desperate poverty of so many Middle Eastern countries.

And then, of course, there was a climate of opinion in the Arab world that began to take shape in the 1980s—a climate that men like Abdullah Azzam, Ayman Zawahiri, and Omar Abdel Rahman both reflected and helped to create. There was a weird, perverse, radical utopianism in the air, fueled by the paranoid conviction that evil enemies, what they referred to as "Jews and Crusaders" especially but Muslim heretics also, lurked everywhere. Those susceptible to that utopianism and that paranoia banded together; they talked mostly to themselves; they formed a society apart with its own values and idols. When Arabs like Atta went to Germany to study, they found common ground in their belief in the surrounding evil and in the possibility of paradise through martyrdom. And they were powerfully encouraged in this by local imams who preached sermons of hatred against the Jews, the Crusaders, the heretics, and who invoked the demagogic authority of sheiks from Egypt and Saudi Arabia, some of them blind men supposedly imbued with brilliant interior visions, who called on all Muslims to slaughter the infidel.

The strange thing, however, is the absence of any evidence that the young Atta, the boy in a Nile Delta village, the adolescent and young man in Cairo, even the student in his early years in Germany, was susceptible to that kind of appeal. In the wake of September 11, journalists from around the world visited the scenes of Atta's early years, talking to his relatives, his friends, his father, and his teachers, and, while they have found a strangely reclusive, serious, intelligent, and meticulous young man, they have found very little to prefigure the suicide terrorist that he would become later.

"It's hard to imagine that such a man could acquire the verve and daring to lead an enterprise as audacious as the September attacks," one journalist, Terry McDermott of the *Los Angeles Times,* wrote. "Maybe we have misconceived the nature of the attacks and build the requisite figure to orchestrate them. Maybe a brilliant general is not what is needed. Maybe the plan wasn't so much difficult as it was detailed, and what it really required was somebody with will and steadfastness to see it through."[4]

Young Mohammed Atta, a bright boy by all indications, was born in an agricultural village called Kafr el Sheik in the north of Egypt. His relatives to this day remember his family, especially his father, Mohammed al-Amir Awad el Sayed Atta, being disdainful of ordinary local people and burning with the ambition to achieve something bigger and grander than could be achieved in a provincial farming settlement lost in the unchanging, overcrowded Nile Delta. And that is why, these relatives say, that when young Atta was nine or ten, the father, a lawyer with a good practice, took the family to a crowded, dilapidated district of Cairo called Abdin. The adolescent Mohammed, as he faced life in the big city, was expected to be ambitious himself. He worked hard at school. He didn't play with the neighborhood children, or, indeed, do anything that would divert him from the important, successful life his father wanted for him.

The Atta family lived in a large, dark apartment in Abdin, a neighborhood of a kind of shabby gentility whose once grand stone apartment buildings have fallen into disrepair. It is the kind of place where midlevel government bureaucrats once lived well on their salaries of $100 a month but now find themselves in a vortex of downward mobility, working second and third jobs to survive. There, the Atta family, more prosperous than others around them, was as aloof and as superior as they had been in Kafr el Sheik. People in Abdin talk of Atta senior as an arrogant man who often passed without a word or a glance at his neighbors.

He was also in his way a modern man. He had the same ambitions for his two daughters as for his only son, Mohammed, sending them all to the same schools and demanding that they work hard and spend no time dallying on the streets. He used to complain that his wife pampered all of the children, especially Mohammed. She treated him like a girl, the father told the reporters who came to see him after September 11. "He was so gentle," the father said of his son. "I used to tell him, 'Toughen up, boy!' "

Mohammed, who was the youngest child, went to school and worked. He didn't hang around with other young boys "chewing pistachios, spitting out the shells," as one neighbor put it.[5] In a high school classroom of twenty-six students—who were grouped together by name, so that boys named Mohammed were put together—the young Atta concentrated on doing his father's bidding, living up to his expectations.

"I never saw him playing," one classmate, Mohammed Hassan Attiya, said. "We did not like him very much, and I think he wanted to play with the rest of the boys, but his family, and I think his father, wanted him to always perform in school in an excellent way."

Mohammed's father seems a psychologist's nightmare, not just coldly, rigidly, and imperiously judgmental, but also utterly unself-aware. There is a smothered sort of fury in the remarks he casually made to journalists that dehumanizes others, makes them not just worthless in his world but almost nonexistent. "We are people who keep to ourselves" is one remark attributed to him. "We don't mix a lot with people, and we are all successful." He expresses this same idea in different ways, and the message he would have conveyed to a child by these words is: "Don't so much care about people as disdain them, regard them as unworthy of your attention." "We keep our doors closed," he said, "and that is why my two daughters and my son are academically and morally excellent."

Mohammed went to Cairo University, a huge rambling institution where students are assigned to subjects on the basis of test results, not individual preference. Atta's sisters went there too, one of them becoming a botanist, the other a cardiologist. Mohammed was assigned to study architecture in the engineering department, a subject reserved for some of the highest-scoring students. He didn't do brilliantly, but he did well. There are signs that, like his father, Mohammed thought himself morally excellent, or, at least, observant of a strict code of morality. One friend said that when he watched television, he used to walk out of the room when a belly-dancing program came on the air. His father said that he began to pray regularly when he was twelve or thirteen, so, clearly, he experienced a strong religious impulse, but he was not a religious radical. He refused to play in a basketball league because it was sponsored by the Islamic Brotherhood, Egypt's largest Islamic party.

Egypt itself was a troubled society. President Anwar Sadat had been assassinated in 1981, and the government's harsh crackdown on Islamic fundamentalism took place in the years after that. Sheltered though he may have been, Atta would surely have felt the turmoil of the street and the disillusionment of his middle-class fellow students who, even after their professional training at Cairo University, often couldn't get jobs. The Muslim Brotherhood recruited actively at Cairo University, including in the engineering department, and, although Mohammed refused to join, he would have heard its appeal and its rhetoric about the Jews and the Crusaders and the Zionists and the heretics and the need to fight back with a purified, revivified Islam. At the time, preachers like Omar Abdel Rahman attracted devoted followings and the audiotapes of Abdullah Azzam, recorded in Peshawar, made the rounds of mosques and associations. Some young men of around Atta's age were heeding his call to do jihad in Afghanistan.

It is of course possible that Atta, in his quiet way, absorbed some of the religious and political fanaticism in the air. His father denies it, saying that when it came to politics, his son was a "donkey." But during his conversations with Western reporters, the father issued streams of invective against Israel and of the West for its moral decadence, so Atta might well have picked up some of the impotent anger that affected much of the Muslim world from his father. Still, none of young Atta's friends or relatives remember him belonging to organizations or even expressing strong political opinions. And even though he was dubious about the moral worth of the West, the elder Atta encouraged his son to study German and English, and, when his years at Cairo University were finished, not to study sharia like Abdullah Azzam had done at Al Azhar University, but to go to some reputable place in Europe for advanced training in engineering and architecture.

"I told him I needed to hear the word 'doctor' in front of his name," his father said. "We told him, 'Your sisters are doctors and their husbands are doctors and you are the man of the family.'"

Atta senior says that young Mohammed was attached to his mother and uninterested in studying abroad, and he was lucky enough to get work with a German company in Cairo. One night, Mohammed's father invited two visitors from Germany to dinner, and Mohammed spoke to them in his fluent German. He won a scholarship to study at the Hamburg Technical University, convinced, it seems, by his father's argument that an advanced degree from a European university would pay large dividends later. He went to the German consulate in Cairo and picked up a visa to Germany, and by 1991, a year after graduating from Cairo University, he arrived in Hamburg. He studied engineering there. He answered a classified ad and was hired part-time at an urban planning firm Plankontor, where his diligence and the careful elegance of his drawings made a good impression.

Everything seemed fine to those who met him. But they weren't fine. If they had been fine, recent history would have been different.

FOUR

The Young Man from Saudi Arabia

There is no eyewitness account of Osama bin Laden's first meeting with Abdullah Azzam, though some things about it can be supposed. Probably it took place in one of the gated houses in Peshawar that Azzam used in his recruitment efforts. The two men would have sat on a carpet on the floor in traditional Arabic fashion, leaning their backs against the wall, drinking sugared tea and, in the spirit of Islamic piety, sprinkling their conversation with references to Allah, phrases like, "God willing," or "Praise be to God." The reports on bin Laden at the time have it that he was charming, modest, deferential. After only a few weeks in Peshawar, he seems to have gone back to Saudi Arabia and raised money for Azzam's cause, and then, when he returned to Pakistan, his largess gained him a reputation as a loyal friend of what were coming to be called the Arab Afghans, the men from all over the Arab world who were making common cause with the Afghan guerrillas in the anti-Soviet struggle.

Bin Laden, who, at six-five was visually striking, doled out gifts—money to bereaved families, cashew nuts and chocolates to wounded fighters, watches or shoes to people who didn't have watches or shoes. He became an emir, an informal title for a man of distinction and substance to whom respect and loyalty are due. Reporters covering the war in Afghanistan began hearing stories of the Saudi Good Samaritan who had imported bulldozers and other equipment to build roads and tunnels in

Afghanistan, even that he used to drive the bulldozers himself, despite the Soviet helicopter gunships that flew overhead.[1] Eventually bin Laden and Azzam settled into a large house on Syed Jalaluddin Afghani Road in University Town, a quiet district of large masonry houses where the bougainvillea cascades over wrought-iron railings and the occasional Mercedes-Benz pulls through the metal security gates of a driveway. The leaders of various Afghan factions took over some of the houses there and they would hold court in them, receiving visitors while all around men in turbans and brown homespun vests worn over flowing tunics sat on rugs and leaned their backs against the walls listening to the visitor and their leader converse. Azzam and bin Laden's house was given the name Beit al-Ansar, House of the Faithful. Bin Laden liked to stay up late there discussing theological matters—the passages in the Koran in which the Prophet expounded on a Muslim's obligations to Allah or the histories of the great warriors of Islamic history, like Saladin, who defeated the Crusaders.

Not far from the Beit al-Ansar in University Town was the American consulate and the American Cultural Center, with its library and cafeteria. There is no record that bin Laden ever visited there, but he might have. His hatred of America seems to have come later. Now, the United States itself was apt to see the anti-Soviet forces in Afghanistan as "freedom fighters," not potential terrorist enemies, so bin Laden and Washington were on the same side. In 1981, as the United States began publicly to support the anti-Soviet war in Afghanistan with money and weapons, President Ronald Reagan dedicated a space shuttle flight to the insurgents who he clearly saw as a Cold War weapon. "We cannot and will not turn our backs on this struggle," Reagan said, making his dedication standing next to an Afghan student named Nahid Mojadidi. At the time, there was no good reason to suspect that a person like bin Laden would be any more hostile than that Afghan student. Indeed, had anybody thought much about him at the time, which nobody did, they would have concluded that he would be a likely American ally. He was from Saudi Arabia, a friendly, moderate Arab country. Unlike most of the Arab fighters who came to the Beit al-Ansar, bin Laden knew the West. He had vacationed in Sweden with his family when he was a boy. He wore bell-bottomed pants that summer and short-sleeved shirts. As a teenager, he had spent a summer in Oxford, England, studying English. Before that, back in Saudi Arabia, he had studied at an elite Western-style school called Al-Thagh, where an English tutor, Brian Fyfield-Shayler, remembers him as a shy boy, tall and good-looking.

"He also stood out as he was singularly gracious and polite," Fyfield-Shayler told an English newspaper, "and had a great deal of inner confidence."[2]

One of the first to come to the Beit al-Ansar was a young Algerian named Boujema Bounouar, who went by the nom de guerre Abdullah Anas. Anas had a long career with bin Laden, beginning in the mid-1980s and lasting until he defected in the 1990s, and he is a rare eyewitness to the program created by Azzam and bin Laden to forge a Muslim international out of the turmoil of the Afghan war. Anas, who told his story in London where he now lives, was a teacher in Algeria in 1984 when he read in a weekly news magazine about a fatwa, a religious ruling, making it a Muslim duty to wage war against the Soviets in Afghanistan. It was the kind of pronouncement that emerged out of the theological netherworld in those days, with religious leaders like Azzam himself drawing on more ancient theories of Islamic revivalism, striving to re-create the glorious days of Saladin and other champions of the faithful who fought and defeated the infidels, especially, in Saladin's case, the Crusader infidels. That year, Anas participated in the hajj, the annual pilgrimage that brings millions of Muslims every year to Mecca, Saudi Arabia, and there, standing in the marble expanse of the Great Mosque with 50,000 others, a friend pointed out Azzam himself. Anas introduced himself. The two men talked. A week later Anas was on a flight from Saudi Arabia to Pakistan.

In Peshawar he called the only number he had, and Azzam offered him a place to stay in his own house, a bustling salon frequented by students and scholars inspired by the battles being fought against godless Communism in Afghanistan. It was there that Anas caught sight of Azzam's youngest daughter, whom he would marry five years later. And it was there that Azzam introduced him to bin Laden, identifying him in the traditional Arabic way, as Abu Abdullah, the father of Azzam's eldest son, Abdullah. Anas had heard of the famous youngest son of the more than twenty sons of the man who owned one of the largest construction companies in the Arab world, the man who was donating his wealth to the Islamic cause.

The two men exchanged pleasantries. They discussed the war and the role in it to be played by volunteers from the Middle East like Anas himself. They talked in particular about how the Middle Easterners could teach the Afghans more about Islam and, indeed, Anas's first role was to teach the Koran to Afghan mujahedeen. The Afghans learned it by rote in Arabic, the holy language of Islam, which none of the Afghans understood. At the time, according to Anas, there were no more than a few dozen Arabs in the country, working with the rebels. None spoke the Afghan languages—Pashtun or Dari or Hazari or Uzbek. After a few months, Anas trekked into Afghanistan to join a combat unit, one of three Arabs traveling with a caravan of six hundred Afghan soldiers. He learned Dari, the Persian dialect that is Afghanistan's lingua franca, and took on the role of mediator, traveling to different rebel camps and trying to smooth over the frequent feuds that erupted among them. He spent most of each year inside Afghanistan, eventually becoming a top aide to Commander Ahmed Shah Massoud, the legendary Uzbek fighter whose troops controlled northern Afghanistan—and who was assassinated in a suicide bombing just days before September 11.

At some point in the mid-1980s, bin Laden, who had commuted back and forth from Pakistan to Saudi Arabia, where he raised money directly and through a burgeoning network of supposedly charitable organizations, moved permanently to Peshawar. "He was one of the guys who came to jihad in Afghanistan," Anas said. "But unlike the others, what he had was a lot of money. He's not very sophisticated politically or organizationally. But he's an activist with great imagination. He ate very little. He slept very little. Very generous. He'd give you his clothes. He'd give you his money."

Bin Laden would sleep at the guest house in Peshawar on a cushion on the floor, and the simplicity of his lifestyle added to his growing reputation. Anas remembers Azzam saying, "You see this man has everything in his country. You see he lives with all the poor people in this room." As Azzam raised money for his Office of Services, dispatching followers or going himself to Islamic centers around the world, including the United States, bin Laden became his chief partner, providing financial support and handling military affairs. He was a natural leader, possessed of a tranquil authority and an unshakable resolve.

"When you sit with Osama, you don't want to leave the meeting," Anas said. "You wish to continue talking to him because he is very calm, very fluent."

In some ways Osama bin Laden is a prototype of a common kind of modern-day political figure, the child of wealth and privilege who devotes himself to overturning the establishment that gave him his privileges in the first place. Others among the dramatis personae in this story share that characteristic. Revolutions are not made by the downtrodden. The downtrodden are too preoccupied with sheer survival to devote themselves to revolutions, which require men and women from the middle class or higher, people with education, ambition, social consciences. And bin Laden was certainly well educated; economically, he was a good deal more than middle class, and he had a keen, if peculiar, social conscience.

His own father, Mohamed Awad bin Laden, was an illiterate bricklayer from the Hadramout Valley in Yemen, blind in one eye, who went to Saudi Arabia as a young man in the way that ambitious young Americans might have gone to Texas at that time—to make his fortune. It was 1930 or 1932; accounts on the exact date differ. Saudi Arabia had only recently been officially promulgated. Its leader was the vigorous Abdul-Aziz ibn Saud, who had combined the strict religious doctrine known as Wahhabism with the conquest of neighboring tribes to unify most of the Arabian Peninsula—except for Yemen in the south and the Gulf principalities to the east—and place it under his rule. The senior bin Laden's first job was as a bricklayer with Aramco, the Arabian-American Oil Company. Soon he started his own construction company and somehow developed a close relationship with Abdul-Aziz, winning a major contract to build a highway from Jeddah, the Saudi capital, to the resort town of Taif. After that, he got a contract to extend the Holy Mosque complex in Mecca, and then a foreign contractor withdrew from a deal to build a highway between Medina and Jeddah, and bin Laden got that job too.

He became exceedingly wealthy. In an interview with the Al Jazeera cable television station in Qatar in 1998, his son Osama told how his father restored the Saudi holy places free of charge, as a sign of his piety, but while he may well not have charged for his work, he does not seem to have been an especially religious man. By the 1970s, he had used his favored standing with the royal family to become the biggest construction magnate in Saudi Arabia, a country where there was a great deal of construction, paid for by the vast quantities of oil money that poured into the national treasury, and into the profligate hands of the many princes of the royal family. It is not clear exactly how rich bin Laden became—some say he was worth about $5 billion. Whatever the exact figure, like many wealthy men of the Middle East and elsewhere, he used his wealth to support his four wives and fifty-two children in lavish style.

Bin Laden senior died in a helicopter crash when Osama was eleven years old and some writers have seen a key to the son's personality in that fact. Various reports on bin Laden give widely different figures for the amount of money that he inherited, anywhere from a few million to $300 million. In any case, he was rich, and over the years he used his money to attach himself to a series of older men, mentors, father figures, for guidance, Abdullah Azzam being among the first and most important of them. Whether or not that is the psychological truth, there was certainly something in Osama that made him different from the other bin Laden children—in fact that made him different from all the other children of the monied Saudi elite. Osama's mother is the only one of Mohamed's four wives who was not Saudi when he married her; she was a Syrian named Hamida, the daughter of a trader. Mohamed's three Saudi wives were permanent, but he changed the fourth wife regularly, dispatching his pilot around the Middle East to bring candidates back to him, some of them as young as fifteen. A French engineer, interviewed by an English newspaper, said that Mohamed "changed wives like you or I change cars."[3]

Hamida was twenty-two years old when Mohamed married her. Unlike the other wives, all of them traditional members of the orthodox Wahhabi sect, she was more inclined to wear Chanel suits than the veil. It is not clear whether Hamida was still married to Mohamed at the time of his death—the available reports differ on this point—but Mohamed was known to treat his former wives very well, setting them up in palaces of their own in Jeddah and Hijaz. Still, the status of his mother is one thing that might have set Osama, Hamida's only child, apart from the children of Mohamed's other wives. As the constantly rotating fourth wife, known as "the slave wife," a foreigner, not devoutly religious, she was an outsider within both Saudi society and the house of bin Laden.

After Mohamed died, the family lived the life of the oil-rich elite, sending

their sons to school abroad, taking European vacations. A family friend
told the *Times* of London that in the nightclubs of Beirut, Osama was
known as "a heavy drinker who often ended up embroiled in shouting
matches and fistfights with young men over an attractive dancer or bar-
maid." But clearly there was something in that life that the teenaged
Osama rejected. Unlike some of his brothers, he did not go to school
abroad. Instead he went to King Abdul Aziz University in Jeddah to study
management and economics, and it seems to be there that he was introduced to Islamic revivalism. He engaged in religious debates. He prayed
and read. He also became a friend of Prince Turki bin-Faisal, a Saudi prince
who later became chief of the Saudi intelligence service. Very likely he listened to tapes of Abdullah Aziz's sermons.

Osama graduated in 1979 with the expectation that, like Mohamed's
other sons, he would go into the family business, now headed by Salem,
his older half brother. But he didn't. Certainly he knew of the exciting,
thrilling, watershed events that took place that year. In February, the Ayatollah Ruhollah Khomeini established an Islamic republic in Iran, and
declared the United States, the supporter of the overthrown former government of Mohammed Reza Shah Pahlavi, to be "the Great Satan." The
importance of Khomeini's rise from years of imprisonment and exile to
being the undisputed ruler of the ancient Persian civilization cannot be
overestimated. Even though Iranian Muslims are Shias—followers of Ali,
a nephew of the Prophet—and have bitter sectarian disputes with the
orthodox Sunni sect, Khomeini was the first religious leader to take political power in centuries in Islam, and his model was a tremendous inspiration for the Islamic movement in general.

"After 1979, there was nobody within the Muslim world or outside it
who was unaware of militant Islamism," Gilles Kepel, a French scholar of
Islam, has written. Khomeini's principle grievance, moreover, was one
that would be adopted by bin Laden and motivate his own campaign.
More than anything else, it was the presence of American soldiers on
Iranian soil, required by Iran's dependence on American military equipment, that led him, as early as 1964, to accuse the shah of treasonously
bartering away Iran's sovereign dignity to the infidel Americans. When he
came to power in 1979 after fifteen years of exile, Khomeini brought with
him bands of followers thrilled with the idea of spreading the Islamic rev-

olution elsewhere, and, among the slowly growing aftereffects of his seizure of power was the growth of Muslim-oriented parties among what had been secular movements.[4] Azzam himself represents just such a tendency inside the Palestinian movement. Within a few years, other armed Islamic groups were emerging with direct Iranian sponsorship, including, most notably, the Hezbollah, or Party of God, of Lebanon, which formed in the Bekaa Valley to fight the country regarded as Islam's main enemy, Israel. Among Khomeini's great contributions to militant Islam, in addition, was the very public humbling of the United States, which took place when Iranian students, tacitly supported by their government, seized the American embassy in Teheran in 1979 and held the fifty-three Americans working there for more than a year. The only American attempt to rescue the hostages, an ill-conceived commando raid using helicopters based on ships in the Persian Gulf, ended disastrously, with the crash of one of the helicopters and the death of eight Americans in the desert. The failure of the rescue effort, with its widely disseminated pictures of Iranian soldiers poking at dead American soldiers with their bayonets, is still celebrated as a national holiday in Iran.

The Iranian revolution thus seemed both to promise a new dawn for the Islamic revival and to demonstrate the weakness of the United States, its existence as what the Chinese leader Mao Zedong used to call a paper tiger. And the prospect of revivalism on one side and decline on the other were surely inspiring to the young bin Laden. But there were other events in 1979 that also had an impact on him. In November, Islamic radicals seized the Holy Mosque in Mecca, and held it until they were defeated by government troops. This was an event that, bin Laden said in later interviews, powerfully affected him. And then, in the last few days of the year, the Soviet Union invaded Muslim Afghanistan, thereby unintentionally giving purpose and mission to the young Osama bin Laden, who, a few months later, turned up at Abdullah Azzam's house in Peshawar.

For several years, as long as the anti-Soviet struggle took everything the foreign Muslims in Pakistan and Afghanistan were able to give it, the cooperation between bin Laden and Azzam seemed smooth. Azzam himself tirelessly set up offices abroad, including the one at the Al Kifah Center in Brooklyn, dispatching a follower named Mustafa Shalabi, an Egyptian, to run it. There, Arabs living in the United States congregated, some of them going to Afghanistan, others discussing the deplorable con-dition of the Arab world. The Al Kifah Center became a kind of Ameri-can echo of Azzam's Beit al-Ansar in Peshawar, a gathering point for disaffected Muslims drawn by the theories and goals of the Islamic Broth-erhood, troubled by the secularism, the poverty, and the dictatorships of the Middle East. They read *Al Jihad,* an Arabic-language magazine put out by Azzam's center in Peshawar but widely circulated in the United States and dedicated to heroic stories, illustrated in color, from the mujahedeen front lines in Afghanistan. According to Steven Emerson, *Al-Jihad* had a circulation of about fifty thousand, half of it in the United States. Azzam himself made an American trip, attending an Islamic conference in Okla-homa City in 1988, where he gave a keynote address exhorting his listen-ers to jihad. Emerson, who has studied videotapes of the conference, reported that Islamic militants from around the world were there, includ-ing representatives of such radical organizations as Hamas and Islamic Jihad, which set up stands for recruitment and fund-raising.[5]

But even as Islamic militants took advantage of the openness of American society to raise money and to recruit followers, divisions were appearing within the Office of Services back in Peshawar. Increasingly, the young Arabs who continued to be drawn there, and who were powerfully disaffected from the regimes that ruled their home countries, became frustrated over Azzam's insistence that the movement support only the Afghan cause, which, it seemed to them, would have little effect on the plight of their own homelands. Azzam aimed in Afghanistan at attaching Arab-Afghans to Afghan guerrilla units headed by Afghan fighters, his belief being that they would be more readily accepted in Afghanistan that way. But the radical Arabs' goal was to form a separate independent front made up of Arab troops who would then be available for other battles. Azzam's vision in this sense was limited. Despite his superheated rhetoric, he seems to have been relatively cautious in action. He hesitated to extend the jihad to other countries, especially to Arab countries, and he knew that separately formed and led Arab fighting units would, as one observer of the debates on this question in Peshawar put it, be "uncontrollable" once the Afghan war was over and they returned to their home coun-tries.[6] But overthrowing those home governments was exactly what the more radical figures who came to Peshawar wanted, and they eventually won the all-important money man, bin Laden, to their point of view.

The quarrel with Azzam brought about several major changes. Among the most important, it gave prominence to the radical Egyptians, more sophisticated than Osama, older, more seasoned in the struggles of Islamic fundamentalism, who were soon to give a new shape to bin Laden's role, to direct his attention from Afghanistan itself to other places in the world. Eventually, the Egyptians came to occupy most of the high positions in bin Laden's terrorist organization Al Qaeda, especially the military positions—and the word *military* in Al Qaeda means terrorist operations, not conventional war. After September 11, the military commanders, most notably Mohammed Atef and the man known as Abu Zubeidah, became top targets of the American war in Afghanistan. But in these early stages, the two men who seem to play the key roles, both in fomenting discord among the Arab-Afghans and bringing jihad to the rest of the world, were Ayman Zawahiri and Omar Abdel Rahman.

Both of them had been implicated, though never convicted, in the assassination of Egyptian president Anwar Sadat in 1981. Both had spent time in Egyptian prisons and, when freed, had made their way to Abdullah Azzam's house in Peshawar. Both believed in expanding the concept of jihad to include the causes of the Palestinians and of the downtrodden masses in Muslim countries ruled over by what they regarded as apostate Arab rulers, like Sadat himself. Zawahiri was a doctor from a distinguished family in Egypt who gave up the easy life to wage religious warfare. Abdel Rahman was a simple preacher from rural Egypt, a blind man, who, though now serving a life sentence in the United States for plotting terror attacks in New York, still has an avid, loyal, worshipful following among militant Muslims around the world.

There is some videotape, shown on a *Frontline* television documentary, of Zawahiri behind bars in Egypt after the Sadat assassination, and only a brief look at it conveys the power of his personality. It was an extraordinary moment in Middle Eastern history. Sadat, the only Arab ruler up to then to make peace with Israel, had been murdered by his own troops during a military parade. The government of his successor, President Hosni Mubarak, began a wholesale roundup of Islamic militants, members of the Muslim Brotherhood and several more radical splinter groups who were suspected of having played roles in the assassination. There were widespread reports, denied by the Egyptian authorities, of torture. But during the trial, with the defendants grouped together behind barred cages, the militants themselves had a chance to speak while the cameras of the international press were rolling.

Zawahiri, the leader of the Egyptian Jihad, one of the radical Islamic groups that had broken away from the Muslim Brotherhood, was deputed to speak for them, and he did, shouting through the prison bars while the other prisoners from time to time interrupted his speech with chants. He wore a white skull cap and severe black-framed glasses. He had a thick black beard, and there is an ardent, urgent quality to his voice as he denounced, in close to perfect English, what he called "injustice, dictatorship, corruption."

"We want to speak to the whole world," he shouted. "Who are we? We are Muslims. We are Muslims who believed in their religion. We tried our best to establish a Muslim state and a Muslim society. We are the real Islamic Front against Zionism, Communism, and imperialism." Zawahiri denounced the treatment of the several hundred men locked up with him. "We suffered the severest inhuman treatment. They kicked us, they beat us, they whipped us with electric cables, they shocked us with electricity, they hanged us from the edges of the door with our hands tied behind our backs."[7] Zawahiri at this point clasped his own hands together behind his back and raised them, imitating the torture. "They arrested our wives, our mothers, our fathers, our sisters and our sons in this trial to put the psychological pressure on these innocent prisoners."

In fact, whether the prisoners were innocent or not is an open question, but there is no question about the righteous fury in Zawahiri's voice. He is, in the words of W. B. Yeats, full of passionate intensity, and, it seems, he had been for most of his life.

Born in 1950 or 1951, Zawahiri came from one of Egypt's best-known families. An uncle was the first secretary-general of the Arab League, his father a professor at Cairo University, his grandfather a famous religious scholar. But, like bin Laden, six years younger, Zawahiri rejected the privileged life he could have led. When he was fifteen years old, he was arrested for membership in the Muslim Brotherhood, which was outlawed in the time of Nasser. He went to medical school at Cairo University and while a student in the 1970s was a founder of the Egyptian

Islamic Jihad, which was bitterly opposed to Sadat's peace agreement with Israel and is believed to have recruited the army officers who assassinated him.

When, after the assassination, Zawahiri finished serving his three-year sentence in Egypt, he went back for a brief time to the practice of medicine near his family's home in Cairo, but in 1984 he left Egypt for Pakistan in order to treat wounded guerrilla fighters. He became a kind of Islamic version of Che Guevara, the Argentine doctor who fought beside Fidel Castro in the Cuban revolution. According to an autobiography Zawahiri wrote and that was published in an Arabic newspaper in London, he set up an office of the Islamic Jihad in Peshawar in 1987 and published a magazine there called *The Conquest*. Like other Arab-Afghans, he made contact with Abdullah Azzam and, through him, met Osama bin Laden. The evidence is that, especially as bin Laden moved away from Azzam, Zawahiri became another of the older men to serve as models and guides for bin Laden.

Zawahiri's own mentor was Omar Abdel Rahman, who, in that videotape of the Cairo trial, is seen sitting quietly in a cage as Zawahiri makes his oration. Abdel Rahman was accused of having issued the fatwa that justified the Sadat assassination. That was not proved at trial and Abdel Rahman went free. In fact, the issue is not whether he approved of the killing of Muslim rulers who do not rule according to sharia—he did, at least in theory. What could not be proved, as his lawyer, Saad Hasaballah, explained, was that he was referring specifically to Sadat.

"They asked for a religious stand about a ruler who is ruling against Islamic law," Hasaballah said. Abdel Rahman replied that such a ruler should be pushed aside, but, according to Hasaballah, "He did not specify Sadat and the members of the Jihad Organization did not specify Sadat for him."

Abdel Rahman was born in 1938 in the village of Al Gamalia, in the Nile Delta. In his autobiography, published in Egypt after the Sadat assassination, he wrote that he became blind when he was just ten months old, a handicap that propelled him into a life devoted to religion. Many Egyptian youngsters lose their sight because of parasites or diseases, and it is common for children with this affliction to be taken to the mosque in the hope that they will have the talent to become preachers.

Abdel Rahman had the talent. By the age of eleven, he had memorized the Koran, a feat that earned him admission to an Islamic boarding school and then to Al Azhar University in Cairo, the apex of the worldwide system of Islamic education. He graduated in 1965 and was sent to preach in a town called Fedemin on the outskirts of Fayoum, a city about sixty miles south of Cairo.

It was there, in a small mosque alongside the main road surrounded by mango trees, that Abdel Rahman first drew the attention of the authorities. In September 1970, Gamel Abdel Nasser, the secular, nationalist president of Egypt, died, and millions of worshipful followers massed in the streets of Egypt's cities to mourn him. But Abdel Rahman, who opposed Nasser's secularism, referring to him as "the wicked Pharaoh," told his followers that it would be sinful to pray for the dead president because he was an infidel. Abdel Rahman's rhetoric is saturated with the profound moral conservatism that is one of the main pillars of Muslim fundamentalism, with the belief that modern society is decadent and corrupt and needs a bracing dose of the old desert purism to cure it.

"The state allows adultery and creates the opportunity for it," he later wrote in his autobiography. "The state organizes nightclubs and prepares special police to protect adulterers and prostitutes. Liquor factories are built by the state. Doesn't this deny God's laws?"

Abdel Rahman spent eight months in Cairo's vast twelfth-century Citadel Prison, where he was detained without charges for his remarks. After his release, he benefited from a shift in the Egyptian government's attitude toward Islam as President Sadat tried to enlist Islamic support in his contest against the Egyptian left. In a way, Sadat made the same mistake that the United States later made regarding Muslim militants in Afghanistan. He tried to enlist their support in Egyptian politics, using them as a counterweight to the pro-Soviet left, strengthening them in the process, only to have the clerics turn against him. In later years, the United States supported radical Muslims in the war against the Soviet Union in Afghanistan, and, with the war over, found that it had armed and supplied a force that was inimical to it. In both instances, Abdel Rahman was at the center of the action.

There is no question that Abdel Rahman had close relations with the Sadat assassins, who were part of a larger group known as the Jihad

Organization that formed in the late 1970s, and, early on, was supported by the Egyptian security police. The group, which was especially powerful in Asyut, had asked Abdel Rahman to serve as its religious leader.

When he was formally accused of involvement in the Sadat assassination and went on trial, Abdel Rahman was able to turn the event to his advantage, using it as a platform to speak for two days before a national audience and giving his vision of Islam. "In court, at his trial, when he defended himself he was very convincing," said Abdel Hamouda, a magazine editor in Cairo. "The prosecutor did not know what he was saying. It was as though he had just prepared for a day or so. But Omar Abdel Rahman had a very strong point of view on Islamic jurisprudence, and he stated it well. Even those who did not sympathize with him had nothing to say in reply."

After a few years preaching in Fayoum, Abdel Rahman rose to further prominence in the late 1980s when he became the spiritual leader of the Arab-Afghans. He never lived in Pakistan or Afghanistan for any length of time, but he went to Peshawar at least twice during the 1980s to urge on the anti-Soviet Arab fighters and he visited the Afghan battlefield itself at least once, in 1985. He is reported to have stayed outside Peshawar at the home of Mohammed Islambouli, an Arab-Afghan who was the brother of the man who organized the army faction that actually carried out the Sadat assassination. Abdel Rahman sent two of his own sons to fight in Afghanistan.

In 1989, after a riot at a mosque in Fayoum, where he was preaching during regular Friday prayers, Abdel Rahman was arrested and put on trial along with forty-eight other defendants. The government argued that he had instigated the riot; witnesses testified that the police had provoked the disturbance, bursting into the mosque during prayers, guns firing. In any case, from that point on, Abdel Rahman lived under virtual house arrest. The Egyptian Association for Human Rights visited his home in December 1989 and found it under what one association member, interviewed in Cairo, called a state of siege.

"He used to go out under guard," said Adel el-Lamouni, his lawyer in Fayoum. "His son would guide him to the mosque for Friday prayers, but whenever he went, he would be followed by two cars full of policemen."

Then early in 1990, Abdel Rahman made what has become, among his supporters in Fayoum, a legendary escape. One man said that the cleric was smuggled past his guards in a washing machine that was being taken out of his home. Another account, told by a resident in the neighboring village of Fedemin, was that the cleric left the house after another man, dressed up to look like the sheik, drew Abdel Rahman's usual guards away from their posts. Abdel Rahman tried to leave Egypt on a pilgrimage to Saudi Arabia, but, according to Egyptian journalists, he was detained at passport control at the Cairo International Airport until after the plane had left. Barred from leaving the country by air, he went overland to the Sudan. There, even though he was on a list of suspected terrorists barred from entry to the United States, he was given a visa at the United States embassy and, after a trip to Pakistan, he arrived in New York in July 1990.

This would seem to have been a failure to be properly vigilant on the part of American authorities. An Islamic militant identified by American intelligence as a terrorist figure, the acknowledged spiritual leader of Zawahiri, the presiding eminence of Egyptian Jihad, was admitted to the United States. He began to preach at mosques in New York and New Jersey. These were the very mosques that served as gathering places for the Muslim immigrants in America who carried out the first major terrorist attack on American soil, the truck bombing of the World Trade Center on February 26, 1993.

According to Abdullah Anas—and Western intelligence agencies agree with him in this—Ayman Zawahiri by the late 1980s was a commanding influence on bin Laden. And from that point on, the move to a broader definition for jihad was unstoppable, one that included the Muslim rulers of countries like Egypt and Saudi Arabia who were to be deemed infidels. Azzam himself quarreled bitterly with the Egyptians. Once, Anas said, he witnessed an argument between Azzam and Omar Abdel Rahman during one of the blind Egyptian's visits to Peshawar, during which Abdel Rahman maintained that Islamic rulers, including Mohammed Zia ul-Haq of Pakistan and Hosni Mubarak of Egypt, were infidels, because they flouted sharia, Islamic law.

By around 1986, bin Laden began to chart a course separate from Azzam's. He established his own training camp for Persian Gulf Arabs, a group of about fifty who lived in tents set apart from the other Afghan fighters. He called the camp Al Masadah—The Lion's Den. And within a little more than a year, bin Laden and the Egyptians had founded Al Qaeda—the "base" for what they hoped would be a global crusade. Azzam confided to Anas that Egyptian ideologues had wooed bin Laden away from him, gaining access to his money.

"He told me one time: 'I'm very upset about Osama. This heaven-sent man, like an angel. I am worried about his future if he stays with these people.'"

"The arguments were very secret," Anas said. "Only three to four people knew about them at the time." Azzam saw little difference between the United States and the Soviet Union, contending in his articles and speeches that both were hostile to Islam, but he nonetheless opposed terrorism against the West, according to Anas. The problem for him, especially by the late 1980s, was that the war against the Soviet Union was becoming less relevant. The United States had stepped up its aid to the Afghan guerrillas, most importantly by providing heat-seeking Stinger missiles that were soon knocking Soviet helicopter gunships out of the sky. Peshawar was still a magnet for disaffected young Muslims, and they still came to Azzam's Beit al-Ansar, but they tended to share the views of the Egyptians and very often they had, in fact, very little concern with Afghanistan.

"Ten people would open a guest house and start issuing fatwas," Anas recalled. "'We are going to make revolution in Jordan, in Egypt, in Syria.' And they haven't got any contact with the real jihad in Afghanistan."

By February 1989, the Soviets had withdrawn, leaving a puppet government in power in Kabul at the mercy of the Afghan guerrillas, who continued to fight, even as the United States lost interest in their factional quarrels. But with thousands of Arab-Afghans still in the region, the stage was set for a new kind of war. Abdullah Azzam's group was splitting up and the radical Egyptians, with bin Laden now in their camp, were in control. It was then that extraordinary developments occurred both in Peshawar and in Brooklyn, New York, events that showed how closely those two places were linked.

FIVE

Glick and Jarrah:

An Open Life and a Closed One

On the morning of September 11, 2001, Jeremy Glick made his second early trip in as many days to Newark Airport. He was supposed to have traveled to San Francisco for a business meeting the day before, on Monday, September 10, and he planned to return home on the red eye on Wednesday morning. That first morning, the Monday, figuring he would be gone for a few days, he helped pack the car for his wife, Lyzbeth, and their twelve-week-old baby girl, Emerson, who were going to spend the time of Jeremy's absence visiting Lyz's parents in Windham, New York, in the Catskill Mountains. But there was a fire at an airport construction site in Newark on September 10, and several flights, including Jeremy's, were canceled. So he went home, about an hour by car from the airport, and there he spent the last night of his life by himself, though he did speak to Lyz several times by phone. And then on Tuesday, September 11, he got up early and drove to the airport again, trying once more to make it to San Francisco—on United Airlines flight 93.

Like most of the passengers on flight 93, indeed, like most Americans, Jeremy Glick led a life striking for its openness. It's not that he had no secrets. It's a safe bet that, like the rest of us, Jeremy had a few little ones, but he lived, like most of us do, in the open. He shared his life with Lyz, his high school sweetheart, his wife, and his best friend, in a comfortable, woody house in Hewitt, New Jersey, with a view of Greenwood Lake across the road. It was the kind of house that was furnished so you could put your feet up on the furniture, with a weather-beaten gazebo up the hill in back and a dock on the lake in front where he and Lyz would lie at night and look at the stars. Jeremy was one of those naturally gregarious people who had lots of friends and admirers, as evidenced by the hundreds of letters that have poured in to Lyz since flight 93 crashed in rural Pennsylvania. There was nothing dark about Jeremy Glick. It was like his judo—he was a past national collegiate champion in the sport. You do judo with open hands, with nothing concealed, with a stress on fairness. Jeremy was what you saw, a big, six-one affable guy and a natural leader who worked hard and knew how to have a good time. There was nothing shadowy about him, nothing hidden about his agenda, no missing periods where it is impossible to know where he was or what he was doing.

And all of that is what puts him in such stark contrast with the group of dark, clandestine figures who killed him and the thirty-nine other people on flight 93 on September 11. We know so little about the four men who hijacked his plane that we can't even be sure in some instances that we know their true names, much less the content of their minds, the state of their spirits. And that seems emblematic of September 11, a reason why the event itself was so dumbfounding. We cannot comprehend the people who perpetrated the crime, even as the people it was perpetrated against seem so guileless, almost innocent of the dark forces that destroyed them.

Glick was born on September 3, 1970, in New York City, the son of a speech therapist and a technology executive. He grew up in Oradell, New Jersey, a typical upper-middle-class suburb within the greater metropolitan region of New York City, and he did the usual things of an American boyhood. He went to private schools, the Elizabeth Morrow Elementary School in Englewood, then grades seven through twelve at the Saddle River Day School. When he was in the ninth grade, his lab partner in Mrs. Treue's biology class was Lyz.

"He sported a big huge Afro back then, and I was kind of taken aback by it," she said later. "He had great, curly, gorgeous hair. Later on, when he was a judo champion, he used to tell me his strength came from his hair."

A decade and a half later, after they had been married for several years, Jeremy remembered what Lyzbeth was wearing when he first saw her that day in the biology lab, a Laura Ashley floral sundress, probably pink, Lyzbeth said.

"After the first day, he went home and told his mom that he had met the greatest girl and that he was going to marry me," she remembered. Lyz and Jeremy were a pair almost from the beginning. Lyz was a gymnast; Jeremy was an all-around athlete. They became pals, best friends, and Lyz still remembers that when Jeremy first asked her on a date, he was so shy about it he couldn't look at her. She agreed to go out with him on one condition, that whatever happened they would always be friends, and they always were.

Jeremy started judo at the age of six, when his parents had put him into a local martial arts academy, and he hated it at first—until he won his first competition when he was about seven, and then he was hooked. In high school, he played soccer and lacrosse and he wrestled. He would tell his friends that he used his big piled-up hairdo to mesmerize his opponents. He lived the life of a kind of good-time teenager in New Jersey, going to lots of parties, trying to get into clubs in New York even though he was underage, attending concerts by the Grateful Dead, breaking up with Lyzbeth and then getting back together with her. But there was always a special thoughtfulness about Jeremy, a kindness. After he died, Lyz got a letter from a man who was a classmate of his in elementary school who invited all of his classmates to go to his bar mitzvah. He wasn't a very popular boy, and none of the classmates showed up—except Jeremy. Many years later, he remembered Jeremy for that gesture.

Jeremy entered the University of Rochester in 1988, where he eventually earned a double major, in English and philosophy, but in his sophomore year, his family ran into some financial difficulties that forced him to drop out and earn some money. Ray Zaykowski, Jr., who met Jeremy when they were both freshmen in the athletes' dorm at Rochester, remembers Jeremy at the age of nineteen getting initiated into the world of real work—unloading cargo trucks at night, for example. When Jeremy had saved enough money to go back to school, he returned a more serious young man, determined to excel academically and athletically.

He did, and perhaps nothing illustrates his toughness more than judo. Busy with college and other sports, he didn't even practice judo for about six years until, in his last year in college, he took it up again. His friend Zaykowski thinks it was because, having dropped out for a while, most of his friends had already graduated and he wanted something else to do. "He did everything on his own," Zaykowski said, "trained, everything." After just a year, he turned up at the national collegiate championships in San Francisco, and he won the title. And then he was modest about it. Lyz says that there is a cabinet full of trophies that Jeremy won over the years, but he never put a trophy on display.

After Rochester, Jeremy went to work in New York, finding himself drawn naturally to the sales departments of several companies. Lyz went to Colorado to get a master's degree in anthropology, and the two of them burned up so much money on airplane tickets and long-distance phone calls that it was clear they'd go bankrupt if they stayed apart. Finally, it was Thanksgiving of 1995. "I called him up and I said, 'You're going to come out here and drive me home,' Lyz said." He did. For a while they lived in New York. They got married in Upstate New York near Lyz's parents' home in Windham. They had everything, the old stone church, the horse and buggy, the cloudless day in a season that had been rainy. They went on a honeymoon in Indonesia—Komodo Island and Bali. Jeremy went to work, ending up at Vividence, a web marketing company, and the couple lived on the Upper East Side of Manhattan. But every weekend, they found themselves leaving the city to indulge their love of the outdoor life, hiking, waterskiing, camping, and they decided they'd be happier in the country, preferably in a house on a lake. That was when they moved to their simple brown house across a small neighborhood road from Greenwood Lake.

And there they were living when Jeremy left on September 11 for a quick sales meeting in San Francisco. They had two dogs, pugs named Eloise and Maxine, and just twelve weeks before flight 93, Emerson was born—named by Jeremy, the philosophy major, after Ralph Waldo Emerson. Emerson came a month early and so she required hourly feeding, and Jeremy cheerfully took the 8 P.M. to 2 A.M. nursing shift so Lyz, who also had a job, could get some sleep. He used a little tube that was attached to a milk bottle on one end and to Jeremy's finger on the other, and Emerson got her milk by sucking on the finger.

"He just knew what to do," Lyz says. "Even if I got up at two in the morning, and Jeremy had been taking care of her all night, he'd stay up with me if she was having difficulty latching on or something. He couldn't have been more in love with her."

There is a photograph on Lyz's wall that tells it all. It shows Jeremy in a plaid shirt, tall and solidly built holding tiny Emerson in his large hands and looking slightly skyward, as if to heaven. In fact, Lyz points out, he was examining some spiderwebs in the rafters of the porch. But never mind. Jeremy had a sense of humor, and he was a man who always knew what he wanted, and he had the wisdom to appreciate his good fortune. He and Lyz were planning to raise Emerson so that she would identify with two traditions, his Jewish one and her Christian one. He had plans, for a big family, for lots of early mornings on the lake, before it got crowded. But Emerson will never know her father in person. She'll know him through the letters that people wrote to her mother after he died, letters that show how many sides there were to him and how much he was liked.

There were forty innocent, unsuspecting people on flight 93, going from Newark to San Francisco, and there is nothing secretive or clandestine about any of them. Alan Beaven, born in New Zealand, was an environmental lawyer with an office in San Francisco, a hardworking, stylistically casual, old-fashioned man who wrote his briefs in longhand and didn't carry a cell phone. John Talignani, bespectacled, tweedy, a thrice-married baseball memorabilia collector, had been a bartender in a Manhattan restaurant and could tell stories of shmoozing with the likes of Donald Trump and Dick Clarke.[1] Christine Snyder was an arborist and landscape designer whose silky blond hair fell over her shoulders. Beaven was off to San Francisco to work on a deal, and after that he was planning to move on to something else in life—going to India with his family to do volunteer work there. Snyder was going to Hawaii, where she worked and where her husband was waiting for her.

But about the hijackers and the murderers of Glick, Talignani, Snyder, Beaven, and the other passengers and crew we have some solid facts, something like a biography, though a brief one, about only one of them. And this is the presumed leader of the group, Ziad al-Jarrah. What we know about him, moreover, makes it seem as though, in very different circumstances, he would even have had a few things in common with Jeremy Glick. Like Glick, Jarrah was born into affluent circumstances,

Glick in 1970 into a middle-class family in New Jersey, Jarrah in the Bekaa Valley of eastern Lebanon in 1975. His father was a government official, his mother a schoolteacher. The two of them, Glick and Jarrah, both loved sports—swimming and basketball in Jarrah's case. Jarrah seemed a modern boy in a country, Lebanon, that was always the most secular, the most European, the most urbane, and one of the most moderate of the Arab countries, a country with a strong cosmopolitan middle class. The Jarrahs themselves were Sunni Muslims, but they believed that education was more important than religion, and they sent Ziad to a Christian school in Beirut, evidently because they wanted him to have a modern education, rather than an Islamic one. Later, when he was of an age, Jarrad drank alcohol, he had girlfriends, he did not go to the mosque. In fact he had a girlfriend right to the end, a Turkish woman he met in Germany to whom he wrote a good-bye letter on September 10.

"No one in the family has this kind of radical belief," an uncle, Jamal Jarrah, said. He meant by the phrase "this kind of radical belief" the kinds of views that suicide terrorists would have. He was expressing skepticism that his nephew was the kind of person who would have made a martyr out of himself while killing others. The Jarrah family comes across like one of those ordinary, socially conservative American families whose son or daughter has inexplicably joined the Hare Krishnas, spending their time in airport waiting rooms chanting and asking for alms, when the family's ambition inclined more toward law or medical school. Who knows what self-defeating rebellion lurks in the hearts of children?

The Jarrahs are from Al Marj in the Bekaa Valley, a lush region where most of Lebanon's fruit and vegetables are grown. One of Ziad's relatives there was a banker, another a senior customs broker. Samir, Ziad's father, had a high post in the Lebanese social security system. It is difficult to see what would have turned Ziad to extremism, though the Bekaa Valley, for all of its verdant beauty, is a stronghold of the Iran-supported, virulently anti-Western, bitterly anti-Israeli and anti-American Hezbollah, or Party of God. Perhaps he picked up some nascent fury, some political radicalism, as a result of the tumult in Lebanon that followed the Israeli invasion of the southern half of the country in 1982, an invasion that had been preceded and was followed by terrible, sanguinary conflicts among Lebanon's several ethnic and religious groups.

Still, like Mohammed Atta, Jarrah showed no inclinations early in his life of becoming a Muslim extremist. Every weekend during his high school years in Beirut, he returned home to Al-Marj to be with his cousin and best friend, Salim. When he graduated in 1995, his family allowed him to pursue what had become his dream, which was to study abroad and become an aeronautical engineer. There are some indications that he actually spent some time in the mid-1990s in the United States, driving a car for a car service company in Brooklyn, New York. A Brooklyn apartment lease bears the name Ziad Jarrah, and landlords in Brooklyn have identified him from his post–September 11 photographs, though his family says he was in Beirut at the time.

That Brooklyn lease could have belonged to another person named Ziad Jarrah, and the photo identifications could be mistaken, but there is no question that the Ziad Jarrah who turned up on flight 93 on September 11 left Lebanon to begin a student career in Germany in 1996. He went together with Salim to Greifswald, a city on the Baltic Sea near the Polish border, to add German to the French and English that were already in his store of foreign languages. He spent his first year in Europe studying German with a language teacher named Gudrun Schimpfky, who told a reporter from the *Los Angeles Times* that Jarrah was "just a lovely, kind young man."[2] It was then that he met his girlfriend, a Turkish student named Aysel Senguen. When, after a year in Greifswald, Jarrah went to Hamburg to begin studying aeronautical engineering at the University of Applied Sciences, Senguen went to the city of Bochem to study medicine.

Unlike Atta, who gave voice to his increasing radicalism, and who was cold, uncommunicative, vaguely hostile, Jarrah seems to have made friends easily and to have been liked. His landlady in Hamburg, Rosemarie Canel, doesn't remember him having a lot of visitors, and Senguen told the German police that Jarrah never talked about Atta or any of the other suspects in the September 11 attacks. His family members, including Salim, now a successful businessman in Greifswald, agree that he was on flight 93, but they deny that he could have been one of the hijackers. In their opinion, he was just another passenger, a victim like the other passengers and crew.[3]

The FBI on the other hand identified Jarrah not only as one of the four hijackers but as the hijacker-pilot of flight 93, and the evidence is convincing on this. Jarrah took flight training in the same town in Florida as Mohammed Atta and Mahmud al-Shehhi, another of the presumed hijacker-pilots. He rented an apartment in Florida together with a Saudi who seems to fit the terror profile perfectly and is believed by the FBI to be another of the hijackers. Like the other suspected hijackers, he took rigorous fitness training in Florida in the months prior to September 11. In Jarrah's case, the fitness training included lessons in street fighting. In addition, while he was still in Germany, he behaved oddly at times. There are periods of time that are not accounted for when, possibly, he was off in Afghanistan getting Al Qaeda training, though this is unproven. It could perhaps be chalked up to coincidence that he lived in Hamburg, Germany, at the same time that Atta and al-Shehhi were living there. It might, at a stretch, even be seen as coincidence that he then turned up in the same city as Atta and al-Shehhi in Florida and that all three of them took flight training. But it's hard to believe that he just happened by coincidence to be on a plane that was hijacked on the very day that Atta and al-Shehhi were hijacking other planes.

So, yes, despite the absence of proof and despite his family's certainty of his innocence, Jarrah was one of the hijackers of flight 93. And while we don't know why exactly, we can be pretty certain that sometime between growing up in the Bekaa Valley in the 1970s and 1980s, the years the international jihad movement was being built in Pakistan and Afghanistan, Jarrah became a dedicated and obedient terrorist.

Less is known of the other three hijackers of United flight 93 and what they were doing in the years prior to the planning and preparation of the attack. The FBI lists them as Ahmed Alhaznawi, twenty, Ahmed Alnami, twenty-four, and Saeed Alghamdi, twenty-five, and all of them are Saudis—or, as the FBI puts it in the case of Alghamdi, he "seems to be Saudi." According to the Saudi newspaper *Al-Watan*, Alhaznawi and Alnami came from impoverished regions in the southwest of Saudi Arabia, the provinces of Asir and Baha near the border with Yemen. These have always been regions of religious dissent and extremism. Many of the schoolteachers of Asir and Baha are Egyptian members of the Egyptian Islamic Jihad, Ayman Zawahiri's organization.[4]

Alnami's father, interviewed in the Saudi press, said that his son left for a pilgrimage to Mecca a year and a half before September 11, and never came back. For the four months prior to the September 11 attack, they had even lost telephone contact with him. Alhaznawi is from Baljurshi, the capital of Baha Province, where his father is a prayer leader. As for Alghamdi, so little is known about him that the FBI lists eleven aliases and four different dates of birth for him, ranging from November 5, 1960, to November 21, 1979, which would seem to make the age listed in the FBI information very uncertain.

The three hijackers in this sense can be understood not as individuals but as representatives of a clear pattern to the September 11 attacks. Three of the presumed leaders of the attacks—Atta, al-Shehhi, and Jarrah—were, respectively, from Egypt, the United Arab Emirates, and Lebanon. The presumed leader of the fourth hijacking, Khalid al-Midhar, is of unknown nationality. But all of the lower-ranking figures in the attacks, those who arrived in the United States late in the plot and who served as its infantrymen, its foot soldiers, were young men from Saudi Arabia. How the first group got into contact with the second group remains unknown. There is simply no record, for example, of Jarrah contacting Alhaznawi, Alnami, and Alghamdi, who were his fellow hijackers of flight 93, or arranging their travel to the United States. The best conjecture is that Osama bin Laden and Al Qaeda chose some recruits they had in their training camps in Afghanistan and sent them to the hijack leaders who needed manpower, and this conjecture gains credibility because 1) there was no shortage of such recruits and 2) videotape of one of them, Ahmed Alhaznawi, announcing his martyrdom, was later found in Afghanistan by American troops. Still, to repeat, this is informed supposition. Except for Alhaznawi, there is no proof at all that any of the other Saudis involved in September 11 ever set foot in Afghanistan. They probably did. Certainly they fit the profile of other young Saudis who did. But we can't be sure.

What can be known with greater certainty is this: whoever the foot soldiers were and however they were recruited, trained, and assigned to their tasks in the September 11 plot, they were all Saudis, and that in turn suggests a political phenomenon of global import. Saudi Arabia, despite its enormous wealth in oil, its extensive welfare system, and the pro-Western position of its government, has furnished a large share of the young men drawn to the calls of Abdullah Azzam and Osama bin Laden, young men eager to do jihad, even to give their lives for it. Saudi intelligence estimates that as many as twenty-five thousand Saudis received training abroad since 1979. Saudis have been involved in many of the major terror attacks against the United States since 1996, in Saudi Arabia itself, in Kenya, Tanzania, and Yemen. The belief of many American officials is that Saudi Arabia actually encouraged its disaffected young men to join the jihadists abroad as a way of deflecting attention away from the problems of corruption, dictatorship, nepotism, and poverty inside the country. Or, as Martin Indyk, an assistant secretary of state for Middle East policy during the Clinton administration, said, "The Saudi policies made the world safer for Saudi Arabia and the Saudi regime."

But there is something beyond expediency in the Saudi role. That Saudi Arabia was the largest pool from which bin Laden's foot soldiers were chosen reflects not only that the Saudi government welcomed an outlet for discontent that might otherwise have been directed inward; it also reflects Saudi Arabia's own long tradition of Islamic strictness. It is not just that Saudi Arabia is the birthplace of Islam itself, but also that it has been the center of Islamic revivalism of a sort that is entirely compatible with the Islam of the international jihad. Saudi Arabia is a country where sharia has been applied for years, where thieves' hands are cut off, where adulterers are stoned, and where the practice of any other religion is a crime punishable by death. It is the birthplace of a brand of strict Islam, known as Wahhabism, after a Saudi reformer named Mohamed Ibn abd al-Wahhab who in the nineteenth century became religious adviser to the House of Saud, the tribe that put most of the Arabian peninsula under its control.

Wahhab, in turn, was inspired by a much earlier fundamentalist figure, Ibn Taymiyya, who lived in what is now Syria in the fourteenth century when the homelands of the Middle East were threatened by the Mongol invasions. Ibn Taymiyya called on Muslims to reject the rule of the Mongols even though they too were Muslims; his argument was that the Mongols had devised their own system of rule and did not observe sharia, Islamic law. Ibn Taymiyya called for a return to the pure, unsullied, uncontaminated roots of Islam, as formulated by the Prophet and other eighth-century forefathers as the basis of an authentic Muslim revival, and among his most important principles was a strict, unyielding application of the law. "Every governor," he declared in his best-known book,

The Book on the Government of the Religious Law, "must be inexorable in the application of the Legal Penalties and inaccessible to pity, because religion is at stake."[5]

Other, more recent Islamic revivalists were also inspired by these ideas, among them the Egyptian schoolteacher Hassan al-Banna who founded the Islamic Brotherhood in 1928, and Sayyid Qutb, the later Islamic Brotherhood leader who was executed by the Egyptian president Gamel Abdel Nasser in 1966. Among the elements that Qutb added to fundamentalism was its powerfully anti-foreign and especially anti-Western flavor. In this sense, much of the fundamentalist movement in the Middle East has been a reaction against the perceived humiliation of a once supremely great civilization fallen prey to the imperial power of outsiders—first the Ottoman Turks, then British and French colonialism, then the Zionists and American armed forces.

"The emergence of the construct we call Islamic extremism, with its penchant for defiance, resentment, and violence, has its roots in the history of the Muslim sense of decline and its unhappy encounter with the dominant West," Abbas Amanat, the chairman of the Council on Middle East Studies at Yale University, has written.[6]

Certainly, the Islam of Osama bin Laden, Ayman Zawahiri, and the other leaders of Al Qaeda is derived from that of Ibn Taymiyya and Wahhab, al-Banna, and Qutb, not only in its emphasis on the duty to kill the enemies of Islam wherever they can be found, but to kill Muslim rulers who do not rule in accordance with sharia. Indeed, there is testimony showing that the example of Taymiyya was very much in the minds of Al Qaeda's leaders as they planned their campaign against the United States. The Al Qaeda defector Al-Fadl remembered one instance in the Sudan when bin Laden and some of his followers were having a discussion on the question of civilian casualties during war, specifically whether is was permitted under Islamic law to carry out an operation if innocent bystanders would be killed. One of the men, known as Abu Hajer al-Iraqi, brought up Taymiyya, al-Fadl said, summarizing al-Iraqi's view of him this way:

"He said anybody around the tartar, he buy something from them and he sell them something, you should kill him. And also, if when you attack the tartar, if anybody around them, anything, or he's not military or that—if you kill him, you don't have to worry about that. If he's a good person, he go to paradise, and if he's a bad person he go to hell."[7]

These ideas, which even rationalize the killing of bystanders, are what the Islamic scholar Fouad Ajami calls a new force in the Muslim world. "It's called *takfir*, which comes from the word *kaffir*, an unbeliever," he said. "It's the idea that you can declare somebody an apostate. This was something new. Generations of Muslims in the late nineteenth and early twentieth centuries never heard of a *takfir* where you get up in the morning and declare somebody your religious enemy. But it's an idea that began to infect political life. It's the idea that killed Sadat."

"This is how the great jurists were outflanked and discarded," Ajami contended. "The new radicals said, 'We have access to the scripture and we don't need the great jurists who, in any case, are hired guns.' These new activists said, 'Not only are the rulers impious and unbelievers, but so are the jurists.' They took Islam to these new mosques that arose everywhere. The religion became portable and the insurgents hijacked it and took it where they wanted to go."

There were many among these "hijackers" of Islam. Among them, for example, were the founders of the Islamic religious schools, or *madrasahs*, set up in the border regions of Pakistan courtesy of donations from wealthy Saudi Arabians. Established in accordance with the strict doctrines of Wahhabism, they catered both to Pakistanis and to the sons of the hundreds of thousands of Afghan refugees who had become semipermanent residents of Pakistan, living in tent cities and shantytowns on the outskirts of Peshawar. The *madrasahs* became gathering points for poor boys with not much in the way of prospects elsewhere. They were taken care of in the school, fed and clothed and educated. They sat on the floor at low tables, looking like dutiful students elsewhere. They memorized the Koran and they were instructed to hate the enemies of Islam and to love jihad. They were *taliban*, which means "student" in Pashtun, the dominant language of northwest Pakistan and southeast Afghanistan, and eventually they would serve as foot soldiers in the Taliban movement that would take over most of Afghanistan in 1996.

Among the other "hijackers" of Islam were the radicals who grouped themselves first around Abdullah Azzam in Peshawar and, after his assassination, Osama bin Laden. With the defeat of the Soviet Union, bin

Laden was soon to want to seize on opportunities to expand his operations to the enemies of Islam elsewhere, and to build an international organization on the foundation laid by Abdullah Azzam. His pool of recruits came initially from the thousands of Arab-Afghans who had gotten at least some basic military training in Afghanistan during the course of the anti-Soviet war.

In Jordan some of these former Arab-Afghans founded a group, Jaish Muhammad, that officials say took aim at King Hussein, whose family claims descent from the Prophet Muhammed. In Algeria, they were among the founders of the Armed Islamic Group, the most radical to emerge after the military government canceled elections there in 1991, fearful that the Islamic parties would win and take power. Known by its French initials, GIA, it began by blowing up military targets and escalating to wholesale massacres of Algerians who did not believe in the jihad. Eventually—though, it seems, possibly not until well into the 1990s—there were cells in Europe, in England, Belgium, Spain, and, most important, Germany, where students from the Middle East like Mohammed Atta mingled with Islamic militants and radical preachers in the mosques and in their bare apartments, plotting to do glorious deeds for Allah.

And then there were those, like Mahmud Abuhalima and el-Sayyid Nosair, who went to the United States, where they mingled with other Arab immigrants at the Al Kifah centers in New York and Texas. They prayed at mosques in Brooklyn and Jersey City, New Jersey, where Sheik Omar Abdel Rahman preached, and some of them began to make plans to attack the country they saw as the root source of evil in the world, the pillar of support for the corrupt, reactionary, un-Islamic regimes they hated back home.

And finally, though we don't know details of their lives, there were men like Ahmed Alnami, Ahmed Alhaznawi, and Saeed Alghamdi, who emerged from the Saudi religious netherworld to wreak havoc in the United States on September 11. We don't know exactly what any of them were doing in the 1980s, but it seems very possible that when Jeremy Glick was becoming a judo master in faraway America, they were being schooled in the hatreds that would lead them to be on the same airplane as Jeremy Glick and the other passengers on flight 93 and to cause them to die.

SIX

Terrorism Arrives in America

On July 2, 1989, FBI agent James P. Fogle watched as several men emerged from the Al Farooq Mosque on Atlantic Avenue in Brooklyn carrying boxes and other objects draped in cloth. Fogle, who was part of a team staking out the mosque, watched as the men loaded their baggage into vans and cars parked nearby. Then he and his fellow agents followed the men all the way to the Calverton Shooting Range near Riverhead on eastern Long Island, about ninety miles from Brooklyn.

There, as the FBI looked on, the men took target practice with AK-47 assault rifles and nine-millimeter semiautomatic pistols. After a while, one of the men casually fired his AK-47 into the ground a few feet ahead of him. Fogle watched as another member of the group disciplined the shooter.

"He came over, grabbed the weapon and like slapped the person for, you know, carelessness," Fogel said later.

The man who slapped the careless shooter was Mahmud Abuhalima, back from Afghanistan and now, it would seem, helping to provide training in weapons and ammunition to men grouped around Mustafa Shalabi's Al Kifah organization in Brooklyn. Also present at the Calverton Shooting Range that July day were Mohammed A. Salameh and Nidal A. Ayyad, two other Arab immigrants who frequented Al Kifah. And then there was the former Egyptian el-Sayyid Nosair, who put his training to

59

use by assassinating Rabbi Meier Kahane, leader of the Jewish Defense League, the following year.

Four years later, on February 26, 1993, Abuhalima, Ayyad, and Salameh, carrying out a plan inspired by Nosair, were among the men who set off the huge truck bomb in the basement of the World Trade Center that unmistakably introduced foreign terrorism to the United States. Given that, it does seem as though that trip to the shooting range in Calverton by members of the Al Kifah circle was the first step in Islamic militancy's long American journey, which culminated in the hijackings and mass killings of September 11. There were to be many turnings along that road and certainly many changes of personnel. The people who grouped themselves around Al Kifah in Brooklyn in the late 1980s made up an entirely separate group from the one that carried out the hijackings out of Boston, Newark, and Washington airports twelve years later. And yet there is a consistency of purpose and a sort of inter-locking network of individuals and groups that tie September 11 with that morning in 1989 when the FBI watched Abuhalima and company shoot their AK-47s on eastern Long Island.

For a reason that has never been explained publicly, the FBI, though aware that the Al Kifah Center in Brooklyn was a recruitment ground for the anti-Soviet war in Afghanistan, did not sustain its surveillance of the group from the Al Farooq Mosque, and this was the first of many intelli-gence failures committed over the years. Indeed, though the failure in this first instance was an understandable one, it would be followed by many other failures, not so minor or understandable, as elements of a foreign army planted themselves on American soil with the intention of doing the country harm. Indeed, for the next twelve years, as we will see, there were many occasions when American intelligence and law enforcement seemed almost to hover over plots directed against the United States and yet was unable to prevent them. Dangerous people, like Abdel Rahman— on a State Department terrorist watch list as of 1987—were not only allowed unimpeded entry into the United States, they were granted visas by the very State Department that had listed them as terrorists. In 1991, though his visa had been revoked by the State Department the year before, Abdel Rahman not only lived openly in Brooklyn and New Jersey, but was also granted permanent residency status by the Immigration and

Naturalization Service.[1] American intelligence knew from Egyptian officials exactly who Abdel Rahman was, especially his presumed role in the Sadat assassination, and for the better part of a year, the FBI used an Egyptian-American informant named Emad Salem to penetrate the circle around Abdel Rahman and the Al Farooq Mosque.

Still, Salem was dismissed in 1992, and the FBI did not learn about the plot to bomb the World Trade Center until every other American learned about it—the day in 1993 when the bomb went off. Before that, American intelligence was also unaware of two important related developments. One of them was the simple fact that as of late 1990, a core of Islamic militants grouped around Omar Abdel Rahman already saw the United States as its primary terrorist target. When, for example, el-Sayyid Nosair assassinated Rabbi Kahane in 1990, the police and FBI did not examine a cache of documents found in the basement of his home. If it had, it would have learned that the same men who wanted Kahane dead were already entertaining grand ambitions for spectacular attacks on the United States itself.

The second development involves the key link between past and present, between the Calverton Shooting Range in 1989 and the four hijackings of September 11. It was that in faraway Peshawar, Pakistan, the organization that Abdullah Azzam had founded to fight the Russians in Afghanistan—and that was therefore at least a tactical American ally— was being taken over by a new, more radical Islamic group that would be unremittingly and violently hostile to the United States. Essentially, Azzam's Office of Services was being transformed into Osama bin Laden's Al Qaeda. The first major act in that transformation took place on a Friday in November 1989, when Azzam himself was assassinated.

This important event took place along a narrow road in Peshawar that Azzam, accompanied by two of his sons and one other person, took to the mosque he attended for the Muslim Friday prayer service. When Azzam got out of his car, planning to walk the remaining distance to the mosque, a bomb planted along the road went off, creating an explosion loud enough to be heard throughout Peshawar and strong enough almost to vaporize the car. Azzam and both of his sons were killed.

The killer of Abdullah Azzam, the inspirational creator of the armed Muslim International, has never been determined, though many possibilities present themselves. The bombing itself was a sophisticated operation, involving careful timing and a good deal of bomb-making expertise. But bomb-making was one of the skills taught in Azzam's own training camps; more generally, it was a skill that many people possessed in Afghanistan and Pakistan during the anti-Soviet war. Nobody was ever arrested or put on trial for the assassination, no group claimed responsibility for it, and the list of Azzam's possible enemies is not a short one. They include, most obviously, the Afghan secret police, loyal to the government in Kabul maintained by Soviet power. But Azzam had foes within the anti-Soviet opposition as well. He was said to be close to the Tajik military commander Ahmed Shah Massoud, the most famous of the anti-Soviet commanders, and may have been providing him with money. Therefore, it is possible that he was wanted dead by one of Massoud's rivals—perhaps Gulbuddin Hekmatyar, the rabidly anti-Western commander of one of the anti-Soviet guerrilla groups fighting in the Kabul area. It was Hekmatyar, it should be noted, who accompanied Sheik Omar Abdel Rahman on his visit to the Afghan battlefield in 1985.[2]

It is also possible that Azzam was killed by one of the Arab factions that he himself had attracted to Peshawar to do jihad, perhaps the Egyptians with whom he was quarreling. (And the Egyptians are said to have been close to Hekmatyar precisely because of his anti-Western feelings.) Or perhaps Azzam was killed in some factional or personal quarrel too obscure for outsiders to fathom. In any case, his death left a vacuum in the Office of Services, a vacuum that was filled by Osama bin Laden and his new Egyptian allies.

One of the most intriguing and suggestive aspects of the assassination of Azzam, moreover, was its similarity with another assassination a bit more than a year later in Brooklyn at the Al Kifah office itself, which Azzam had set up under Mustafa Shalabi. Al Kifah, located along a stretch of Atlantic Avenue between Third and Fourth Avenues, was in the midst of a neighborhood of restaurants, groceries, bookstores, and mosques where many Arab immigrants first went when they came to the United States. Shalabi's office was a few doors away from the Al Farooq Mosque, where several thousand Muslim faithful congregated during Friday prayers.

He probably recruited about two hundred young Arab immigrants to go to Peshawar. They paid their own airfare, about $500 to $600 for tickets—one way. Once they arrived in Peshawar, they contacted Azzam's Office of Services, which found them a place to stay and arranged for them to get military training in Afghanistan itself.

In 1990, when Omar Abdel Rahman escaped from house arrest in Egypt and arrived in New York (having been given a multiple-entry visa in Khartoum and having not been stopped at immigration control), he received a hero's welcome on Atlantic Avenue. Shalabi went to Kennedy International Airport to greet him, and he assigned Mahmud Abuhalima to be his part-time driver. For a while, Shalabi and Abdel Rahman ran the recruiting center together. And then things soured. There were quarrels over money and power.

"At stake in the battle over the Al Kifah was a transnational Islamic militant power base—the de facto control over hundreds of thousands of dollars and a network of thousands of jihad veterans and future jihad volunteers," Steven Emerson has written. "Shalabi wanted to plow the money back into the Afghanistan effort, while Sheik Abdul Rahman wanted to expend the funds on jihad in Egypt and new jihad fronts around the globe."[3]

By early 1990, just a couple of months after Azzam's assassination, Shalabi was receiving threats from Abdel Rahman's followers who accused him of having pilfered some $2 million from Al Kifah's treasury. Shalabi himself made plans to leave New York and go to Pakistan where he apparently felt he would receive protection at the Office of Services under Azzam's successor. But on February 26, 1991, Shalabi, according to the police, opened his door to somebody he knew. He was shot once in the head and stabbed several times. His body was found in the apartment several days later.

The Shalabi murder, like the Azzam assassination, was never solved. At the time, suspicion fell on several men, including both Abdel Rahman and Abuhalima, both of whom denied responsibility for the murder. In any case, nobody was arrested and nobody claimed credit. But, also like the Azzam murder, the elimination of Shalabi left the radical Egyptian faction, headed in the United States by Abdel Rahman, in sole charge of the recruitment office and its money.

Several meanings can be drawn, retroactively, from the history of Al Kifah. For one, the United States, like Jordan and Algeria, Egypt and Saudi Arabia, was also a place where the Arab-Afghans were being dispatched in what was to become an organized campaign of terror. Mahmud Abuhalima, the Egyptian who had fought in Afghanistan, is a perfect illustration of that, a militant Arab immigrant who received training in Afghanistan and then turned toward a new jihadist purpose in the United States. Second, Abdel Rahman's presence in the United States meant that there would be close links between the Arab-Afghans in the United States and radical Muslims in Pakistan, still the headquarters of the Muslim International.

It is not clear exactly when the Arab-Afghans in the United States transformed themselves into an active terrorist cell. We know from later investigations that the first major action of the Brooklyn group, the 1993 bombing of the World Trade Center, was being discussed by el-Sayyid Nosair as early as 1991 or early 1992. But we also know that no concrete steps were taken toward an attack on Americans in America until one of the key and still most mysterious figures involved in the history of global Muslim terrorism arrived in the United States, bringing with him the technical know-how and the organizational ability to get the job done. This person, who had several identities, is generally known as Ramzi Ahmed Yousef, and he arrived in New York two years after Abdel Rahman, on September 1, 1992, on a flight from Peshawar, Pakistan. But no sooner did Yousef arrive than the Al Kifah group—and especially Salameh, Ayyad, and Abuhalima—were enlisted in a plot to carry out the worst foreign terrorist attack to take place in the United States in the years leading up to September 11.

Exactly who Yousef is, where he was born, what the details are of his biography, have never really become clear, even now several years after he was arrested and jailed in the United States. Lengthy biographical sketches have been written about him, stating that he had a Palestinian mother and a Pakistani father and that he studied engineering at Swansea University in Wales. But are these details true? Some of them are true of a man named Abdul Basit, a Kuwaiti whose passport was one of those that

Yousef used, and some have concluded that Abdul Basit and Ramzi Yousef were the same person. But the terrorism expert Laurie Mylroie has demonstrated almost beyond any doubt that that conclusion is incorrect. She believes—and she is supported in this conclusion by experts in the FBI and the CIA—that Abdul Basit's passport was stolen, most likely by Iraqi intelligence during the brief Iraqi occupation of Kuwait in 1990 and 1991, and used to provide Yousef with a false identity.[4] Was he an Islamic fundamentalist? Again there is no decisive evidence on that question one way or the other, though there are certainly indications that he himself was not deeply religious. Many students of terrorism, most notably Mylroie, believe that he was in the tradition of secular extremists—like the Palestinian terrorist Abu Nidal, or like Iraqi president Saddam Hussein—and not in that of religious extremists like Zawahiri and bin Laden.

Yousef arrived in the United States on a flight from Pakistan in September 1992. He carried an Iraqi passport. He had no visa. He applied for political asylum, claiming that he had run afoul of the Iraqi secret police in connection with Iraq's invasion of Kuwait in 1991 and was threatened with torture and persecution if forced to return to his native country. Martha Morales was the immigration inspector who interviewed Yousef. She noted that he was oddly dressed, in what she later called a colorful Middle East costume made out of silk, with "puffed sleeves" and "harem pants." But Morales was suspicious of him not because of his costume but because Yousef had identification papers in his baggage with two names other than his own. She recommended that he be refused asylum status and advised the Immigration and Naturalization Service to take Yousef into custody. But INS officials ignored her advice and released Yousef on his own recognizance. He vowed to return for a hearing on his political asylum request. Needless to say, he didn't. Allowing Yousef into the country and failing to keep tabs on him was another, and this time very costly, failure to be vigilant against the terrorist threat.

Once in the country, Yousef made contact with Salameh, Ayyad, and Abuhalima, all of whom lived in New Jersey. Together they, and a fifth man, Abdul Rahman Yasin, who is almost certainly now living in Iraq, made a 1,200-to 1,500-pound urea-nitrate bomb in a house in New Jersey. They rented a van from a Ryder Rental Agency in Jersey City, loaded the homemade explosive device onto it, and, early in the morning of February 26, drove it through the Holland Tunnel into Manhattan. They drove the van down the ramp leading from West Street into the basement of the World Trade Center and parked it in the subterranean garage about eight feet from the south wall of the north tower, near a support column known as K31/8. At 12:18 P.M., the bomb went off. Six people were killed, a thousand were injured. Approximately fifty thousand people—unwittingly rehearsing what would happen on September 11 eight years later—were evacuated via the three sets of emergency stairs in each tower.

The blast blew an immense hole in the underground portions of the Trade Center five stories deep and 180 feet in diameter. Certainly it shocked New York and the United States, which experienced Middle East–type violence for the first time. But judging from the placement of the bomb, the terrorists' goal had been to destroy the Trade Center altogether by toppling the north tower onto the south tower, killing many thousands in the process. So, from their standpoint, the mission had been a failure—or, at best, a limited success. From the American point of view, of course, the terrorists had succeeded all too well. From the moment that first World Trade Center bomb went off, it was clear that the country faced a new and potent danger, though a danger from exactly what and exactly whom wasn't clear. The determination of ultimate responsibility for the 1993 attack—who ordered it, who paid for it, who sponsored it—has never been made. Was Ramzi Yousef a creature of Osama bin Laden and the newly emergent Islamic International based in Peshawar? Or was he an independent operator taking orders from somebody else who used the Al-Kifah men for the simple reason that they were there and they shared his objectives?

Many writers on this subject have made a direct connection between Yousef and bin Laden, in particular by citing reports that Yousef lived in a safe house financed by bin Laden in Peshawar. But though these reports have been widely repeated in the press, the original source of them is buried in fog and they have never been verified. Indeed, some reports have it that Yousef lived in a bin Laden guest house in Peshawar, others that he was living in a bin Laden guest house in Islamabad, the capital of Pakistan, where he was captured two years after the 1993 bombing. Clearly, Yousef was a well-traveled international terrorist with money to spend and big plans to spend it on. He arrived in New York from Peshawar in

1992, and Peshawar was still probably the global center of armed Muslim extremism—though by then bin Laden himself had left Pakistan and was living in Sudan. Most probably, Yousef's main employer was Iraqi intelligence, but he knew that there was a rich source of money and manpower inside the Muslim movement revitalized and radicalized in Peshawar and Afghanistan, and he went there to gain support for his plans.

There are in this sense parallels also between Yousef and Mohammed Atta, the young middle-class Egyptian and Al Qaeda operative who arrived in the United States in 2001 and succeeded where Yousef had failed—in bringing down that greatest symbol of American commercial power, the World Trade Center. Both men became part of the jihadist army abroad; both came to the United States to carry out a terrorist mission. Both had money; both traveled a good deal, speaking foreign languages, able to cross borders with ease; both got funds to cover their expenses from some master terrorist or terrorists outside the country. There is no clear evidence that either of them ever had direct contact with bin Laden, though, in Atta's case, bin Laden certainly gave both critical support and sanction for his actions.

There are important and obvious differences between Atta and Yousef as well. Atta was a suicide bomber and Yousef was not, and that is a very big difference, because it suggests that one was a deeply religious Muslim seeking eternal reward for slaying the enemies of Allah, while the other had secular political objectives. Indeed, while Atta came to the United States to die, Yousef came to carry out a mission and then to escape so that he could move on to other endeavors. Yousef and bin Laden certainly shared a hatred of the United States and a desire to harm it. Yousef, however, does not fit the profile of an Al Qaeda operative even if he used elements of the Muslim International spawned by Abdullah Azzam and taken over by Osama bin Laden to achieve his purpose.

Yousef himself later told FBI agents that he had watched the World Trade Center bomb go off from a vantage point across the Hudson River in New Jersey, and then he got on a plane to Pakistan using the Kuwaiti passport of Abdul Basit and disappeared, for a while. He left behind the other members of the terror team—except for Yasin, who left before the explosion and went to Iraq—and they were quickly arrested. At some point after that, probably in 1994, Yousef went to Bangkok, and by

December of that year, he was in Manila, the Philippines, where there is no doubt about his activities. Using the alias Haddad, he rented an apartment—for $478 a month—and, with a friend named Ahmed, began planning a new terrorist assault—placing bombs on about a dozen American airlines going from Asia to the United States, so that all of the planes would blow up in midair on the same day.

But while the operation was still being planned, some chemicals that Yousef or Ahmed were mixing in their Manila apartment caught fire. When neighbors investigated, Yousef and Ahmed tried to reassure them that it was nothing—just firecrackers they were preparing for a delayed New Year's celebration that had accidentally ignited. But a security guard at the building insisted on calling the police and fire department. Yousef and Ahmed decamped, never to return. The police conducted a search of the apartment and found many interesting things—chemicals and other bomb-making supplies, like wires, timing devices, and a soldering gun. They also found a computer and computer disks on which Yousef had indicated plans to kill the pope—due in Manila a few days later—and to put bombs on those twelve or so American airlines. His pool of recruits this time was the so-called Abu Sayyef group, an Islamic terrorist gang in Mindanao Province of the Philippines where a violent Muslim independence movement has simmered for decades.

There are some stronger signs at this point in his career that Yousef did have a connection with Osama bin Laden. American investigators have said that notes for a plan to attack the American Central Intelligence Agency in Langley, Virginia, were on the computer Yousef left behind in Manila. The plan was to hijack a plane and crash it into the CIA's building, a possible foreshadowing of the September 11 plot. Second, investigators believe that one of the financial backers of Yousef when he was in the Philippines was Mohammed Khalifa, a brother-in-law of bin Laden.

In any case, Yousef, understanding that the jig was up, made his way back to Pakistan. The United States announced a $2 million reward for information leading to his capture, and the next month, his whereabouts were disclosed by two South African Muslims who were living in the Su Casa rooming house in Islamabad across the hall from Yousef.

The South Africans called the American embassy, which, acting quickly, contacted the Pakistani authorities, and law enforcement agents of the two countries grabbed Yousef. He was flown to the United States and convicted in two separate trials—one for masterminding the World Trade Center attack, the other for attempting to blow up airliners from his base in the Philippines. He was sentenced to life in prison in both cases and he is now serving his term at a maximum-security federal prison in Colorado. The South African informants were flown to the United States and entered into the witness protection program.

If bin Laden did not directly sponsor Yousef and the 1993 Trade Center attack, clearly he picked up the relay after Yousef's failures. As one terrorism expert, Rohan Gunaratna, has written, "Osama operationalized Yousef's plan." Moreover, for the next several years, a certain coming-and-going indicates an ongoing cross-fertilization between the former members of Al Kifah and Osama bin Laden. As we will see later, at least two men with close ties to Al Kifah later turned up as important operatives in Al Qaeda. Certainly, by the time of the 1993 attack, bin Laden was well advanced in what had become his ambition. It was to create a kind of Terrorist Inc., an organization fed by donations and profits from business that would redirect the Holy War away from Afghanistan and toward the "infidel" Arab regimes and their American backers.

SEVEN

Harry Ramos and Victor Wald:
The Courage of Strangers

For the most part, the victims of September 11 didn't know each other, though they passed each other in the lobby, or sat next to each other on the plaza outside at lunchtime in nice weather, or they rode the elevators together and then went into different offices. And then when their places of work were hit by terrorist-commandeered planes, they helped each other, and they died together, and in a few cases it turned out that they sacrificed themselves for each other. Such was the case with Harry Ramos and Victor Wald, two men in the New York financial world who couldn't have been more different—and, in a way, couldn't have been more alike.

Wald was an Orthodox Jew, born in 1952, who spent just about his entire life within a twenty-block radius of the Upper West Side of Manhattan. He was a serious man, not the kind of man to go out drinking with colleagues, heavyset and bearded, so impassioned about what he regarded as the hostility of the world to Jews that he was once—though no longer—an active supporter of the extremist, anti-Arab leader of the Jewish Defense League, Meier Kahane.

Ramos, of Puerto Rican ancestry, was exactly the kind of man who did like to go drinking with the guys. Where Wald was overweight and serious, Ramos was slim, a natty dresser, and a natural comedian. His brother Henry says that Harry was so naturally gregarious and entertaining that his bosses and customers used to pay his way to Las Vegas just to have his company. He even got a ringside seat at a Mike Tyson heavy-weight championship match that way. "He loved schmoozing," Henry said. "And he was good at it. He loved his job."

In fact, there was a kind of sociological similarity between Victor Wald and Harry Ramos, an up-from-modest beginnings ambitiousness about them that landed them both high in the sky in offices in the south tower. Victor, born in Manhattan, had parents who were Jewish refugees from Germany and Austria; Harry, born in Brooklyn, had parents who immigrated from Puerto Rico. They both worked hard; they were family men, with two children each—two daughters for Victor, two sons for Harry. One of Harry's daughters and one of Victor's sons had the same name, Alex. Both Harry and Victor represented the Great American Mobility Machine, and the basic indifference of that machine—especially in the world of finance—to such matters as national origin or religious belief. They were individuals, in I. B. Singer's sense of the word, not blended into any homogeneous mix.

There was an outsized quality to Wald, an intensity to him something close to voraciousness in the variety and quality of his many interests. His life fits a certain American archetype, like a character from a novel by Chaim Potok, the boy from a strictly Orthodox background who rebels against that strictness as a man even while remaining powerfully attached to the Orthodox traditions. He and his family were the kinds of Jews who strictly observed the daylong fast on Yom Kippur, the Day of Atonement, and then would break the fast by ordering in from unkosher Hunan Balcony or Empire Szechuan. The apartment he shared with his wife, Rebecca, and their two daughters was full of religious articles—mezuzahs hung in the doorway to each room; twenty menorahs gleamed from display cabi-nets alongside translucent glass vases bought in Jerusalem, and illumi-nated Torah manuscripts lined the walls of the hallway. But there was also a vast music collection, as weighted toward Bob Marley, the Who, Edith Piaf, and Harry Chapin as to Puccini and Debussy. Victor was an avid and serious stamp collector, and the bookshelves of the apartment were also crammed with binders whose spines bore such exotic name places as the Marshall Islands, San Marino, and Slovenia—some fifty volumes in all as of September 11, 2001, though from time to time he had sold previous col-lections in order to raise money for new ones. In the last months of his life he had developed an interest in feng-shui, which added to an interest in kabbalah, Jewish mystical interpretations of the holy scripts.

And so, Victor was passionate and large and full of benign contradictions. Even though he had more than a passing flirtation with the extreme anti-Arab Judaism of Meier Kahane, he was a great reader of American history, and, along with the binders full of stamps, the bookshelves contained a large library of biographies of the great statesmen and presidents as well as many works on the Civil War. Victor had taken trips to several of the battlefields—Antietam, Fredericksburg, and Gettysburg. This sort of cultural and spiritual eclecticism was evident from an early age. Once as a youth he spent a week at a kibbutz in Israel where his job was feeding the turkeys. His supervisor told him to play classical music to soothe the birds, but Victor rebelliously played Led Zepellin instead, and he was not invited to return to that kibbutz.

Victor went from second through twelfth grades to the Jewish Ramaz Schools across Central Park. He played soccer after school in the park, did Jewish studies at City College as an undergraduate, and then got a master's degree in both foreign affairs and business administration from Columbia University.

He was a smart and curious boy, immersed even then in history, already a Civil War buff, and yet he was a mediocre student because he simply didn't pay very close attention to his studies. And then there was his attraction to Meier Kahane, who was rejected by most of the Jewish establishment, including most Orthodox rabbis, but Wald attended several demonstrations in his favor, even getting into fistfights with Arab counter-demonstrators on one or two occasions. But, Rebecca said, he mellowed by the time he finished graduate school and went to such demonstrations no more. Along with his stamps, he collected coins and baseball cards as well, all with a connoisseur's eye for detail and a childlike pride in his collections. He was sickly at times, especially as a child when he once spent six months in bed with rheumatic fever, and as an adult he sometimes wheezed with asthma. In his middle age he was a stout 250 pounds. But when he was in school, he showed a certain muscularity. He even worked as a service processor during school breaks, delivering summonses and subpoenas to people who often didn't want to get them. With the money he earned in one month he could fly to Europe and Israel for the remainder of the summer.

As he got a bit older, and especially after he graduated from business school, he became more interested in worldly success than in rabble rousing—though he did keep to his strong opinions on the Middle East and was always ready for a debate. He started professional life as an account executive for Gray Advertising, managing such high-profile clients as Cointreau and Club Med. But he had creative longings, a desire to be a writer, and after a year he took off to write a book, which he described as a biography of God. "It's a cynical view of the Orthodox take on Judaism," his wife, Rebecca, said of her husband's neatly typed, but unpublished, two-hundred-page manuscript. "There were lots of references to the Torah." And so it was that Wald joined the legions of people who try to realize a literary dream, to write the great American novel, and then, realizing that they probably don't have quite what it takes, return to something more ordinary. In Wald's case it was to return to advertising for a while. But then, a friend of his named David Landau came along to exert a major influence on his life.

Landau urged Wald to become a stock broker, where the real money was, and that's what he did. He studied for the broker's exam and then, in 1981, went to work for Prudential Bache at 666 Fifth Avenue. He liked it. The work was more gratifying, more interesting, than advertising, he felt, and the monetary reward was greater.

And then there was Rebecca Brandstetter, who was Landau's cousin. Victor met her at a dinner hosted by Landau at Teacher's Too, a well-known Upper West Side eatery, long since gone out of business. They seemed an unlikely match at first. Rebecca, who was nine years younger than Victor, who was thirty in 1982, thought he was too old. She thought he was too Jewish also, or at least he looked too Jewish, she felt. She moved to San Francisco only a month after meeting Victor, but he was ardent, not to be denied. He phoned her frequently for three months before going to San Francisco and proposing to her in September 1984. She accepted, and they were married the following March.

Victor was doing well, newly married and thriving in his new career, but he was also running into problems. A rapid climb up the ladder required a certain gregariousness that wasn't natural to him. He didn't belong to the boys' club, drinking after work, cultivating managers and executives, playing the game of buddyship and conviviality, and that, in his view, led him to be passed over for advancements to which he was otherwise entitled.

He left Prudential Bache after the stock market crash in 1987 and moved to the Oppenheimer Fund. But he encountered the same problems there as he had at Prudential Bache. "He didn't go out with the guys," Rebecca said. "He came home." Their daughters, Alexandra and Daniella, were born in 1987 and 1990. "It was very important to have family outings," Rebecca said.

Wald made a risky move in 1995, trying to get away from the partial satisfaction of life at a major brokerage to win the fuller satisfaction of doing business on his own. He and several others started up their own specialty investment bank, Continuum Capital, with an office on Third Avenue and Thirty-ninth Street. Wald became a minor partner in the new enterprise, but when one of the major partners withdrew his stake in Continuum the company effectively collapsed.

Wald then went to work for another brokerage firm, Coleman & Company, in 1999, but Coleman, like most firms dependent on Wall Street, ran into the market downturn of 2000 and 2001. For a time, Wald took his computer home and cleared trades in an office he set up in Alexandra's room, not even going into the office. And, in 2001, only a few months before September 11, the principle partners at Coleman advised him to find a position at Avalon Partners, a stock brokerage that they had plans to take over, promising to make Victor a manager once they did.

And that is how Victor Wald went to work on September 11, 2001, taking the express elevator to the 79th-floor Sky Lobby in the north tower and the local to the 84th floor, where Avalon Partners had its offices. He took the subway from the Ninety-sixth Street station, only a block or so away from his apartment on Ninety-seventh Street, and, while it was a straight shot from there to Cortland Street, the World Trade Center stop, maybe twenty minutes altogether, he felt that his way of getting to work was something of a comedown for a man who used to be able to afford taxis in the morning. But his career had faltered somewhat and he had private-school tuition to pay for his two daughters and a new job that didn't provide the same cash flow as the old one. Rebecca thinks he was depressed, though perhaps he was going through what is commonly called the mid-life crisis.

"In the past year he became frustrated," Rebecca said. "He worked very hard, but we had a hard time making enough for tuition."

And so, on September 11, Victor Wald went to work like many, maybe even most, middle-aged New Yorkers that morning, bearing the burdens of his responsibilities, anxious about money in a city where the expenses seem to come out of nowhere and you're no longer young enough to start all over. Life doesn't always fulfill all the expectations you have for it. But still, you make the most of it, and you try not to complain, and you know that you're going to have to keep going, barring the unforeseen.

Harry Ramos worked only three floors above Victor, though the two men never met before September 11. Ramos had spent a couple of decades as a Wall Street trader and he had become a trusted pro—"his word was his bond," as John DeVito, a senior colleague at his last job at May Davis put it—though he got to his profession by an indirect, almost accidental route. Harry was born in Brooklyn in 1955, the youngest of the four children of Napoleon and Bertha Ramos, who emigrated from Puerto Rico in 1937 and 1943. He grew up in the Fort Green projects, which is another way of saying that he came from modest beginnings, no silver spoons there.

"Harry and I, we're about one and a half years apart," his brother and best friend Henry said. "Our mother kept a close eye on us when we were growing up. All the other kids in the neighborhood would be going to the movies and our mom would always say no."

But the two Ramos brothers, both skinny boys, would slip out of the house and go down to the movie theater anyway, crawling under the gates at the back door (where they put newspaper on the ground because men in the movie house came out there to relieve themselves) and watching their favorite kung-fu epics.

Harry graduated from Westinghouse High School in 1973. He was lively and active in his school years, a good dancer, the singer for a salsa band that once performed at Yankee Stadium after a game. He was also good with his hands. He built his own stereo equipment; he was a carpenter; he was also both a natty dresser and a jokester, a kid with a gift for making other kids laugh.

"He would make a joke out of anything," Henry said. "He was very well liked. He touched a lot of people even back then. He would see someone sad and he would walk right up to them and talk to them to get them to talk about it, or even just to get their minds off of things."

But Harry's father, who worked in a hotel, died suddenly of a massive cerebral hemorrhage the year Harry graduated from high school, and Harry had to go to work. His handiness got him his first job, which was building display cabinets for the Rolex watch company. Then, in the early 1980s, a friend who had a job at the brokerage house Lehman Brothers asked him to join the stock trading team there. Harry did, not staying long at Lehman, but moving around to several different jobs on Wall Street, and doing well, making money.

Harry's family moved to Staten Island in 1974, and Harry lived there while he was a bachelor. But one night he went to a party and saw a green-eyed eighteen-year-old named Migdalia Cruz, who, as it happened, was so morose over having broken up with her boyfriend that she had turned down a series of young men who had asked her to dance. Finally, her girlfriends, tired of trying to cheer her up, said, "If you don't dance with the next person who asks you, we're going to embarrass you." The next boy was Harry.

"He was a great dancer," Migdalia said. "He had a lot of hustle."

When Migdalia told Harry that she was Puerto Rican, he made his decision, right then, on the spot. "I have to marry you then," he said, startling her, almost scaring her away, "because I've been looking for a Puerto Rican girl with green eyes." He even took out a photograph and showed her that his two brothers had both married green-eyed Puerto Ricans.

Migdalia, thinking this was a little forward, considered giving him a fake phone number so he couldn't call her, but she didn't, and the two then dated for eight years before they got married in 1986. They had two boys, Eugene Harry in 1996 and Alex George just a few months before September 11.

What Victor Wald couldn't do was Harry Ramos's forte. He was a born schmoozer, a natural at corporate socializing and fitting in. When he joined the May Davis Group, a minority-owned investment bank, in 2001, he didn't like the office he was given. But rather than complain, he found a storage space that was vacant, and he built a new workspace himself. It was on the 87th floor of the north tower, and he got to work early.

"The guys on Wall Street used to call Harry 'the Godfather,'" Henry said, "because he was always dressed so sharp. I mean he would buy a new suit every few weeks, and a new $75 tie! Some of his bosses and customers would take him to Vegas for the weekend, all expenses paid because he was pure entertainment. Like he would get to go to the Tyson fight, ringside seats. They used to call him 'mobile comedy' because he was just that, he was mobile and he was funny."

On the morning of September 11, while Victor Wald was morose on his way to the 84th floor of the north tower, Harry Ramos was his usual cheerful self as he set off for the 87th floor. Henry drove him from his home to Pennsylvania Station in Newark as he did every morning. But Harry too had a few things on his mind. Migdalia had recently lost her mother, so Henry gave Harry a bit of a talking to, reminding him that Migdalia would need him more than ever, and maybe he'd have to spend more time at home, rather than go out with the boys so often. And then there was the contractor who he went to see that morning at a coffee shop before going to work. Harry was building a new house and the contractor was working too slowly. After Harry's meeting with the contractor, he told Henry that he was annoyed, but he was also stuck, since the old house was sold already, and, while he could stay there for a while, he needed to get the new house ready quickly if he was going to have a place to live for the family. So as the brothers arrived at the station, Harry too carried some of the ordinary burdens of life in the Big City. But as always Harry told Henry he loved him, and he gave him a high five and got out of the car.

"And the last thing I saw him do was point out some guy who was funny-looking, piling into the station to get on the train," Henry said. "He always did that, point some goofy-looking person out so I could laugh to myself as I drove away."

Was there anything in the life of Harry Ramos to that point showing that he would risk his own life to help somebody else, especially somebody he didn't know, had never met before, and was about as different from him as it is possible to be? Probably none of us shows advance signs of something like that, or maybe if somebody does, it turns out that the signs were false and that he was the kind of person who runs away. Heroism just comes, or it doesn't, with the occasion, and, for Harry Ramos, the occasion was only a train ride and an hour or so away.

EIGHT

"In Time of War There Is No Death"

It was 10:30 on the hot morning of August 7, 1998, when Mohammed Rashed Daoud al-'Owhali and a man known only as Azzam were riding down Haile Selassie Avenue, a main commercial thoroughfare in Nairobi, Kenya. The men wove through the heavy morning traffic in a light brown truck listening to inspirational poetic chants in Arabic on the radio. This was to help them maintain their courage, not to lose faith, as they faced what both believed would be the last minutes of their lives.

Their freight, carried on the truck bed behind them, consisted of four hundred pounds of mixed aluminum nitrate, aluminum powder, and TNT packed into wooden crates and wired through a battery to a detonator button in the cab. Their target was the American embassy, and they were carrying out the worst terrorist assault up to that point sponsored by Osama bin Laden and his Al Qaeda organization. Indeed, the terrorist assault of that day, against two American embassies in Africa simultaneously, marked the final transformation of bin Laden's organization from a locally based faction in the anti-Soviet struggle in Afghanistan into a global terrorist network with global ambitions. It sees bin Laden himself making a strange round-trip from Afghanistan to the Sudan and back to Afghanistan, and that round-trip parallels another story, the transformation of Afghanistan itself from an arena of Cold War conflict against the Soviet Union into a base of operations for the world's largest terrorist network as it embarked on a war against the United States.

In 1989, with the Soviets beginning to escape from their lethal quagmire in Afghanistan, bin Laden returned for a time to his native Saudi Arabia. The next year, on August 2, 1990, Saddam Hussein, the dictator of Iraq, occupied the neighboring oil-rich country of Kuwait. In response, bin Laden had a plan. He sent a message to the Saudi leadership proposing that they allow him to raise an army of thirty thousand Afghan-war veterans, and, using them, to drive Iraq away. The request was denied. Instead, in a decision that was to infuriate bin Laden and to make him a sworn enemy of the Saudi government forever after, the United States was invited to send an expeditionary force to Saudi Arabia from which it would launch its land invasion of Iraq in 1991. As a consequence of that, the United States established permanent military bases in Saudi Arabia—what bin Laden called "the land of the two holy places," Mecca and Medina. Bin Laden, far from seeing himself elevated to the status of protector of Islam, was thrust aside by the Saudi monarchy, which chose instead to rely for its defense on an infidel power. From that point on, like the Ayatollah Khomeini in Iran, incensed over an American military presence in Iran, bin Laden became a determined foe of the United States, and of any Arab government that remained linked to it.

Still, it was not a good time for bin Laden. With the war against the Soviet Union winding down in Afghanistan, there was little for him to do there. Or, as Jamal Ahmed al-Fadl, a longtime Al Qaeda member, put it in later court testimony, "In Afghanistan, we don't have too much work because the Russians, they left." Still, disappointed in his native country, bin Laden returned to Peshawar for a time in 1990 and 1991, and he seems to have been there when a golden opportunity presented itself.[1]

Toward the end of 1990 or early in 1991, Hassan Turabi, the spiritual leader of the Islamic Salvation Front, which had taken power in Sudan after a military coup in 1989, invited bin Laden to move to his own country, and to bring Al Qaeda and its training operations there. Al-Fadl was present at the deliberations that ensued at bin Laden's Peshawar headquarters. Who was this Turabi and could he be trusted? Some Al Qaeda leaders were concerned over reports that Turabi had studied at the Sorbonne in Paris—reports that were true—and might therefore not be a true Muslim, but bin Laden sent a delegation of his lieutenants to Sudan itself to investigate Turabi's invitation, and, when they came back, he decided to accept it.[2]

And so, in a complicated logistical operation, bin Laden moved himself and the entire top Al Qaeda leadership to Sudan. Al-Fadl himself was dispatched with money to rent (and eventually buy) farms and houses— the farms to serve both as businesses and training camps, the houses to accommodate the Al Qaeda members who made the move to the new location. Bin Laden paid $250,000 for one farm north of Khartoum, Sudan's capital, the money given to al-Fadl, who made the purchase in his own name, by Ayman Zawahiri. Then he paid $180,000 for a salt farm on the Red Sea, about 800 miles from Khartoum, where, he said, military training took place. In fact, at one point, neighbors complained to the police of the noise of explosions at the farm, leading the police to arrest several Al Qaeda members. But Al Qaeda quickly contacted the Sudanese intelligence service, which arranged for the men to be released.

Over the next five years, to the casual observer, bin Laden would have appeared to be a legitimate businessman, doing in the Sudan what the main family business had long done in Saudi Arabia. He created a company called Wadi al-Aqiq, which ran a diverse portfolio of enterprises. There was a trading company called Laden International, a construction company called Hijra Construction, an international currency trading outfit called Taba Investment. Al-Themar al-Mubaraka grew and marketed sesame seeds, peanuts, and white corn on a farm near Damazine. There was a fruit and vegetable company, a trucking business, a tannery, and a $50 million investment in a new Islamic Bank in Khartoum. At first the company rented an eight- or nine-room office on McNimr Street in Khartoum with secretaries, a reception room, and an office for bin Laden, the first room on the left. It then moved to larger quarters in Riyadh City, a subdivision of Khartoum.

In the town of Soba, near the Blue Nile, bin Laden bought four farms, one of them with an airport hangar–like building where he could store supplies. He bought a three-story guest house in Khartoum, with a room for himself on the second floor and where he held lectures and discussions every Thursday about jihad and what bin Laden called "our agenda." He had a letter signed by Omar Hassan Ahmad al-Bashir, the Sudanese president, giving him the right to import goods from abroad without customs inspections or customs duties. He delegated a liaison man to work for Sudanese intelligence to provide information on Islamic groups that, like Al Qaeda, wanted to set up shop in Sudan.

Military training for the thousands of jihad soldiers who now came to Sudan was conducted at bin Laden's farms. Bin Laden himself began issuing fatwas calling on Muslims to fight the American presence in the Gulf region. Meanwhile, Egyptian veterans of the Afghan jihad who had returned to their homeland engaged in a spree of assassinations there. This led Egyptian president Hosni Mubarak to ask Saudi Arabia to take action against bin Laden, and it did, stripping him of his citizenship and making it impossible for him ever to return to his homeland.

In 1995, prosecutors in the Southern District of Manhattan, who handled all of the early cases of terrorism, including the World Trade Center attack of 1993 and Omar Abdel Rahman's plan to blow up other New York City landmarks, indicted bin Laden for what they claimed was his role in the attacks on American servicemen in Somalia in 1993. Somalia, on the horn of Africa, was a country ruled by a collection of rival warlords who were obstructing efforts by relief agencies to deliver food to a starving population, and the American troops, dispatched in the waning days of the first Bush administration, were intended at first to assure that the supplies would get through. This part of the mission succeeded, saving uncountable lives. But then, the Clinton administration, which had taken office in the meantime, was reluctant to leave Somalia in the hands of the same warlords who had caused the problem in the first place, and it ordered American forces to move against the most notorious of those figures, Mohammed Farah Aidid. It was then, October 3, 1993, that an American Black Hawk helicopter was shot down and eighteen servicemen were killed, their bodies dragged through the streets of Mogadishu by a furious mob.

Was bin Laden ultimately behind the Black Hawk attack? American prosecutors believe that he was, and so do some of the former Al Qaeda operatives who have given information to American investigators. According to al-Fadl, for example, bin Laden repeatedly expressed concerns that the American move into Somalia was a geo-strategic move, not a humanitarian act, that threatened to have a kind of domino effect elsewhere in Africa. From Somalia, bin Laden told his followers, the

United States could expand its influence to South Sudan, where Christians were in a state of rebellion against the Muslim government of the north, and the end result would be ever greater American influence in the Islamic world.

"He say about American army now they came to the Horn of Africa, and we have to stop the head of the snake," al-Fadl later testified during a trial in New York in 2001. "He said that the snake is America, and we have to stop them. We have to cut the head and stop them, what they doing now in Horn of Africa."[3]

American press reports have cited intelligence sources to the effect that bin Laden trained the Somalian groups that attacked American troops in Mogadishu. This remains unproved, but there are two findings, aside from the statements by bin Laden overheard by al-Fadl, that indicate a role in Somalia for Al Qaeda. Al-Fadl himself testified that bin Laden sent several of his people to Somalia, including Mohammed Atef, an Egyptian who was later to emerge as Al Qaeda's military chief. Upon returning to Sudan, Atef reported at a meeting at the Khartoum guest house attended by al-Fadl that "everything happening in Somalia, it's our responsibility." Al-Fadl reported that Atef had difficulty getting out of Somalia after the anti-American attack, but that he was spirited back to Sudan by members of the Afar tribe, who gave him a spot on a small plane they used for transporting khat, the intoxicating plant that is in widespread use in Somalia.[4]

Several years later, in 1997, American investigators discovered a letter, written by an Al Qaeda operative in Nairobi warning the bin Laden organization in Kenya that American intelligence was closing in on them. In the letter, the writer, believed to be one Harun Fazul, who will play a key role later on in the story of Islamic terrorism, refers specifically to the "members" of the Al Qaeda cell in Nairobi, who were "the ones who killed the Americans in Somalia."[5]

But whether bin Laden had a hand in the Somalia disaster or not, there is no mistake that he was expanding elsewhere in Africa. In 1991 or 1992, al-Fadl was dispatched to Nairobi where he handed over an envelope full of money to two operatives who picked him up at the airport. American prosecutors in later terrorism cases have maintained that bin Laden's creation of a cell in Nairobi was aimed at giving him a gateway to the

Horn of Africa, specifically Somalia. But his plans went beyond Somalia. By 1993, bin Laden already had in mind targets against American interests in other African countries as well. That year he sent an agent to Nairobi to take pictures of the American embassy there, pictures that bin Laden personally scrutinized looking for a way to inflict as much harm as possible.

But bin Laden's plans for a major attack in Africa were postponed when he himself, once again, had to change his address. During his time in Sudan, bin Laden, as we have seen, was particularly affronted by two events in the early 1990s: the stationing of American troops in Saudi Arabia and the dispatch of American marines to Somalia. It was then that bin Laden began talking to followers like al-Fadl in the Khartoum guest house of the need to cut off the head of the American snake. And it was then too that bin Laden began to take on greater importance in the American view of things. American officials came to the belief that he played a role in the disastrous attack on American troops in Somalia. Then, in 1995, there were two bomb attacks on Americans in Saudi Arabia—one at a military training center in Riyadh, another at a barracks for American troops in Dhahran, killing a total of twenty-four American servicemen. Bin Laden was suspected of responsibility in those attacks, though nothing has ever been proved against him in those incidents, and the most common belief now is that they were carried out independently of him, very likely by Iranian-backed Saudis. Still, alerted to the increased danger of terrorism, the Americans were putting intense pressure on Sudan to expel bin Laden. Sudan capitulated; having invited bin Laden to move his operations to Sudan five years earlier, it now invited him to leave, and it took possession of its share of his Sudanese assets when he did so.[6]

It was then that bin Laden returned to an Afghanistan much changed since the days of jihad against the Soviet Union. According to one account, Turabi, the Sudanese religious leader, contacted the Sudanese ambassador to Afghanistan, who persuaded several commanders in the Jalalabad region to give protection to bin Laden. Bin Laden flew to Jalalabad in May 1996 on a special plane with three of his wives, a number of his children, and about one hundred Arab fighters. But the commanders whom he expected to see had been defeated by the rising Taliban army, and bin Laden quickly made contact with the Taliban instead, meeting with the mayor of Kabul, Mohammed Rabbani, and promising him his support.[7]

The Taliban had grown out of a local movement in the southwestern Afghan city of Kandahar where it was led by a reclusive religious teacher known as Mullah Omar. From modest beginnings as a kind of law-and-order religious party, the Taliban, helped by Pakistan, which provided money, arms, and training, began to extend its sway over the rest of the country. The Pakistani involvement seems to have been motivated by a combination of religious and political goals. Pakistan wanted a compliant Afghanistan on its northern frontier, which it could use, in part, as a base area for its support of guerrilla forces in Kashmir, control over which is fiercely disputed between it and India. In addition, some figures within Pakistani intelligence, Inter Services Intelligence, or ISI, were sympathetic to the fundamentalist brand of Islam represented by Mullah Omar. The Islamic schools that sprang up along the Pakistani side of the border, each of them led by its own bearded sheik, became, in essence, boot camps that provided recruits for Taliban military units. Students would study jihad in the classroom and then they could cross the border into Afghanistan and fight in a real jihad as allies of the Taliban.

Afghanistan itself had fragmented. Mutually suspicious military factions, each under its own warlord, often divided along ethnic lines, occupied chunks of territory. Technically, the president of Afghanistan—or, at least, the Afghanistan that held a seat in the United Nations and had the diplomatic recognition of a majority of countries—was Burhanuddin Rabbani, who was supported by the most famous of the former anti-Soviet commanders, Ahmed Shah Massoud. But both Rabbani and Massoud were Tajik, an ethnic minority from the north whose members speak a dialect of Persian, and they were not recognized by many of the southern commanders, most of whom were Pashtuns, who speak the same language as their cousins across the border in the Northwest Territories of Pakistan.

As the Taliban extended its control from Kandahar, defeating some warlords militarily, buying others off with money supplied by Pakistan, a natural alliance sprang up with bin Laden. "He had money in his pocket," Mohammed Khaksar, a senior Taliban official, said later, after the United

States had helped an anti-Taliban alliance take power late in 2001. "Any time he wanted, he would just pull it out and give it to them." Bin Laden, Khaksar said, gave fancy cars and other valuables to Taliban leaders. He supplied pickup trucks for military operations.[8]

The money cemented a relationship between bin Laden and the mysterious Mullah Omar that seems based not just on money but on common aspirations as well, a common vision. In the early years, Mullah Omar seems to have had no interest in anything outside of Afghanistan itself, but under bin Laden's tutelage, he too began to think about a global mission. The two men would talk by the light of kerosene lamps late into the night about restoring the greatness of Islam. Sometime in late 2000 or early 2001, bin Laden swore a "bayat," an oath, to Omar in which he swore his fealty to the Afghan leader, and, in videotapes and conversations, he began referring to him as the commander of the faithful, or the caliph, terms that have powerful connotations in Islam. Bin Laden was recognizing Omar as a figure of world historical significance. Those titles recognized him as the future leader of a renascent Islam, the bearer of the title of Saladin who conquered the Crusaders, the man who would realize the great dream of Wahhab and other Muslim revivalists for a unified Islamic state governed in accordance with sharia, Islamic law.

Meanwhile, bin Laden was given free reign to recruit abroad, to bring Islamic fighters to camps throughout Taliban-controlled Afghanistan, and to build a kind of state within a state, to become one of the country's most powerful warlords in his own right. Bin Laden organized a network of about a dozen different training camps, bringing together several different groups, in addition to Al Qaeda. These included the Pakistani group Harkat ul-Mujahadeen and the Islamic Movement of Uzbekistan, which aimed to create a vast Muslim state out of several former Soviet republics and the west Chinese region of Xinjiang. Recruits came from about twenty different countries, including Pakistan, Kyrgyzstan, Syria, Egypt, Morocco, Turkey, Saudi Arabia, Libya, Somalia, China, and the Philippines, as well as Canada, the United States, Britain, and Russia. In the wake of the American-led war in Afghanistan after September 11, *New York Times* reporters uncovered large caches of documents in Al Qaeda safe houses and training camps—letters, notebooks, diaries, instruction manuals, magazines, inspirational audio- and videotapes, personnel records,

and even American military training manuals—that give a detailed picture of life within the Al Qaeda state-within-a-state.

Most of the recruits received basic infantry training, whose purpose
seems not to have been international terrorism but the ongoing trench
war in Afghanistan between the Taliban and its main rival, the Northern
Alliance led by Massoud. The documents in this sense confirm that bin
Laden became indispensable to the Taliban because he provided them
with a substantial core of religiously committed and well-trained troops.
The average recruit was a young, unmarried man who had studied, or
perhaps memorized, the Koran, and, in many cases, belonged to a fundamentalist group in his native country. Whether the young man had
received permission to join the jihad from his parents was carefully noted
in personnel records. Each *mujahid*, or holy warrior, was given a code
name so that even his fellow recruits generally did not know his real
name. Each was supposed to be equipped with a uniform, boots, a belt, a
hat, a handkerchief, a flashlight, batteries, soap, a pencil, some jackets,
gloves, and medicines. Every day began with a rigorous program of calis-
thenics—sit-ups, push-ups, crawling, and running—followed by training
in the Kalashnikov assault rifle, rocket-propelled grenades, mortars, map
reading, and what military experts found to be sophisticated coordinated
infantry tactics in which infantrymen advance just behind covering fire
provided by units on their flanks. The training, not surprisingly, was
accompanied by steady infusions of Islamic fervor, in the form of Koran
study, movies, lectures, and pamphlets. There was great stress on the
glory of giving one's life for Allah, and the two greatest prohibitions, the
most mortal spiritual sins, were what was called "love of the world" and
"hatred of death." A key slogan was "In time of war there is no death." A
document found in an Al Qaeda house established these as the organization's chief goals and objectives:

1. Establishing the rule of God on earth.
2. Attaining martyrdom in the cause of God.
3. Purification of the ranks of Islam from the elements of depravity.

It was a smaller, more elite group that got additional, specialized
training in the techniques of terrorism. Presumably this was the pool of

young men willing to die from which the Al Qaeda terror task forces were drawn. After completing the basic infantry training of the ordinary recruits, they got lessons in surveillance, assassinations, hijackings, and bomb-making. They learned about secure communications, manufacturing and handling nitroglycerine and the plastique explosives C-3 and C-4, the uses of electronic components like diodes, resistors, and switches, and how to convert a radio-controlled toy boat into a remote detonator. The elite groups also seem to have had the honor of an audience with "Abu Abdullah," bin Laden himself. Some of them made martyrdom videotapes, reading texts prepared for them and claiming to be members of an organization whose name was provided for them. The system was a kind of theological Leninism. It consisted of a disciplined party organization broken up into small cells that reported to higher ups and whose members were expected to be obedient literally unto death, to do whatever their commanding officers demanded of them. At the same time they received heavy doses of ideological indoctrination in the form of radical Islamic principles. "God Almighty has ordered us to terrorize his enemies," began one manual found in Afghanistan. The standard oath that every recruit was required to sign pledged him to "slaughter infidels my entire life." One text was a paperback by bin Laden himself entitled, "Announcement of Jihad Against the Americans Occupying the Land of the Holy Places," on the cover of which was a map of Saudi Arabia surrounded by American, French, and British flags.

As for Afghanistan itself, it is hard to be sure whether bin Laden was a guest of Mullah Omar or whether Mullah Omar became the titular leader in an Afghanistan where bin Laden increasingly controlled the most powerful military force.

A strange episode in this regard has to do with an effort in 1998 by Prince Turki bin Faisal, who was Saudi Arabia's intelligence chief at the time, to persuade Omar to drop his support of bin Laden and to extradite him to Saudi Arabia on charges of attempting to overthrow the monarchy. Saudi Arabia was one of only two countries that officially recognized the Taliban—Pakistan was the other—and Saudi money heavily subsidized Taliban rule. One would think, given that, that the Taliban would be amenable to Saudi persuasion. And, indeed, according to bin Faisal, when he visited Omar in June 1998, Omar promised to turn bin Laden over to the

Saudis sometime later. But when bin Faisal returned to see Omar a second time in September, a month after the bombing of the American embassies in Africa, Omar had reversed his decision.

"Mullah Omar started using harsh language against the kingdom," bin Faisal said. "He used the same words that bin Laden uses, about the presence of infidel troops despoiling the land of the two holy mosques and people have a right to declare a jihad to liberate the holy land from these infidel operators."

According to American intelligence officials, Pakistani intelligence also helped to consolidate bin Laden's position inside Afghanistan. The ISI, they said, trained some of the covert operatives it sent to fight Indian control of Kashmir in Al Qaeda camps. Thus, not only did Pakistan have a special relationship with the Taliban, it maintained a degree of cooperation with bin Laden at a time when bin Laden was seen in the United States as a terrorist menace. When President Bill Clinton was contemplating a trip to Pakistan in 2000, the Secret Service adamantly opposed it, on the grounds that the ISI was so penetrated by extremist groups that secret details of the president's whereabouts and itinerary might be leaked to assassins. When Clinton insisted on going to Pakistan, Air Force One was flown empty into the country as a decoy, while the president traveled on an unmarked plane.

Accounts that filtered out of Afghanistan after the American-sponsored overthrow of the Taliban indicate that bin Laden's Al Qaeda became a kind of Praetorian Guard for the Taliban, its shock troops, its version of the SS, helping as the Taliban went about establishing a harsh Islamic dictatorship, enforced by the Ministry for the Promotion of Virtue and Prevention of Vice. The Taliban banned women from the streets, from schools, and from jobs. Shopkeepers were jailed for doing business during Friday prayers. Music, dancing, pool and billiards, chess, television, VCRs, nail polish, satellite dishes, firecrackers, sewing catalogues, photographs, and statues—all were made illegal by the Taliban, which banned keeping pigeons and flying kites as well, both favorite Afghan pastimes. The once heavily agricultural Shamali Plain north of Kabul, an area previously occupied by non-Pashtun groups, was ethnically cleansed, its villages and orchards burned. Thousands of Hazaris, Shiite Muslims who had lived for centuries in Bamiyan, northwest of Kabul, were killed and buried in mass graves.

In the wake of the Taliban's fall late in 2001, Afghans in Kabul told reporters that the Arab and Pakistani soldiers who arrived in Afghanistan by the thousands, many of them part of bin Laden's network, imposed a kind of foreign occupation on the country. The Arabs especially were even fiercer in their practice of Islam than the Taliban itself and they roamed the streets of the cities enforcing their own moral and religious code on the population. They got the best houses in the cities, thanks to Taliban generosity. They were given local girls as brides. According to some Afghans, it was the foreign troops that persuaded the Taliban to destroy the ancient Buddhist statues in the Hazara territory of Bamiyan, which were blown up in March 2001, and to prosecute eight European and American aid workers for proselytizing Christianity.

Afghanistan, in short, wasn't exactly an occupied country, but it was colonized by a group of extremists that needed a safe and supportive territory from which to base its operations, and in Mullah Omar, bin Laden had found the perfect, willing, and very likely dependent partner. There was a kind of escalation in bin Laden's rhetoric and activity as the months in Afghanistan went by, traced by *Frontline*, the television documentary series. In 1995, when still in Sudan, bin Laden said in an interview with a French journalist, "I did not fight against the communist threat while forgetting the peril from the West." A few months later, in an "Open Letter to King Fahd," the Saudi ruler, he called for a guerrilla war to drive American troops out of Saudi Arabia. "The Saudis now know their real enemy is America," he said in July 1996.

After being expelled from the Sudan, bin Laden turned to an unmistakable declaration of war against the United States. "Muslims burn with anger at America," he said on August 23, 1996. A year later, in an interview with CNN, he said: "We declared jihad against the U.S. government because the U.S. government is unjust, criminal, and tyrannical. It has committed acts that are extremely unjust, hideous, and criminal whether directly or through its support of the Israeli occupation." Then came his most extreme utterance. He announced not only that the American government and military would be the targets of his wrath, but so would any Americans wherever they could be struck. The occasion for this declaration was the formation of a united front between Al Qaeda and Ayman Zawahiri's group, Egyptian Jihad. Or, as bin Laden called the new organization, "The International Islamic Front for Jihad Against the Jews and Crusaders." It is worth quoting this declaration at some length:

We—with God's help—call on every Muslim who believes in God and wishes to be rewarded to comply with God's order to kill the Americans and plunder their money wherever and whenever they find it. We also call on Muslim ulema [the traditional Muslim religious conclave], leaders, youths, and soldiers to launch the raid on Satan's U.S. troops and the devil's supporters allying with them, and to displace those who are behind them so that they may learn a lesson.

The ruling to kill the Americans and their allies—civilians and military—is an individual duty for every Muslim who can do it in any country in which it is possible to do it, in order to liberate the Al Aqsa Mosque [in Jerusalem] and the Holy Mosque [in Mecca] from their grip, and in order for their armies to move out of all the lands of Islam, defeated and unable to threaten any Muslim.[9]

This declaration was called a fatwa by bin Laden, a religious order. A few years earlier, the Ayatollah Khomeini in Iran had issued a fatwa calling it a religious obligation to kill the writer Salman Rushdie. Now bin Laden was saying, in essence, that there was a similar religious obligation to kill Americans anyplace they could be found. It was a kind of theological blank check, an open invitation issued by the acknowledged leader of the armed Muslim International. The bombing of the embassies in Africa was bin Laden's way of announcing to the world that the program announced in this fatwa was operational.

Nobody better illustrates the way bin Laden's ambitions were realized than that young man, Mohammed 'Owhali, who on August 7, 1998, was sitting in the passenger seat of that bomb-laden truck driving toward the American embassy in Nairobi.[10] 'Owhali is the perfect embodiment of Al Qaeda's methods of recruitment and training and its selection of members of a small elite force for special martyrdom operations. He was born in 1977 (in Liverpool, England, where his father was a student in a master's degree program at a British university) and given a strict religious upbringing back home in Saudi Arabia. He read magazines like *Al Jihad*, which was being published by Abdullah Azzam in Peshawar, and *Al Mujahedeen*, or "Holy Warriors," and he read books like *Love and Hour of the Martyrs* that glorified the sacrifices made by the soldiers of Allah. He remembered listening to one videotape in particular, recorded by a man named Abdul

Rachman al-Howari, that made mention of something called the Kissinger Promise, which he described as the American secretary of state's plan to occupy the Arabian Peninsula.

Eventually, like other young Saudis, like Osama bin Laden some years before him, 'Owhali found his way to Afghanistan where he received military training and theological indoctrination in an Al Qaeda camp called Khalden. He got the standard training in light weaponry, demolition, and artillery, and the standard religious training as well—especially in the fatwas calling on Muslims to kill rulers who did not rule in accordance with Islamic law.

At a certain point, to reward his skills and enthusiasm, 'Owhali was chosen to be part of a group to have an audience with bin Laden himself, often referred to as "the emir." Bin Laden impressed upon his listeners the importance of fighting against the Americans and casting them out of Saudi Arabia. He also encouraged them to get further training, and 'Owhali did, going to a succession of camps in Afghanistan and studying an advanced terrorist curriculum. He learned how to gather intelligence and how to prevent intelligence from being divulged, how to conduct hijackings of buses and planes and how to carry out kidnappings.

'Owhali met others in Al Qaeda. Azzam, another Saudi whom he met at the Khalden Camp, became a kind of mentor, assuring him that they would do great and important things. He met a man he knew by the name of Khalid who was of higher rank than Azzam. He saw action, fighting in the Kabul region alongside the Taliban, and his bravery earned him certain privileges, most important the privilege of carrying his rifle anywhere he went in camp including in the presence of bin Laden himself. One day his friend Azzam asked him if he wanted to undertake something more important than fighting with the Taliban. When 'Owhali answered that he did, he became part of the mission to blow up the American embassy in Nairobi.

For this, he received the advanced training that was given to only a small elite group in Al Qaeda. He learned about the operation and management of cells, the small groups of operatives that Al Qaeda was establishing outside of Afghanistan. He learned that the person who is the intelligence chief of a cell is also the cell's overall commander. He studied surveillance techniques along with still- and video-camera photography. His training complete, he was told to shave his beard, so as not to look like an Islamic

militant. Furnished with an Iraqi passport in the name of Abdul Ali Latif, he
was sent over the border to Peshawar and from there on a commercial flight
to Yemen where he got a Yemeni passport in still another name—Khaled
Salim Saleh bin Rashid. He returned for three months to Pakistan where,
under orders from Azzam and Khalid, he made a martyrdom video, identifying himself in front of a camera as a member of the Third Martyrs Barracks First Squad of the El Bara Bin Malik Division of the Army of
Liberating the Islamic Holy Lands.[11] Then, using his Yemeni passport, he
went from Peshawar to Nairobi passing through Karachi, Muscat, and Abu
Dhabi, arriving early in the morning of August 2.

In Nairobi, he was reunited with his friends Azzam and Khalid, and
he began to rehearse the glorious mission that would be his life's work.
He lived at the house of a man called Harun and took instruction from
another man named Saleh, who was described to him as the leader of the
Nairobi Al-Qaeda cell. It was Saleh who showed 'Owhali the brown truck,
parked at Harun's house, with the bomb already assembled and installed
in back. Saleh also gave 'Owhali his instructions: first, that he would ride
in the passenger seat in the truck, which would be driven by Azzam, to
the embassy. When they arrived, he was to jump out and force the guard
to open the gate by threatening him with a pistol; second, he was to
throw some stun grenades, which he would wear on his belt, to get people to scatter from the area; and, three, if the electrical detonator failed to
work, he was to throw a stun grenade into the back of the truck and cause
the bomb to explode manually.

Saleh also explained the choice of the American embassy in Nairobi,
and this tells volumes about Al Qaeda's vision of the world. First, he said,
there was a large American presence in Nairobi; second, the American
ambassador there was a woman and therefore if the bomb resulted in her
being killed, it would further the publicity aroused by the attack; third,
that some of the embassy personnel in Nairobi were responsible for work
in Sudan, from which bin Laden had been expelled; four, that there were
a number of Christian missionaries at the embassy; and, fifth, it was an
easy target.

On the day of the bombing, at about 9:20, 'Owhali made a last telephone call, to a friend in Yemen. A few minutes later, at 9:45, he and
Azzam got into the truck and left Harun's house. 'Owhali was wearing
black shoes, blue jeans, a white short-sleeved shirt, and a blue cotton

jacket inside of which was his pistol. He attached four stun grenades to his belt. Harun led the way in a white pickup truck, turning away at a roundabout before reaching the target. In a fateful move, an illustration of a kind of terrorists' Murphy's Law, Azzam told 'Owhali that the jacket he was wearing might make it difficult for him to reach the stun grenades on his belt, so 'Owhali took the jacket off.

At the embassy, Azzam drove the truck into an alley between the embassy itself and the seven-story Ufundi Cooperative House, which housed a secretarial school, in full session at that hour, and some commercial offices. The alley led to the parking garage behind the embassy, barred by a drop gate controlled by a Kenyan security guard. When the Kenyan refused the two suicide bombers permission to entry, 'Owhali, according to plan, jumped out to threaten the guard with his pistol and force him to open the gate. But as he did so, he realized that his pistol was in the pocket of the jacket he had left in the truck. Without any means of threatening the guard, he tossed a stun grenade instead. People began to run, including the guard and 'Owhali himself, who suddenly had second thoughts about suicide. Or, as he put this to an FBI agent who interrogated him in Nairobi, he realized that his mission was complete, that there was nothing further for him to do. To die while carrying out the mission would be a martyrdom, he felt, but to die uselessly after the mission is complete would be suicide, and suicide is not acceptable in Islam. And so he ran and as he did so Azzam gamely carried on. He detonated the bomb, and suddenly a peaceful morning in Nairobi became a scene of carnage, foreshadowing what was to come on a similarly bright morning in New York and Washington, D.C., four years later.

Outside on Haile Selassie Avenue more than 1,600 people were immediately wounded, almost all of them Kenyans. The dismembered bodies of 15 people were later found on the street outside the embassy. The Ufundi Cooperative House collapsed in on itself, killing dozens of people inside and leaving people on the outside crawling over the mountain of cement and steel and clawing at the debris to free people trapped inside and calling for help. In all 250 people were killed, including twelve Americans inside the embassy. Ambassador Bushnell, who was meeting with a Kenyan minister in a building adjacent to the embassy—and who had written letters pleading with the State Department to build a safer, more terrorist-proof embassy—was cut by falling glass. In the Solar Building, across the street from the embassy, Beatrice Ngeru, a twenty-three-year-old secretary, happened to be standing next to a window. She heard what sounded to her like a gunshot, and she looked across the street. In the next instant, the window exploded, raking her arms, face, and chest with glass. In the hours that followed, rescue workers managed to pull four survivors out of the rubble, but hopes that more would be found were dimming.

They didn't know it in Nairobi at the time, but minutes before the Nairobi blast, the bomb placed in a truck and pulled up near the front entrance of the American embassy in Dar es Salaam exploded as planned, killing seven people, none of them American.

Back in Nairobi, 'Owhali himself was knocked over by the blast, suffering some injuries, but he was able to make it on his own steam to the clinic. There, he threw his last remaining stun grenade into a trash can and deposited the keys to the truck, and three bullets to the pistol, on a ledge in the men's room. He had no money and, since he was supposed to die, no plan to get away from Nairobi. He took a taxi back to the Ramada Hotel, where he told the reception clerk that he had been injured in the embassy blast and lost his money. He persuaded the clerk to loan him the money to pay for his taxi and to give him a room, promising to pay for everything after he had contacted some friends who would send him money.

Some time later, he did get some money, sent to him by the very friend in Yemen he had called before setting off for the embassy. But when he went to a hospital to receive treatment for the cuts he had received in the bomb blast, he came under suspicion when he was unable to produce any identity papers. He was arrested by the Kenyan police on August 12 and interrogated by both Kenyan and American law enforcement personnel. In January 2001, he pleaded innocent to charges of carrying out the bombing of the Nairobi embassy. He was found guilty and sentenced to life in prison.

NINE

Yeneneh Betru:
Medicine for the Neediest

Around the time that Osama bin Laden was leaving his native Saudi Arabia for the path of jihad, a young man from Addis Ababa named Yeneneh Betru, who was born in Ethiopia in 1966, was on a path toward the fulfillment of a promise he made to his grandmother when he was a boy. He told her way back then that he would become a doctor so he could take care of her if she fell ill. It's the sort of childhood vow that is ardently made at the time and then usually forgotten. But when, in 1981, the fifteen-year-old Yeneneh left Addis to attend high school at the Abbey School in Cañon City, Colorado, he already knew what his purpose was in life, and he never wavered from it.

The Holy Cross Abbey School in Cañon City—which is near Colorado Springs on the edge of the Rocky Mountains—is a Catholic school that recruited Yeneneh in Saudi Arabia, where the Betru family lived for several years. Yeneneh's father, Betru Tensay, worked in the marketing department for several airlines and moved the whole family to Jeddah, the Saudi capital, in search of a better job. He and his wife, Sara Tesheberu, who belonged to the Ethiopian Orthodox Church, had four children altogether, Yeneneh first, followed by two more sons, Sirak and Aron, and a daughter, Ruth. It was a close family, surrounded by uncles and aunts and cousins. The photo albums in the Betru household in California, where Yeneneh's parents now live, are full of pictures of Yeneneh with the other children of the clan, and with his brothers and sister. One shows him and Sirak dressed in similar suits for a birthday. Yeneneh went to a private school in Ethiopia through the fifth grade, then he was in Saudi Arabia for four years, and then, as the oldest child, he was the first to go to high school in the United States, where his brothers and sister all followed.

"We all attended American schools because our parents wanted us to get the best education possible," Sirak said, "and they knew that English was a very important language to know."

Yeneneh was a good student and an athlete. He was also the star forward on the Abbey soccer team—one of the best players in the school's history, said Sirak. He went horseback riding in the Colorado countryside and competed as a *Vaqueros*, a trick horseback rider. Years later, his family, living in a wood-paneled stucco home in Los Angeles, still had his trophies—for baseball tournaments in Saudi Arabia and for *Vaqueros* competitions in Colorado. "Even though he was a really good student, he wasn't just a bookworm," Aron said. But when he went on to Loyola Marymount University in Los Angeles, where he got a degree in biology, with honors, in 1988, and then to medical school at the University of Michigan, there wasn't much time for extracurricular activities.

"He set a high mark for us," Ruth said. "We owe our professional success to him. One time when I was an undergrad at UC Berkeley, I went out to Michigan to see him, to get away from studying." Yeneneh was then in medical school. "And you know what he did? The minute I got there, he sent me to the library to study! I ended up sleeping on a couch, but he studied while I slept."

Yeneneh, in other words, worked hard, doing what many immigrants and nonimmigrants have done since time began in American life, using the schools to get ahead. And he pursued his medical career with devotion. His mother recalled that even when he was taken to the hospital in Addis Ababa when he was three years old, he would say he wanted to be a doctor, maybe because he liked the medical attire, she thought. Or maybe it was because of his vow to his grandmother. It certainly wasn't to get rich. When Aron once told Yeneneh that he also wanted to be a doctor because doctors made lots of money, he got a fraternal reprimand about the spiritual thinness of the pursuit of wealth.

"He said that was not a good reason," Aron said. "He said you should always find a passion and enjoy what you do. For him it was definitely the passion of helping people."

Yeneneh did his internship and residency in Los Angeles, and eventually joined a group called Consultants for Lung Diseases / Institute for Better Breathing in Burbank, California. He was a hospitalist, a physician who works only in a hospital, not in an office or private practice. "Betru was on the cutting edge of what a hospitalist should do," said Earl Gomberg, executive director of the Consultants for Lung Diseases. "He went around the country training doctors on how they should deal with hospitalists. But Betru also loved patient interaction so he did rounds on the weekends. He didn't want to lose patient contact."

He never lost touch with his Ethiopian roots, whether that meant calling his mother and asking to come over for some of his favorite Ethiopian dishes, or giving medical advice to members of St. Mary's Ethiopian Church, which his family attended. Once when Ruth had to do some community work as part of her graduate studies at UCLA, Yeneneh suggested that she organize an Ethiopian health fair. He and other volunteer doctors provided free medical care and advice to the three hundred or so low-income people who attended.

He lived in Burbank in a single-story, two-bedroom house with white stone walls and a manicured lawn. It was sparsely decorated with modern furniture and ethnic artifacts. There were three paintings of an Ethiopian boy playing musical instruments, two wooden statues of an Ethiopian warrior and his wife, and many Ethiopian crosses on display, along with American Indian pottery on the bookshelves on either side of the fireplace.

And in the garage of the Burbank house were four refurbished kidney dialysis machines along with a water filtration system, needles, gauze, and other supplies he was planning to ship to Ethiopia, and therein lies the key to understanding Yeneneh Betru's passion for helping others. When he died, he was in the midst of a long, difficult effort to create the first kidney dialysis center in Ethiopia, a project that, for him, epitomized what he wanted his life to mean.

It was his beloved grandmother back home who prompted him to undertake this mission. In 1998, he got word that she had fallen desperately ill. Yeneneh called her doctors in Ethiopia to find out what he could about their diagnosis, which he realized was incorrect.

"The doctors over there thought it was some type of urinary tract infection or something," Ruth remembers, "but after talking to my grandmother, he realized that she had had a stroke. He got all the medication that he could in the U.S. and he flew, with my mom, to Ethiopia. But by the time they got there, my grandmother had a blood clot and was suffering even more."

Yeneneh, contrary to his boyhood pledge, was unable to help her, but he vowed to do something about the primitive state of medicine in Ethiopia. He spoke to doctors there, and they told him that what the country needed most urgently was dialysis machines, since kidney disease was an important cause of death in Ethiopia and yet there wasn't a single dialysis center. Yeneneh began using his contacts with American kidney specialists to collect used dialysis machines, six of them altogether. At the same time he began negotiations with Ethiopia to set up a dialysis center at the Tikur Anbessa Hospital in Addis Ababa, Ethiopia's largest hospital and the center of its most important medical faculty.

"He wanted to do something big for his home country before he got married," said Jim Stramoski, a technician who rebuilds used dialysis machines for hospitals in California. Betru, helped by Stramoski, was able to put together his six machines for only about $15,000, an eighth of what the same machines would have cost new.[1]

"He didn't want to help the rich," the *Addis Tribune*, an Ethiopian newspaper, wrote, "but the poor, the ones who can't help themselves."

It wasn't the first time that Yeneneh wanted to help the poor. When he was a resident at the University of Southern California Medical Center, he had some patients who were so poor they paid him with live chickens or ducks, which he brought home to the house he was sharing with Ruth in Los Angeles. "We built a small fence one year to house these chickens that Yeneneh would get," Ruth said. "At one point, we were worried that our neighbors would call animal control or something to complain about all the livestock we had in our backyard."

In the meantime, Yeneneh's American career was advancing. In 1999, he became director of medical affairs for In-Patient Consultants, which recruits and trains hospitalists and advises hospitals on using their services. At the same time, for the three years after his grandmother's death—until September 11, 2001—he traveled frequently to Ethiopia, consulting with local doctors and meeting with government officials in his effort to create his dialysis center at the Tikur Anbessa Hospital. It wasn't easy. Ethiopia is a country of bureaucratic red tape, a country that didn't have a single dialysis machine and yet imposed prohibitively high tariffs on refurbished machinery.

"He never showed any frustration with the roadblocks he faced in his dealings with the machines," Gomberg said. "He just plodded along and kept trying to get the quest done."

"He was such a good person and he was only thirty-five years old," Yeneneh's brother Aron said. "He was a visionary. He had a lot of ideas. He was at the point where he was going to break free and do so much more."

In January 2001, Yeneneh and Sirak went to Ethiopia for vacation and in his last few days there he met a young women. He didn't say much about her to his family, not wanting to make her too much of a subject before he knew what would happen between them. She agreed to go to the United States so the two of them could get to know each other better, and in the last weeks of his life, he went, accompanied by his mother, to Ethiopia to bring her back with him. He flew back from Ethiopia to Washington and deposited the young woman with a sister of hers who lived in Washington. Yeneneh was supposed to stay for a couple of days in Washington and fly back to work in California on September 12, but he was anxious to get home and back to work, and so he went to the airport to see if he could get on a flight standby. He did. The flight that had seats available was American Airlines flight 77, bound for Los Angeles.

TEN

The Cell in Hamburg

People who knew Mohammed Atta when he began to study engineering at the Technical University of Hamburg in 1992 recall a young man similar to the younger one who studied architecture and engineering in Cairo. He was intense, polite, neatly dressed, distant, narrow in his interests. One lecturer at the university who knew Atta, Alptekin Ozdemir, a Turk who advises foreign students, told a reporter he saw no signs that Atta was "a fanatical Muslim," at least not in his early German period.

Still, being an alien in an alien country does seem to have induced Atta to be more religiously observant than he had been before. In Cairo, he said his daily prayers, but nobody remembers him going to the mosque. In Hamburg he went often. He drank no alcohol and ate no pork. He checked the ingredients of everything, even medicines, to be sure there wasn't anything in them that violated the Islamic dietary laws. He scraped icing off of cakes for fear that lard might be an ingredient. He argued about religion with his landlady, who was one of the two people from Germany that his father had had to dinner in Cairo, telling her that the Koran was the only truth.[1]

Atta at first lived rent-free with his father's friends, but he moved out after a year and then stayed in university housing for the next several years where, contrary to the impression others had of him as neat and meticulous, his roommates found him slovenly, closed in, and inconsiderate.

"We never shared food," one of them said. "We shared dishes. Mostly, he messed them up and I cleaned them."[2] Atta was cool to the point of hostility to women, including the girlfriend of one of his roommates, who taunted him by putting a reproduction of a Degas nude above the toilet in the bathroom. After three months, Atta asked that she remove it. He was ascetic, uninterested in the pleasures of life, even the small ones, like eating well. He used to prepare a meal consisting of a large mound of boiled and mashed potatoes. He would eat some of it, put the rest in the refrigerator, and then, at another meal, eat some more without heating up the dish. He would walk into the common room of the dormitory without acknowledging anybody's presence, somewhat the way his father used to ignore his neighbors in Cairo. His fellow high school students back home didn't like him, and neither did his roommates in Hamburg. There was something oblivious about him, something disconnected, indifferent, so filled with the importance of his own thoughts and activities that those who did not share them scarcely existed.

Hamburg itself is a magnificent European port city, stately, discreet, elegant, a place of old commercial money, prestige hotels, churches with mighty spires, opulent shops. It is also a place with plenty to alienate a religiously conservative person like Atta, lots of sex shops and prostitutes (some of them on the same street as the Al Quds Mosque where Atta often went) and an active homosexual life.

When he first arrived in Germany, Atta's intention was to study at Hamburg University, the city's most prestigious institution of higher learning, but his application was turned down. This led Atta's father, who believed that the rejection was due to racism, to send his son money to mount a discrimination lawsuit. But in the end nothing was done and Atta was accepted at the Technical University, which is across the Elbe River in Harburg, an old industrial suburb that most Hamburgers themselves have never visited. It was where the immigrants, Turkish, African, and Arab, lived, not exactly in a world apart but in a world unincorporated into the German mainstream.

It is no secret that Muslims in Germany receive a chilly reception from some local people, "real Germans" as it were, especially "real Germans" caught up in the anxiety that Germany has too many immigrants. It would have been difficult for Atta, one of just a handful of Arab

students at the Technical University, which had about five thousand students altogether, to feel at home. The main Muslim immigrant group in
Hamburg is Turkish, and the mosques closest to Atta's campus were
dominated by Turks, who were deemed by many of the Arabs in Hamburg as insufficiently devout and too sympathetic to the United States and
Israel. Atta prayed sometimes at the Arabic-language Al Tauhid Mosque,
which was the back room of a small shop. The imam who preached there,
Ahmed Emam, proclaimed that America was an enemy of Islam and a
country "unloved in the world." After September 11, he was one of those
who insisted that the hijackings and the World Trade Center attacks had
been carried out by the Jews in a plot to frame the Arabs.

Atta's main academic interest was urban restoration and renewal,
especially the restoration and renewal of ancient Muslim cities, and he
had a sympathetic teacher in Dittmar Machule, the dean of the faculty of
construction engineering who had a strong interest in the Arab world
himself. According to Machule, Atta was a good student, "polite, very
religious and with a highly developed critical faculty." Machule had for
years supervised an excavation in northern Syria near Aleppo, and in 1994,
Atta visited both the excavation and Aleppo itself, a city dating back to the
time of Alexander the Great. He was aggrieved at the modern treatment
of Aleppo, where the Syrian government had put in new roads through
old neighborhoods.

"That was the only thing I ever saw him get emotional about," a
Syrian engineer, Razan Abdel-Wahab, who works in the Aleppo redevelopment project, said. "He was very angry at the destruction of our old
heritage."[3]

In 1995, Atta went on a pilgrimage to Mecca. He also returned for a
time to Cairo to study urban renovation projects being undertaken near
the old city gates, Bab al-Nasr and Bab al-Futuh. As in Aleppo, he became
upset over the Cairo projects, feeling that they involved little more than
tearing down poor neighborhoods to improve the views for tourists.

"It made him angry," said Ralph Bodenstein, a German student in the
program. "He said it was a completely absurd way to develop the city, to
make a Disney World out of it."

One only gets isolated glimpses of Atta in his Hamburg years coming
from the few people who had contact with him. He lived an isolated

existence—and those really close to him are not given to talking to for-eign reporters—so it is almost impossible to trace his mental trajectory in close detail. But the arc of it is clear. Atta gradually became both more religious and more politically outspoken. He nurtured resentment until it blossomed into a dark fury that led him to want to strike a fantastic blow against his enemies, even if it meant giving up his life in the process. In an early sign of this inclination toward self-sacrifice, he used to tell his friend Bodenstein and another German student, Volker Hauth, who was with him in Cairo, that his increasingly religious outlook would keep him from getting a good job in his country when he finished his studies in Germany. Atta already suspected, in other words, that he had forfeited his career prospects for the sake of his convictions, and, along with his career prospects, the possibility of satisfying his demanding father. Maybe sacri-ficing himself to a cause was a way of getting Atta senior off his back.

Atta returned to Hamburg in 1996, but Machule says that for the better part of 1997 he didn't see him at all, and some investigators and journalists have speculated that he went to Afghanistan for military training during this missing period, presumably, like other young Egyptians at that time, getting indoctrinated into the Al Qaeda point of view. There is other cir-cumstantial evidence on that point as well. Late in 1999, a few months before coming to the United States, Atta and two other September 11 con-spirators, al-Shehhi and Jarrah, claimed that their passports had been lost and applied for new ones. Investigators have speculated that they wanted to get rid of their old passports to conceal suspicious travel—specifically to Afghanistan—and therefore facilitate their entry into the United States.

Before that, in 1996, Atta went on a second pilgrimage to Mecca, and this seems to have been a transforming experience for him. When he returned, he wore the full beard and long tunic of an orthodox Muslim. He petitioned the university for a prayer room and founded an Islamic student group. "Something changed in him," Ozdemir, the Turkish stu-dent adviser, said. And certainly we know, because of what happened on September 11, that Atta became an extremist, a member of an Al Qaeda cell in Hamburg, and, finally, a suicide terrorist. For such a person to take a trip to Afghanistan for training would not have been surprising.

Still, there is no evidence that Atta had any direct contact with Osama bin Laden, or that he went to Afghanistan in 1997 or any other year. The

hypothesis that he "lost" his passport in 1999 in order to conceal evidence
of a trip to Afghanistan is not entirely convincing, if only because when
an Arab-Afghan went to Afghanistan, it's not likely that he had his passport stamped in the way passports are stamped when one goes to other
countries. The young men who went to join Al Qaeda in Afghanistan
went first to Peshawar in Pakistan and were taken across the porous border into Afghanistan by guides. They didn't walk up to a recognized border post and show their papers to an immigration official. So even if Atta
did go to Afghanistan, the only stamp he would have in his passport
would be one to Pakistan, which he may have felt would be of enough
interest to an American consulate official to deny him a visa. Certainly the
"loss" of Atta's passport—which became known to German authorities
because he, al-Shehhi, and Jarrah applied for new German visas—was
aimed at concealing something about him—ditto for al-Shehhi and Jarrah, the other two suspected hijackers who were living in Hamburg at the
time. The stamps they wanted to hide might have shown travel to Pakistan, but they might also have indicated visits to Iran or to Iraq. As we
will see, there is intriguing, though inconclusive, evidence of a link
between Atta and Iraqi intelligence.

    In any case, Atta may not have been absent from Hamburg for all of
1997. A report in the *Los Angeles Times* shows that for much of the year, he
lived in a redbrick housing project on an island called Wilhelmsburg in the
middle of the Elbe River, a decrepit place whose inhabitants are mostly
Turkish immigrants. According to Helga Link, a resident of Wilhelmsburg and a neighbor of Atta, he occupied a third-floor walk-up with a
group of other Arab men who talked late into the night and then disappeared during the day. The *Los Angeles Times* also found indications that
Atta taught in a series of seminars organized by the group that had earlier
financed his study trip to Cairo, and that his schedule would not have
allowed him to leave the Hamburg area for longer than a few weeks at a
time.[4] That, of course, doesn't mean that Atta couldn't have made a short
trip, or even several short trips, to Afghanistan. Perhaps his lost passport
was intended to hide not one but several trips to Pakistan, and several
trips to Pakistan by a young Egyptian would raise more suspicions than a
single trip. It's possible that the witnesses cited by the *Los Angeles Times*
about Atta's Hamburg appearances are mistaken. They were remembering Atta, presumably from the pictures of him that were published after

September 11, and after-the-fact identifications of that sort are notoriously unreliable. In other words, unlike others who mounted Al Qaeda terrorist operations, like al-'Owhali or al-Fadl, Atta and his exact movements remain obscure.

In 1998, according to the neighbors who identified them for the *Los Angeles Times,* the Arab men who had stayed in Wilhelmsburg suddenly departed, leaving only their mattresses behind, eleven of them. Whether Atta was among these men or not, he almost certainly moved around that time into an apartment in a faded yellow building on a narrow, sloping street called Marienstrasse near the university in Harburg, again sharing the place with other Arab men. Among these was his inseparable companion Marwan al-Shehhi. According to some reports, Ziad Jarrah also lived on Marienstrasse, though this is not at all certain. There is much stronger evidence on the presence there of two other Arab men, one named Said Bahaji and the other Ramzi Mohammed Abdullah bin al-Shibh.

The men at Marienstrasse were close and they were busy. Their landlord, Thorsten Albrecht, described how the plotters equipped each of the apartment's three bedrooms with a table and a computer hooked up to high-speed data lines. They paid their rent on time. They dressed, sometimes in Arab robes, sometimes in somewhat outmoded Western clothes, like beige bell-bottoms. A large number of Arab men visited them. All the evidence indicates that this was the headquarters for the early planning of the September 11 plot.

Strangely, despite his slow absorption into terrorism, Atta did not abandon his other activities. Early in 1999, he reappeared in Machule's office wanting to resume work on his thesis, telling Machule that he had had some family problems and that's why he had not been at the university for so long. A year or so later, he turned in a 152-page work on Aleppo, which was accepted with honors. Atta had graduated. In 1999 he also returned home to Cairo where he got engaged to a local girl. The parents of his betrothed insisted that their daughter never leave Egypt, so Atta, presumably having promised that he would return to Cairo when his studies were complete, went back to Hamburg with a wedding in his future. In fact, he never did return to Egypt and there never was a wedding, because, quite clearly, something else was brewing in Atta's life.

The amazing thing is that Atta and some of the others he lived with
in the apartment on Marienstrasse in Harburg were, in 1998 and 1999,
actually under surveillance by the German police. This part of the story
has to do with a slender dark thread that runs from Atta through the
African embassy bombings of 1998 to the well-dispersed international Al
Qaeda network. One of the Al Qaeda operatives indicted in the embassy
bombings was a man named Mamdouh Mahmud Salim, now in prison in
the United States. Salim was in Nairobi in the days leading up to the truck
bombing of the American embassy there, but he fled a day or so before
the actual attack. A month later he turned up in Munich where he was
arrested by the German police acting at the behest of the United States.
Salim was extradited and, as of this writing, was being held in Manhattan's Metropolitan Corrections Center awaiting trial in the 1998 attacks. In
2000, he stabbed a prison guard through the eye with a comb, causing permanent severe brain damage.

The German police, examining Salim's cell phone, found the name
and number of one Mamoun Darkazanli, a dapper Syrian businessman living in Hamburg. It turned out that Darkazanli had power of attorney over
Salim's bank account in Germany and helped him buy radio equipment for
Al Qaeda in 1995, so he too seemed to have links to the Al Qaeda network.
The German police's interest in Darkazanli, who attended the Al Quds
Mosque, led them to be interested in some of the others who also
attended that mosque. One of them was Said Bahaji, an electrical engineer
and an associate of Darkazanli who was living at 54 Marienstrasse.

The police surveillance of the Atta–al-Shehhi–Bahaji apartment did not
last long and did not produce any startling information. But the Darkazanli-
Bahaji connection provides not only indirect evidence that Atta himself had
been drawn into the Al Qaeda network by early 1998; it also provides some
clues about the way Al Qaeda spreads its tentacles. Darkazanli knew Salim
who helped to blow up the American embassy in Nairobi; Bahaji knew
Darkazanli; Atta lived with Bahaji. After September 11, Darkazanli was
interrogated by German police and his apartment was searched, but he was
not arrested. Early in September, according to his father-in-law, Bahaji suddenly decided to go to Pakistan to study computers. He left his wife behind
in Hamburg and has not been seen or heard from since.

Al-Shibh moved into the Marienstrasse apartment after Bahaji left to get married. Al-Shibh, a Yemeni who also disappeared after September 11, transferred $2,000 from his account in Hamburg to a bank in Florida in August 2000, and he tried at least five times to get a visa for the United States so he could attend flight training, but he was turned down every time. The FBI assumes that al-Shibh had been designated to be one of the hijackers, the twentieth. This claim is substantiated by a videotape found in an Al Qaeda house in Afghanistan after the American military campaign there. It shows five Al Qaeda operatives, al-Shibh among them, taking a vow of martyrdom. Al-Shibh then, unlike Atta, left traces in Afghanistan. The martyrdom videotape proves that he was trained and indoctrinated at an Al Qaeda camp. Like 'Owhali, the would-be Nairobi suicide bomber, he was asked to make a statement on videotape that would presumably be used in Al Qaeda propaganda later.

This, in turn, is a clue as to how the September 11 plot took shape. There are those who surmise that Al Qaeda operates like a foundation, funding projects that are brought to its attention by groups or individuals eager to carry out an exploit for jihad, but not necessarily originating them or controlling them or perhaps not even knowing exactly what they are. Al-Shibh's martyrdom videotape indicates the contrary—that he was dispatched from Afghanistan, like 'Owhali was to Africa before him, already part of a plan and that plan was well-known and approved by Al Qaeda headquarters in Afghanistan.

The plan to hijack airplanes and to crash them into the most visible symbols of American prestige and power was, in other words, being hatched in both Afghanistan and Hamburg, where three of the hijackers—Atta, al-Shehhi, and Jarrah—lived, along with a would-be additional hijacker, al-Shibh, who made a martyrdom videotape under Al Qaeda supervision. But, obviously, whatever plans were made in Germany had to be carried out in the United States, and the three men all arrived there in the middle of 2000, about fourteen months before the September 11 plot was actually carried out. Atta himself came on a flight from Prague on June 3, 2000. Why Prague? That, as we will see, relates to one of the most intriguing unsolved mysteries of the entire September 11 plot. On May 30, 2000, Atta flew from Germany to Prague, but, because he had failed to get a visa for the Czech Republic, which is required of Egyptian citizens, he was denied entry and forced to fly straight back to Germany. He then did get a Czech visa, took a bus to Prague, spent one night there, and then flew to the United States, arriving in Newark and giving the Lexington Hotel in New York City as his destination, though, in fact, he never showed up there. After September 11, some Czech newspapers said that on his brief visit in 2000, Atta met with an Iraqi intelligence agent named Ahmed Khalil Ibrahim Samir al-Ani, but Czech officials said they had no evidence of a meeting between the two men at that time.

Four days earlier, Atta's usually inseparable companion Marwan al-Shehhi flew from Munich to Newark. A few weeks later, on June 27, Jarrah flew from Munich to Atlanta. Clearly, the three men took care not to enter the United States together, or even from the same points of origin or to the same points of entry, though within weeks, all three of them had set up housekeeping in Florida and begun to take flight lessons at two different flight schools.

Atta, al-Shehhi, and Jarrah represent the leaders of three of the hijacking teams. They are presumed to have piloted three of the commandeered planes. The fourth team arrived separately, trained in separate places, and was made up of men who do not seem to have had any contact with Atta, al-Shehhi, and Jarrah before they were all in place in the United States—or, at least, there is no evidence of any earlier contacts. One of the members of that team was Hani Hanjour, who was, the FBI has concluded, the hijacker-pilot of the fourth plane commandeered on September 11. Two other members of that team were Khalid al-Midhar and Salem Alhamzi. All three of them arrived in the United States even before Atta, al-Shehhi, and Jarrah.

Hani Hanjour seems to have come for the first time as early as 1990. His brother, Abdul Hanjour, a wealthy businessman who traveled frequently between Saudi Arabia and Arizona, brought him along one year. He signed up to study English at the University of Arizona's Center for English as a Second Language, returned home for a few years, and then came back in 1996 for the purpose—what else?—of learning how to fly. A friend of his brother's, Susan Khalil, who lived in Florida, helped him apply to school, and eventually he ended up at CRM Airline Training near Phoenix.[5]

Al-Midhar and Alhamzi had more sinister connections. Indeed, of all of the leaders of the September 11 plot, only they had a clear record of previous links to Al Qaeda. In late 1999 or possibly January 2000, both men were in Kuala Lumpur, Malaysia, where, the local intelligence service later reported to the United States, they attended a meeting of members of bin Laden's Southeast Asia branch. Since the September 11 attacks, the size and importance of the Southeast Asia group has become evident. But even earlier, there were signs that Muslim terrorists enjoyed support in Southeast Asia. For one, Ramzi Yousef seems to have counted on drawing from Filipino Muslims in his plot to blow up eleven American airlines crossing the Pacific on the same day. While there are no clear indications that Yousef associated with bin Laden earlier, American investigators say that by 1995, when he was living in Manila, he was receiving funds from Mohammed Khalifa, bin Laden's brother-in-law, who headed a charitable organization in the Philippines.

Al Qaeda seems also to have had cells operating in Indonesia and Malaysia made up of men grouped around radical Muslim clergy in those countries. After September 11, Singapore police arrested thirteen men who, they said, were members of an extensive Al Qaeda network in Asia—rivaling the network in Europe in its extent and ambitions—that was planning to blow up the embassies of the United States, Israel, Britain, and Australia. So the presence of al-Midhar and Alhamzi among these groups at the end of 1999 signals that they too were already part of the terrorist Islamic International. When on October 12, 2000, an Al Qaeda team blew up the USS *Cole*, an American destroyer anchored in Aden Harbor, Malaysian intelligence identified one of the men involved in that attack as having attended the Kuala Lumpur meeting with al-Midhar and Alhamzi.

That connection would turn out to be important, for it would provoke a manhunt for al-Midhar and Alhamzi in the United States just weeks before September 11. But that came later. For now, the important thing is that by the end of June 2000, the men who would become the leaders of all four of the September 11 hijack teams were already in place. The next months would see them handling a variety of matters, from learning how to fly airplanes to inquiring about crop-dusting planes to getting photo identifications and driver's licenses, as the plan discussed in Hamburg (and possibly in Afghanistan) was slowly being implemented in the country of the Great Satan itself.

ELEVEN

John Ogonowski:
Salt of the Earth

To the passengers of American Airlines transcontinental flights, John Ogonowski was one of those confidence-inducing figures in pilots' dress uniform who come on the public address system early in the flight and say, essentially, "Don't worry, you're in good hands." But Ogonowski had many roles in his life. At American Airlines he was a familiar figure, a senior pilot with twenty-three years of service, most recently on Boeing 767 aircraft. To his family, which included his three daughters and his wife, Peggy, he was known as John Deere Johnny, because he was an inveterate and indefatigable maintainer of the machinery he kept on the 150-acre farm he ran in Dracut, Massachusetts, near the New Hampshire border—a real working farm, not a city slicker's weekend retreat where the farming was done by somebody else. To the Cambodian refugee immigrants who farmed land that Ogonowski owned, and whom he mentored in the practices and techniques of New England, as opposed to Southeast Asian farming, he was a benefactor, a friend, a man who wanted to help.

Ogonowski was—to put this simply and directly and with no nod to journalistic neutrality—a great guy, the kind of guy you would like to have met. "They got some of our best," Mrs. Ogonowski said of the September 11 terrorists, and she is right. Twelve days a month, her husband flew transcontinental flights. The rest of the time, he tended the peach orchard and the fields of hay, corn, pumpkins, and blueberries on his beloved farm. He had the manner of both of his vocations—imposing in his captain's uniform; weather-beaten, ruddy, rugged, and callused, wearing the scuffed, nondesigner dungarees of a farmer. From their front door the Ogonowski family could see the rolling hills of New Hampshire, whose border with Massachusetts ran just a few hundred yards from the farm, and Ogonowski farmed in part because he had a love of that view and that land.

Certainly he didn't farm for the money, because, basically, there wasn't any. Without his skills, a farm like his in northern Massachusetts would bankrupt a person with far deeper pockets than he had. But Ogonowski had farming down to something midway between a hard science and an abstract art. His nighttime reading was journals with names like *Implement and Tractor*, *Farm Journal*, and *Highbush Blueberry Production Guide*. Peggy used to say that his John Deere 740 tractor, stored in the barn, was "John's other 767." In September 2001, the barn, with its green aluminum roof, creaking as it expanded in the heat of the sun, was piled high with some fifteen thousand bales of hay stacked to the rafters, and it wasn't just any old hay. It was soft—green—and without any dust at all. "It looks like it came out of a garden," Frank Panek, Ogonowski's cousin, said. "You won't find hay like this ever, ever again in life."

A few years ago, Ogonowski got a call from a friend in the Agriculture Department asking if he'd help in a new program—a joint effort between the government and some universities called the New Entry Farmer Project—that would give Cambodian arrivals a new start in the United States. Ogonowski was the perfect person for a project like that, a person for whom farming was what sculpting marble or playing golf would be to somebody else, something that you do well for its intrinsic value. He immediately turned over fifteen acres of his own fields right away. He was the kind of guy, in other words, who lived the life that he consciously designed, as a pilot, a farmer, an environmentalist, and a good friend to twelve Cambodian farmers who grew Asian vegetables on his land, and for which he always seemed to "forget" to collect the rent that, technically, was owed him. Ogonowski's family came from Poland to be farmers in America a century ago, and John saw the Cambodians who came to Massachusetts doing the same thing a hundred years later.

So he extended a welcome to people very different from him, and he did a lot more than that. He plowed, manured, and harrowed land for them; he made water available for them from a pond on his land; he helped build a greenhouse for seedlings; he taught them about marketing; he applied for grant assistance to help them expand. He found twelve more acres to add to the fifteen he donated, so that alongside his crops, very familiar in traditional New England, there were pea tendrils, peppers, water spinach, taro root, and a dozen or so more, sold at an Asian farmer's market to Lowell's growing Vietnamese and Cambodian communities. It's not too much to say that John Ogonowski was a kind of living Jeffersonian ideal, the sturdily independent farmer who engaged in public life and took seriously the obligations of citizenship.

Rechhat Proum, a Cambodian from Kompong Thom, who came to Dracut in 1988, remembers that in his first year on a plot on the southwest corner of the Ogonowski farm, nothing of his grew. The conditions of northern Massachusetts were too different from those that he knew in tropical Southeast Asia. But John showed him how modern irrigation could come close enough, and the next year Asian cucumbers, lemon grass, taro root, water spinach, and other vegetables not generally seen in Massachusetts sprang from the ground.

"John never took money from me," Proum said. "I give him vegetables instead."

Ogonowski did an interview with National Public Radio only a few weeks before he died in which he explained the link he made between his own Polish ancestors and the immigrants from Cambodia. He called helping them "a good chance" for himself. His brother, Jim Ogonowski, was always amazed that John, who had too much to do already, took on the whole, time-consuming farmer-to-farmer project. "That was the kind of guy he was," Jim said. "You can't imagine what he did with them. It's incredible."

Ogonowski was born in Lowell, Massachusetts, not far from Dracut where he later set up his farm. He went to Catholic schools until college, beginning at St. Stanislaus Elementary School in Lowell, then Keith Academy for high school, where he liked wearing a smart schoolboy uniform and a tie. He was a good student although not especially talkative, self-contained, not interested in winning popularity contests, more interested in farming than in sports. He went to Lowell Technical College, which later became a branch of the University of Massachusetts, and got a B.S.

in nuclear engineering. It was the era of Vietnam War protests and a kind of chic cultural rebellion, but that did not attract him. He enrolled in ROTC and joined the air force when he graduated in 1972. He got his flight training at a base in Texas and then was stationed at Charleston Air Force Base in South Carolina.

And then suddenly he was half a world away, piloting enormous C-141 transport planes across the Pacific to Vietnam, laden with equipment and materiel, and sometimes, on the return trip, with the bodies of American soldiers who had died in the war. He stayed in the air force for a few years after the American withdrawal from Vietnam, rose to the rank of captain, and, in 1978, left to take a job as a commercial airline pilot.

As a junior pilot, he flew a variety of different routes with a variety of crews. One day, while filling out some paperwork before a flight, John got to talking with Margaret LaValle, a pretty flight attendant who was also based in Boston. Peggy, as she was called, remembers he had an air of authority about him, and she is straightforward about her initial reaction.

"There weren't a lot of single pilots at the time. He was cute and I liked him," she said.

They were married the year after they met. John was thirty-two and Peggy was twenty-nine, and both wanted children. They moved into a condominium that Peggy owned in Brighton, Massachusetts, outside Boston, while they renovated an old house John owned in Pelham, New Hampshire. John knew from the beginning of their marriage that he missed farming, the beauty of the land, the cycle of the seasons, the annual miracle of fruit and vegetables, and, luckily for him, his schedule as a pilot, with both work and nonwork days clustered together, gave him the stretches of nonflying days he needed to take care of a farm and fly commercial jets both.

The combined career was in itself a family tradition. John's father, Alexander Ogonowski, drove a truck for forty years, and worked a 120-acre farm on the side, so John himself and his two brothers and two sisters had pitched in when they were growing up. An uncle, Albert Ogonowski, who ran a farm down the road, had recently retired after a long career as a dentist. John's own first step was to buy some rundown fields in Dracut in the 1980s, just two miles from his parents' farm. It was called White Gate Farm. He drained and reseeded his land, trying to convert what had been fallow into productive land again, and over the years he built it up. He studied the craft of farming with the precision of a doctor studying a medical journal. He knew about things like satellite imaging, where the dry spots were and the wet spots, and he traveled far and often to farm shows, in Iowa, Indiana, and Upstate New York.

"If he had a layover in California and there was a farm show out there, he'd rent a car and go to it," Peggy Ogonowski said. Farms like the Ogonowskis' weren't tiny, but they were more labors of love than labors of economic prosperity, and none of them made enough income to support the families that lived on them. "People do it as a second career, as an avocation," Peggy said, though it was an avocation that took a lot of hard work. "He was down and dirty," Peggy said of John. "He'd walk in the house covered in oil and everything else. He did all of the heavy, heavy labor. He worked as many, or more, hours as a farmer as he did as an airline pilot, which was a full-time job."

For Peggy, a city girl, not a country girl, farming was, let's say, an acquired taste. "Do you remember *Green Acres*?" she said. The reference is to the 1960s sitcom in which Eva Gabor played a prissy aristocrat stuck on a farm. "I'm Eva."

Still, Peggy saw what made John happy, what kept his mind and body productive and engaged, and she willingly went along with his choice to live on the farm. She watched him as he planted crops that flourished and repaired the farm's heavy machinery.

"Every piece of equipment ran perfectly," said his brother Jim. And everything was kept clean and ordered, except for his green Chevy pickup truck, which had layers of caked-on dust.

Three daughters came along in those years also, first Laura, then Caroline twenty months later, and finally Mary-Kate three years after that. With three growing daughters, Peggy and John, who had been living just over the border in Pelham, New Hampshire, decided that it would be better to build a home on the farm, which would give them more space and cut down on their travel time between the farm and their house.

John took on the new house like he took on everything else, studying every detail, even the finer points of stone masonry and slate, since the sides of the house were built of fieldstone and the roof from slate taken from a church hall in town that was being dismantled. The back steps were the granite stairs from a theater in Lowell where, as it happens,

Bette Davis performed as a young woman. A three-season porch on one side of the house looked out onto the surrounding property. There were Adirondack chairs on the lawn. John's eye for materials and enthusiasm brought all these elements together in a spacious dream house.

He rarely set foot in a shopping mall and generally wasn't much interested in buying things, except for the tools, material, and equipment he needed to keep the farm going. He built two barns and, in general, was a consummate tinkerer. As a big-time commercial airline pilot, he had all the necessary social graces but he never sought an audience beyond his family. He had no artifice, wore no jewerly or fancy clothes, drove a pickup truck, and was more comfortable talking to other farmers than he would have been talking to college professors. He never liked New York, and when Peggy, the Long Island native, would take her daughters there, he would jokingly reprimand her for it.

"The worst thing he'd say is he sometimes asked, 'Do you got two minutes to help me?'" his brother Jim remembers. These "two-minute" projects often stretched into two-hour mechanical ordeals, and that's how he came to get his family name, John Deere Johnny.

There is a New England picture-postcard quality to the Ogonowskis' life in Dracut, where the colonial houses are smart and well kept and the main street, Broadway, is lined with American flags. On a very clear day, through some trees on the Ogonowski property, you can see Boston's Prudential and John Hancock towers, but generally the place seems far from Boston. The Ogonowski family life centered on the house. They ate dinner together every night that John was in town and he'd help the girls with their homework. Later in the evening, instead of watching television, he read technical journals on agriculture and heavy equipment. He learned the minutiae of machines from bulldozers to backhoes to 767s. He was what Peggy calls a "regular dad," who took his daughters to farm shows and outings in the country.

At American Airlines, Ogonowski became a captain in 1989. He was a respected, sure-handed, reliable veteran. Back in Dracut, he was a founder of the Dracut Land Trust, which sought to buy land and keep it out of the hands of developers. And then there were the Cambodian refugees participating in the Farmer-to-Farmer program. "He got to know a few of them," Peggy said. "He respected the fact that they were hardworking and dedicated. Most of them, like John, work full-time jobs. They're only farming an acre or two. They don't have big heavy equipment. They relied on John to do the initial plowing and the like to get the fields ready for planting. So they're supplementing their income in farming and hopefully eventually it will take off."

John himself said in his NPR interview that, in his view, once a person is a farmer, they're a farmer for life. "They're hooked," he said. "I don't know if the children of these farmers are going to be so active in it, but they may be because these Cambodians, they bring their whole families out here. You'll see the kids out there weeding and picking the crops. So they may take a liking to it."

The interviewer asked Ogonowski about his own children, and whether they would continue in farming.

"I hope so," he replied. "I have three daughters, and they're good workers. They pick blueberries and sell pumpkins. And, hopefully, they'll continue, so I can retire."

John Ogonowski never had that chance. On the morning of September 11, he left his house at 5:30 A.M. for the scheduled 7:58 takeoff of American Airlines flight 11. He was often the pilot of that particular early-morning flight from Logan Airport to Los Angeles, and, in fact, Peggy, in her days as a flight attendant, had worked that flight often also—"thousands of times," she said. Peggy didn't get up to see him off; there was no reason to; this was an ordinary occurrence in the Ogonowski household, just another transcontinental flight by one of American Airline's most experienced pilots.

"I just said good-bye," she said.

We don't know what John was thinking as he got in his pickup for the drive to Boston, less than an hour away in that traffic-free early morning. Maybe he thought of the fifteen thousand bales of the best hay in the world stacked in his barn; maybe he thought about the pumpkin harvest still coming up. The weather was beautiful, perfect for the picnic he was planning for that weekend at the farm. Well, maybe he was thinking of something else, we don't know, but it's nice to think that he was thinking about the 150 acres he had carved out of fallow land and made scientifically productive, because, as we know, he was never to see White Gate Farm again.

TWELVE

While America Slept

The African bombings did what no other terrorist attack and no intelligence finding had done until then. They made Al Qaeda and Osama bin Laden the most urgent national security matters of the federal government's agenda. Two weeks after they took place, on Thursday, August 20, 1998, President Bill Clinton went to a high school auditorium on Martha's Vineyard, where he was on vacation with his family. Only three days before, on the previous Monday, Clinton had gone on national television to admit what he had long denied, namely that he had had an intimate relationship with the suddenly world-famous White House intern Monica Lewinski. Indeed, the Clinton administration was in such deep political trouble as a result of the scandal—and the largely negative reaction across the country to his Monday admission—that some reporters called to the Martha's Vineyard auditorium expected Clinton to announce his resignation. Instead, he told the country that he had ordered a strike against the terrorists.

Two targets, a terrorist camp in Afghanistan and a chemical weapons factory in Sudan, had been hit by about seventy-five Tomahawk cruise missiles fired from ships in the Persian Gulf and the Red Sea.

In the days that followed, administration spokesmen argued that the raids had served to forestall planned future terrorist atrocities. Defense Secretary William Cohen said that the American retaliation would "reduce the ability of these terrorist organizations to train and equip their misguided followers or to acquire weapons of mass destruction for their use in campaigns of terror." Later Cohen explained that the cruise missiles had destroyed targets at the Zhawar Kili al-Badre Camp near Khost in Afghanistan where a high-level meeting of terrorists had been planned for that day. Bin Laden's whereabouts at that point, whether he was alive or dead, were unknown, but Cohen declared, "The attacks have significantly disrupted the capability to use these camps as terrorist training facilities."

Soon it became clear that the American retaliation did not achieve its major goal, the liquidation of bin Laden himself, who, it seems, had left the target area a few hours before the cruise missiles struck. The American raids did signal a new stage in the fight against bin Laden, and that fight continued to be waged for the remainder of the Clinton years in office. Still, within a few days of the assault, questions started to be raised, especially about the destruction of the Shifa Pharmaceuticals Industries Company, which was in an industrial suburb of Khartoum. The administration claimed that the plant was actually a disguised chemical weapons factory. Administration officials said that soil samples taken outside the plant had showed the presence of a substance known as Empta, whose only function was to make the nerve gas VX. The plant, moreover, was heavily guarded, the administration said, and it showed a suspicious lack of ordinary commercial activities.

"I'm not sure that anyone visibly can identify what chemicals might be in and around the vicinity," Sandy Berger said in a television interview, responding to requests for proof that the plant was what the administration said it was. "There is no question in our mind that that facility, that factory, was used to produce a chemical that is used in the manufacture of VX nerve gas and has no other commercial distribution as far as we understand." Berger added, "We have physical evidence of that fact, and very, very little doubt of it."

But a British engineer, Thomas Carnaffin, who worked as a technical manager during the plant's construction between 1992 and 1996, emerged to tell reporters that there was nothing secret or heavily guarded about the plant at all, and that he never saw any evidence of the production of an ingredient needed for nerve gas. The group that monitors compliance with the treaty banning chemical weapons announced that Empta did have legitimate commercial purposes in the manufacture of fungicides and antibiotics. The owner of the Shifa factory gave interviews in which he emphatically denied that the plant was used for anything other than pharmaceuticals, and there was never persuasive evidence to contradict his assertion. At the same time, members of the administration retreated from claims they made earlier that Osama bin Laden had what Cohen called "a financial interest in contributing to this particular facility." It turned out that no direct financial relationship between bin Laden and the plant could be established. At the same time, the administration, now clearly embarrassed by its inclusion of Sudan in its retaliatory strikes, refused to release the intelligence on which it based its conclusions about Empta; the refusal led to a widespread suspicion that a terrible mistake had been made that it was unwilling to admit.

As for the attack on Afghanistan, it is difficult to see that it played much of a role in forestalling future terrorist attacks by bin Laden or members of his group. It is true that several assaults planned for 2000 and 2001 were discovered and prevented—including a plot to set off a bomb at Los Angeles International Airport and another plot to attack the American embassy in Paris—but this success was thanks to good intelligence, good police work, and some very good luck. Indeed, there is a painful irony about the Clinton administration's multifaceted effort to arrest or liquidate bin Laden. Remember that by 1998, Mohammed Atta, Mahmud al-Shehhi, and Ziad Jarrah were all installed in Hamburg, Germany, and that a fourth figure, Ramzi bin al-Shihb, was striving mightily to get a visa to go to the United States. Starting in 1998, the quest by Clinton and, later, Bush to hunt down bin Laden and destroy Al Qaeda, which failed, coincided with the planning and execution of the September 11 terror assault, which succeeded.

It is not that nobody was warning that a devastating attack could occur. In a moment that has become famous in the history of American law enforcement, at a 1997 conference held in Chicago attended by agents of both the FBI and the CIA, John O'Neill, the head of counterterrorism in the New York office of the FBI, predicted almost exactly what happened four years later. A lot of militant terrorist groups were operating on

American soil, O'Neill said, especially Islamic fundamentalist groups, some of whose members had passed through the forge of the Afghan jihad and who were now ready to deploy their skills in and against the United States. They had the "support infrastructure" they needed, O'Neill said, and they could strike, "if they chose to."

O'Neill was speaking of what law enforcement officials and reporters were calling blowback, the idea that the United States had supplied arms, money, and training during the anti-Soviet struggle to groups that were now becoming American enemies. Two reasons explain why O'Neill's statement in 1997 is famous. First, it was among the most direct of numerous warnings that a devastating terror attack on American soil was likely, and second, O'Neill himself, a well-known figure in New York, a habitué of Elaine's, a bar and restaurant popular among writers, journalists, and figures in the arts, and a friend of network television correspondents and newspaper reporters, was killed in the World Trade Center when he went into one of the towers to help get people out.

O'Neill, who was probably the bureau's single most informed student of bin Laden and Al Qaeda, knew what he was talking about, though he was not alone in making his prediction. Rick Rescorla, as we have seen, worried out loud and in public about the likelihood of a devastating attack, and over the course of the 1990s, there were various commissions and studies that made recommendations about steps needed to tighten airport security or do a better job of following up on immigrants who came into the country on student visas but then never went to any language institute, college, or university.

On September 11, Richard C. Clarke, who had been the White House counterterrorism chief in the Clinton years, remembered the warnings made over the years about terrorists striking on American soil. Clarke was another of the officials warning about the terrorist danger. He was commonly reported to be frustrated at the administration's failure to make terrorism a top priority, or even to follow up on the security recommendations that were made, especially in the aftermath of the World Trade Center attack of 1993. When he heard on the morning of September 11 that American Airlines flight 77 had struck the Pentagon, he reached a quick conclusion: "This is Al Qaeda," he said.

"Everybody in the business knew," James Kallstrom, a former head of the FBI's New York office, said, referring to law enforcement and intelligence agents who kept track of terrorism. "Everybody knew it was going to happen. Not exactly where or when, but nobody was surprised."

And yet, though everybody knew, the responses of the American government, both under President Clinton and in the early months of the Bush administration, were confused, uncertain, and sporadic, despite the warnings, issued not only by American intelligence agencies but by the terrorists themselves. After all, hadn't bin Laden said himself that it was the duty of Muslims to kill Americans wherever they could find them? When the Clinton administration, retaliating for the African embassy bombings in 1998, attacked Al Qaeda camps in Afghanistan with cruise missiles, Ayman Zawahiri called a Pakistani journalist and said: "The war has started. Americans should wait for the answer."

The Clinton administration did take bin Laden seriously. It made several covert efforts to assassinate him, or to find Afghan proxies to do that job, but these initiatives took place against a background of political hesitation, uncertainties about the reliability of intelligence, and paralyzing debates about the proper response to make.

When Bill Clinton took office in January 1993, terrorism was a back-burner issue, a problem to be dealt with among others but not the problem producing the keenest sense of urgency. At the top of the Clinton administration national-security agenda in 1993 were other matters—gays in the military, instability in post-Soviet Russia, peace between Israel and the Arabs, and guarding against rogue states, like Iraq and North Korea. The 1993 attack on the World Trade Center, which took place a month after the Clinton administration took office, was a clear lesson in the new dangers confronting the country, but it was dealt with mostly as a matter of police detection and criminal prosecution, not as a terrorist war against the United States. Suspects were rounded up, put on trial, and convicted, while those who had escaped the dragnet were pursued internationally. But Clinton never visited the site of the attacks; there was no public effort to find the higher-ups who had ordered and financed the bombing; there were no orders to law enforcement agencies to do a better job of sharing information, no big efforts to hire more Arabic-speaking intelligence agents, no warnings to other countries that supporting terrorism was the same as perpetrating it, no calls to the public to be more vigilant; no overall strategy for protecting the United States against the new kind of threat that was signaled by the 1993 bombing.

"It wasn't the kind of thing where you walked into a staff meeting and people asked, 'What are we doing today in the war against terrorism?' " said George Stephanopoulos, the president's adviser for policy and strategy in his first term.

One of the reasons, Stephanopoulos said, is that the 1993 bombing was in its way unsuccessful; it was a shock, but the total death toll of six was relatively small and did not create an intense atmosphere of public concern. And, in the absence of an apocalyptic event like September 11, it was difficult for the government to gear up a response commensurate with the warnings of John O'Neill or the threats of bin Laden. The men arrested in the crime seemed like small-time criminals, not global menaces, and since nobody higher up was ever publicly named—in part because, while Iraq was suspected, there was no hard proof that any government had been involved—there was no sense of some large, outside force that posed a grave danger for the future.

Even later, when bin Laden publicly emerged, there was always something so overblown, so bombastic about his rhetoric that skepticism about his real capabilities seemed natural. He could do damage, but even after the African embassy bombings in 1998, how many people believed he could mount an attack on American territory that would claim thousands of lives? Not very many.

Intelligence on bin Laden and terrorism was collected, but much of it went unshared among agencies, and it was never incorporated into a comprehensive program of anti-terror defense. Diplomatic pressures were brought to bear—on Sudan in particular—to expel bin Laden or to restrict his activities, but the administration did not move firmly to arrest him and bring him to trial, fearing that there wasn't enough clear, courtroom-ready evidence to convict him. The African embassy bombings put bin Laden and Al Qaeda among the administration's national security priorities, and the Clinton administration made several highly secret and still-classified attempts to destroy bin Laden and his network. Still, they were sporadic and unsuccessful, and without a commitment to the sort of major, concerted, long-range military enterprise that the Pentagon was saying would be necessary to ensure success.

"From August 1998, bin Laden was Enemy No. 1," said Sandy Berger, Clinton's second-term national security adviser. Still, the impression remains that the effort to nail bin Laden—which the president undertook at the height of the Monica Lewinski–impeachment scandal—was made on the cheap, as it were, without a major expenditure of resources and without any risks to American lives.

As Clarke put the problem: "Democracies don't prepare well for things that have never happened before," and, until September 11, it hadn't happened.

Moreover, before September 11 there were political risks to undertaking a full fight against terrorism and no political pressure to do so, not from within Clinton's party and not from Republicans. The anti-terrorism fight wasn't an issue in the presidential campaigns of either 1996 or 2000. The question "What would you do to protect the country against terrorism?" was never asked in any of the presidential debates. The words "bin Laden" and "Al Qaeda" were never uttered during the course of either campaign and the general public was unfamiliar with them. In 2000, candidate George W. Bush accused the Clinton administration of letting the military deteriorate, but he was speaking of conventional forces facing conventional threats and not of the special forces used against terrorists. There were few, if any, calls in newspaper editorials for a genuine war against terrorism. It would seem that, except for law enforcement or counterterrorism professionals like O'Neill and Clarke—and the warnings by private students of Islamic terrorism like Steven Emerson—there were very few Americans who really believed that bin Laden would be able to carry out his threats. According to Leon E. Panetta, chief of staff in the last part of Clinton's first term, the president's senior aides saw terrorism as only one of several pressing problems.

"Clinton was aware of the threat and sometimes he would mention it," he said. But the "big issues" of the first term were "Russia, Eastern bloc, Middle East peace, human rights, rogue nations, and then terrorism."

And yet, this history is littered with what seem clear in retrospect to be missed opportunities, missed signals, and close calls. The 1990s present a history in which the United States government became ever more aware of bin Laden, Al Qaeda, and the emergence of a new type of warfare, but, before the cataclysmic event of September 11, it did not develop a means to act decisively and effectively. The war on terrorism in this sense is a kind of unhappy thriller in which the good guys, the American government, the FBI, and other agencies, were often close on the trail of dangerous and ruthless foes, but they never were able to catch up with them.

━━━━━

The first major indication of bin Laden's importance came after the World Trade Center bombing of 1993. As we have seen, there has never been any clear evidence that bin Laden was directly involved in that operation. But as part of the investigation that followed the Trade Center blast, the FBI and New York City police examined a cache of materials that had been in their possession for two and a half years, and only then did they became aware of the shape the new terrorist threat was taking. The materials had actually been seized in 1990 from el-Sayyid Nosair, the radical Egyptian, after he assassinated Rabbi Meier Kahane, the founder of the Jewish Defense League. At the time, they didn't seem to have any forensic value, so they were put aside. Now they were astonished to discover a kind of blueprint for Muslim terrorism against the United States, and it had been in their possession all along.

The cache, for example, contained a note written by Nosair himself in which he called for striking at the "enemies of God by means of destroying and blowing up the towers that constitute the pillars of their civilization such as the tourist attractions they are so proud of and the high buildings they are so proud of." The FBI also discovered that the Al Kifah Center was linked to radical Muslims in Peshawar, and the link went beyond recruitment for jihad in Afghanistan. There were tape recordings of conversations between the Brooklyn group and Sheik Omar Abdel Rahman, who was in Peshawar at the time, in which Abdel Rahman encouraged Nosair's ambitions. In other words, already three years before the Trade Center bombing, Abdel Rahman and Nosair were contemplating the sort of attack that then took place in 1993—a strike at one of those tall buildings Americans are so proud of.

At the time, bin Laden was known to American intelligence as a figure in the Peshawar-based jihad movement, and, according to FBI officials active in the investigation, the FBI was aware of him too. But the first person to provide a full portrait of him and his position in the international terrorist movement was a mysterious double agent named Ali A. Mohammed who, in the early to mid-1980s, was both an officer in the Egyptian army and a secret member of Islamic Jihad, which, three years earlier, had assassinated Egyptian president Anwar Sadat. In 1984, Mohammed approached the CIA volunteering to be a spy, and he was put on the payroll. The CIA was trying to collect information on Lebanese groups, especially Hezbollah, that were holding Americans hostage in Beirut, and they hoped that Mohammed could help them. But then the CIA learned that when Mohammed did make contact with a Hezbollah cell in Germany, he revealed that he was working for the CIA, which fired him. Moreover, suspecting that Mohammed was a terrorist himself who had tried to become a double agent, the CIA warned the State Department, which put him on a "watch list" of people not to be allowed into the United States.

Nonetheless, Mohammed applied for a visa at the American embassy in Cairo, and received one. He joined the army, becoming a supply sergeant at the army's Special Warfare School at Fort Bragg, North Carolina, the place where the anti-terrorist Delta Force is trained. He was even used as a kind of character actor in a Special Forces training video, where his role was intended to convey an idea of how Islamic radicals felt about the world.

In 1989, Mohammed was one of the men observed by the FBI giving training to Nosair, Salameh, and Abuhalima at that firing range on Long Island. It seems that while he was a U.S. Army sergeant, he spent weekends helping members of the Al Kifah Center, staying with Nosair while he was in New York. In other words, on the one hand he was connected with the anti-terrorist Delta Force at Fort Bragg; on the other he was helping to train people who were planning a spectacular act of terror against the United States. In November 1989, he was honorably discharged from the army. He also became a citizen that year and, by 1991, began traveling regularly to Pakistan and Afghanistan, where he became a military trainer at an Al Qaeda camp. That year he helped bin Laden make his move from Afghanistan to Sudan, in part by helping to obtain the false documents needed by some of the Al Qaeda team to transit through third countries under assumed identities. Once bin Laden was installed in Sudan, Mohammed trained his personal bodyguards and coordinated with Sudanese intelligence agents who were responsible for bin Laden's security when he ventured outside his compound.

In short, Mohammed knew the members of the Islamic terror network in New York and was also close to Osama bin Laden. This was the case in 1991, two years before the 1993 World Trade Center explosion. In fact, Mohammed was never implicated in that, and, despite his links to the Al-Kifah Center, there is no evidence that he knew about it. But soon after it occurred, in 1994, he was stopped crossing the border into the United States from Canada in the company of a man who was carrying false documents. Questioned by the FBI, Mohammed told them of his ties to bin Laden. And soon after that, he was leading a remarkable double life. He was an informer for the FBI, whose agents he met in Santa Clara, California, where he was living, telling them about bin Laden's operation in the Sudan. At the same time he continued serving bin Laden in the Sudan. He was the man bin Laden had sent to Nairobi in 1993 to case out potential terrorist targets.

"I took pictures, drew diagrams, and wrote a report," he recounted of that trip, speaking in a later court appearance in New York. He gathered information on the American, French, and Israeli embassies and then returned to Khartoum, where he was debriefed by bin Laden himself. "Bin Laden looked at the picture of the American embassy and pointed to where a truck could go as a suicide bomber," Mohammed testified.

By about 1996, bin Laden was considered enough of a threat for the CIA to create a virtual station, code-named Alex, to track his movements and activities around the world. The State Department issued a white paper that it circulated to Middle Eastern governments describing bin Laden as a financier of terrorist movements worldwide. For the first time, bin Laden was said to have been behind the Somali attackers of American troops in Mogadishu in 1993. The State Department also pressed Sudan to expel him, but when Sudan hinted that it was willing to turn him over to American authorities, a Justice Department review of that possibility in the spring of 1996 concluded that there wasn't enough evidence on the Somali attack to convict him in an American court. When Sudan did expel him that year, forcing him to go back to Afghanistan, Berger, the national security adviser, declared, "He lost his base and his momentum."

In fact, bin Laden wasn't losing either a base or momentum. While he was in the Sudan, he was at least under the control of a government that was responsive to American pressure; in Afghanistan he wasn't. Indeed, in Afghanistan he was far freer to recruit new members, to set up training camps, and to mount ever more costly attacks. Moreover, the United States was well aware of the expansion of his network. In 1977, the former Al Qaeda operative Jamal Ahmed al-Fadl emerged to tell American investigators that bin Laden's aim was no longer just overthrowing Saudi Arabia and other "infidel" Middle Eastern governments, but taking jihad to the United States itself.

Al-Fadl, who introduced himself to a consular official while on a visa line at an American embassy in Africa, also told the FBI that the bin Laden group "might try to make bomb against some embassy." He recounted the story of bin Laden's move to Sudan, of his wish to bring harm to American forces in Somalia, and the growth of his empire, which used legitimate business as a way of raising money for jihad. It seems that al-Fadl also prompted American intelligence to begin watching the Al Qaeda cell in Nairobi, and this in turn led to one of the most extraordinary facts of the war on terrorism: it is that for more than a year before the African embassy bombings, American intelligence was not only aware of the Nairobi cell, but it was also monitoring some of its communications. The bombings, in other words, took place under the very noses of American intelligence agents.

The surveillance included National Security Agency taps on telephone lines used by Al Qaeda members in Kenya that enabled the agency to overhear members of the Nairobi group talking by cell phone to bin Laden in Afghanistan. It was around this time that John O'Neill made his now famous prediction about terror attacks on the United States. O'Neill's warnings coincided almost exactly with those of al-Fadl. In addition, the CIA investigated three other warnings—coming either from Arab informants or from the intelligence services of other countries—that an embassy in Africa was going to be targeted for a terrorist attack.

It was also in 1997 that FBI agents searched the Nairobi home of Wadi el-Hage, a naturalized American citizen from Lebanon who worked for bin Laden. El-Hage's name had surfaced earlier. He knew Mahmud Abuhalima, one of the 1993 World Trade Center bombers, and other members of Al Kifah in Brooklyn. Indeed, at one point, though he lived in Houston, Texas, he was named as the person who would take over leadership of Al-Kifah after its founder, Mustafa Shalabi, had gone to Pakistan. But Shalabi, as we have seen, was assassinated and El-Hage never did come to New York.

El-Hage did go to Nairobi, however, where he was a close associate of Osama bin Laden. He claimed in a court proceeding in 2001 that he only handled legitimate business for bin Laden and didn't know of the activities of Al Qaeda, but the jury didn't believe him. One reason for not believing him was that the FBI found a letter in his office computer written by a certain Fazul Abdullah Mohammed. This is the real name of the person that the Nairobi bomber 'Owhali knew as Harun, in whose house he stayed in Nairobi when he arrived there from Afghanistan a few days before the bombing and who seemed to 'Owhali to be in charge. A text of Harun's letter, which was obtained by the television documentary program *Frontline*, is written to an unidentified person called Brother Sharif. It is the letter that we have already seen making reference to the role played by Al Qaeda in the 1993 attack against American servicemen in Somalia. It also warns members of the cell that American intelligence has learned of the Al-Qaeda presence in Nairobi.

"My recommendation to my brothers in East Africa was to not be complacent regarding security matters," Harun's letter said, "and that they should know that now they have become America's primary target and that they should know that there is an American-Kenyan-Egyptian intelligence activity in [Na]irobi aiming to identify the names and residences of the members who are associated with the Shaykh since America knows well that the youth who lived in Somalia and were members of the Shaykh's cell are the ones who killed the Americans in Somalia."[1]

Harun was good at taking his own advice, since under his direction, a bomb was built, installed in a truck, kept at a house in Nairobi that he rented, and used to blow away the façade of the American embassy even though American intelligence was monitoring telephone calls and faxes to and from the Al Qaeda cell in Nairobi right up to August 7, 1998, the date of the bombing.

How could it have happened that American intelligence was able to have penetrated the Al Qaeda cell in Nairobi but failed to prevent the embassy bombings? The historian Roberta Wohlstetter, writing about intelligence during World War II, might provide an explanation for this conundrum. Wohlstetter uses the term "static" to describe the confusion, inconsistencies, and sheer volume of intelligence, which makes it very difficult to pick out ahead of time the few items that seem in retrospect to be crucial. American intelligence received thousands of warnings of terrorist attacks. Which ones to pay attention to and which ones are "static" is extremely difficult to decide.

Moreover, in the case of the African embassy bombings, the very effort to get intelligence may have undermined the value of the intelligence itself. We know, for example, that the FBI interviewed el-Hage several times in Nairobi. That would have signaled to el-Hage that the American authorities had at least some strong suspicions about the Al Qaeda network in Africa. Not long after that, Harun's letter, which warns that American intelligence is hot on Al Qaeda's trail, turned up in el-Hage's computer. It seems reasonable to surmise, in other words, that after being interrogated, el-Hage informed Harun of the FBI's interest in him, and that is what led to Harun's warning. From that point on, it seems that Harun took extraordinary measures to keep information about the bomb plot from leaking. The death of 224 people in Nairobi and Dar es Salaam is proof of how well he succeeded.

After the embassy bombings of August, Clinton himself signed three Memoranda of Notification that authorized the American government to capture or to kill bin Laden and his senior associates. The CIA stepped up its efforts to locate bin Laden, and warships were stationed in the Indian Ocean and the Persian Gulf to fire missiles if his whereabouts could be precisely determined. In September 2000, an unarmed "Predator" spy plane, secretly based in Uzbekistan, was flown over Afghanistan, showing what officials believed to be real-time information on bin Laden's movements. But the Predators were unarmed and several hours were needed between the time bin Laden could be definitively located and missiles from American ships could strike him. Moreover, each time a strike was approved against bin Laden, George Tenet, the director of Central Intelligence, called the president to say that the information was not reliable enough to be used in an attack, and, after the immediate retaliation for the embassy bombings in August, no further attack on bin Laden was launched—until after September 11.[2]

Indeed, before September 11, no administration—and this includes the Bush administration in its first nine months—was willing to undertake major military and diplomatic moves that would have been necessary to destroy Al Qaeda. And in the absence of a very clear threat, conventional wisdom was that such moves would be so costly in lives and money that the public wouldn't support them. Some inside the administration favored stronger diplomatic efforts, like putting pressure on Pakistan to end its support for both the Taliban and bin Laden. But senior officials determined that the risk to the American relationship with Pakistan was too great, and a good relationship with Pakistan was deemed important to forestall a nuclear exchange with India. The result is that a traditionally friendly country and a critical one, Pakistan, continued, through its military and intelligence agencies, to give support to the very figure that the national security adviser, Berger, declared to be Public Enemy Number One.

Meanwhile, the White House asked the Joint Chiefs of Staff to develop plans for a commando raid to kill or capture bin Laden, but the military determined that for a commando raid to be successful, bin Laden's whereabouts would have to be determined twelve to twenty-four hours in advance, a near impossibility.

The chairman of the Joint Chiefs, General Henry H. Shelton, rejected the possibility of striking at bin Laden with just a small commando team and said that only a full-scale invasion of Afghanistan involving many thousands of American troops would do the job. Proposals were made that the Taliban's only remaining enemy in the field in Afghanistan, the Northern Alliance, be helped with money and materials. But this option too was rejected on the grounds that it would involve the United States too deeply in Afghan politics and, in any case, would be opposed by the Taliban's main backer, Pakistan.

Throughout the Clinton adminstration's time in office, a group of officials pressed for strong action. Some wanted to finance and arm the Northern Alliance despite expected Pakistani objections. After the *Cole* attack in October 2000, Richard C. Clarke, the White House counterterrorism director, pushed for bombing bin Laden's largest training camps again, but the Clinton administration had been politically wounded the first time it had struck those camps, and it was unwilling to try again. Clinton, politically weakened by the White House sex scandal, had also been deeply embarrassed by the public reaction to the 1998 bombing of the Sudanese pharmaceuticals plant.

When the George W. Bush administration came to power in January 2001, it inherited the Clinton problem: A private group controlled by bin Laden had succeeded in attacking two American embassies in Aden Harbor and the USS *Cole,* but it had no clear and effective way of responding. The Bush administration did draft a plan for dealing with terrorism. It chose the Northern Alliance option, and its centerpiece was a $200 million CIA program to arm the Taliban's enemies, but the plan did not include putting American troops on the ground or supporting the Northern Alliance with advisers or air power. The Bush administration, moreover, did not treat the problem with urgency. In August, Bush was briefed by the CIA and told that bin Laden himself might have a plan to hijack American airliners, but no connection was made between that general warning and any specific plot. Meanwhile, the draft plan was approved by Bush's advisers on September 4 and it was to be presented to the president on the tenth, but Bush was traveling that day and it was never given to him. The next day was September 11, and the entire world, and the American attitude toward bin Laden, changed forever.

This history seems to show that over more than twenty years of terrorist assaults on the United States, no administration had ever found a strong, effective response. One could say that the history began in 1979 when Iranian militants, clearly supported by the revolutionary Iranian government, seized fifty-three hostages from the American embassy and held them for more than a year. Except for a commando raid that turned out to be a disaster for the United States and a propaganda triumph for Iran, there was no retaliation. During the 1980s, terrorists blew up a marine barracks in Lebanon, killing 225; they bombed the American embassies in both West Beirut and East Beirut, and seized several hostages, most of whom were held for several years. Again, the United States found no way to exact a price.

In 1994, Iraq's Saddam Hussein attempted to assassinate former president Bush during a visit to Kuwait. The response of the Clinton administration was to attack the Iraqi intelligence agency with cruise missiles, at night when the building was empty. During the 1990s, Saddam expelled United Nations arms inspectors investigating Iraq's nuclear, biological, and chemical weapons plants, and the United States took no action to ensure that the inspections would continue, and, eventually, they were abandoned. In 1993, eighteen American servicemen were killed and dragged through the streets of Mogadishu, and the American response was to withdraw its forces. In 1995, twenty-three American servicemen were killed in two attacks on an American training center and a barracks in Saudi Arabia. Though the attacks were traced to Iran-backed groups, no retaliation was attempted. Then came the African embassy bombings in 1998 and the *Cole* bombing of 2000—total Americans dead: twenty-nine.

It's no wonder that Osama bin Laden probably assumed that the United States was too soft, too worried about casualties, too lacking in political conviction to respond to terrorist attacks.

THIRTEEN

Richard A. Penney:
Project Renewal

For Richard A. Penney, it can be fairly said that life had not worked out as he would have expected, or as anyone would have expected for so gifted a man. In the late 1980s, Penney was a member of the army of the homeless in New York City, one of those many people who used both to frighten and trouble the liberal conscience. He had served time in jail, separated from his wife, and lost touch with his only son, Richard Penney, Jr.; he was depressed, and he had essentially stayed indoors from 1976 until the late 1980s. He needed help.

And yet, years before, Penney, who grew up on Green Street in the Bedford-Stuyvesant section of Brooklyn, had been the valedictorian of his class at Metropolitan High School in Manhattan, where he graduated in 1966. He was the star of the block, where his parents, Allie and Inez Penney, a retired construction worker and a domestic for a Manhattan family, owned the four-story house where Richard grew up. He was an athlete and a scholar, captain of the varsity handball team, and a two-time finalist in the city-wide handball championship tournament. There is no more quintessentially urban a sport than handball, played ardently, fiercely in small pocket-sized parks throughout the five boroughs, and to be a champion, or, certainly, the best player in your neighborhood, conferred a lot of prestige, and to be a handball star and a valedictorian at the same time meant that you were exceptional.

Penney had many college scholarship awards, but he elected to go to a technical school in Brooklyn instead. The year after finishing high school he married his childhood sweetheart, Valada Porter, and in 1968, when the country was being torn both by anti–Vietnam War protests and racial demonstrations, Richard, Jr., was born. That same year, Richard, Sr., finished at the RCA Institute, where he studied electronics, and he went to work as a communication craftsman for AT&T, remaining in the job for the next seven years.

But things started to go wrong. Richard and Valada separated in 1970, and Richard and his son moved into the top floor of Allie and Inez Penney's brownstone on Green Street.

"It was a perfect situation, since my grandparents lived below us," Richard, Jr., recalled later, "good for babysitting and such."

Clearly, though he didn't show it to those close to him, Richard, Sr., was a troubled man. In 1975, he quit his job at AT&T, began to associate with criminals, and started shooting heroin. That year, he was arrested for holding up a token booth, and, like a lot of people who get into drugs, he dragged those closest to him down. His parents mortgaged their brownstone to pay for defense lawyers. But Penney was convicted anyway and went to prison.

He got out on parole the next year, but by then too much of his life had fallen apart to put it back together. Valada moved to Virginia, taking Richard, Jr., with her. And though Richard and Valada remained on good terms—and Richard, Jr., went regularly to visit his father—Penney seemed strangely unengaged. "He was a recluse," Richard, Jr., said. "He was depressed, I think, and just stayed in the house. I mean, to think he stayed indoors from 1976 to the late eighties! Prison life changed him and there wasn't much the family could do about it."

Sometime in the mid-1980s, after the death of his father, Penney learned that he had been adopted, that his birth father was Jewish and his mother an African American acquaintance of the family. The news devastated him. When his adoptive mother died, he didn't even go to the funeral. Around that time, Valada and Richard, Jr., went to New York to see Penney. They talked for many hours trying to persuade Penney to move to Virginia and, as Richard, Jr., put this, "to start a new life with us, to start over."

"I had already graduated from high school, so I figured while I went to college, me and my dad could get a place together, some place where he could get some support," Richard, Jr., said. "You see, my family is quite old, so all of my dad's cousins and nephews are much older than he is. So nobody really was around after my grandmother died. She was his family. But even after pleading with him, he refused to come with us."

Valada and Richard, Jr., went home. A cousin of Penney's arranged a room for him in Brooklyn, but after he got back to Virginia, Richard, Jr., realized that he no longer had his father's address or telephone number, and the two lost contact permanently.

"Back then," he said, "I was really hurt, really hurt that my dad didn't come with us. I was so disappointed that he wouldn't come. Even though I knew he had a lot of problems, we still had a great relationship. I knew I was important to him, but I immediately thought that I wasn't important enough to convince him to come down, spend some time with me, to get to know me as a grown man. It really hurt."

But when Richard, Jr., contacted his father's cousin in order to get back in touch, he learned that Penney had left the room where he was living and disappeared.

"I thought maybe I pressed him too hard," Richard, Jr., said. "Maybe he got angry with me. It was maybe, maybe, maybe. I figured I would give him some time, and I figured someone, or something, will come up and I would get back in touch with him again. But after a few months, I still hadn't heard from him. I knew I had to do something. So I started to look for him. It was the early '90s and we weren't hooked up with computers back then. I started out by calling information, asking for any Penney in the Brooklyn area, and my search went wider and wider and wider from there."

Unknown to his son, Penney had become part of what was called "the problem of homelessness." In fact, for the three years after his disappearance in 1987, nobody even knew what homeless shelter he was in, or whether he went to a shelter at all, or whether he slept on the street in some cardboard box next to the doors of a church or over a metal grate or in one of the underground archways of Grand Central Station. His disappearance not only from the world of his son but from the world altogether seems to have been complete. And then, in 1990, he turned up at the Harlem Men's Shelter on 155th Street and he seems to have stayed there, at least some of the time, until 1994.

It was then that Penney met Jon Bunge, now a staff member of the Hope Program, a nonprofit agency that helps homeless people find jobs and get their lives back together. Penney had applied to the Hope Program for a work internship and his application was referred to Bunge by the Harlem Men's Shelter.

"He came across as shy and there was little eye contact," Bunge recalls. "He seemed very intelligent but something was a little off. He wasn't social and wouldn't mingle with the other people in the program at all. But he was definitely a sweet, nice guy."

Penney worked hard. He showed up every day and did an internship at the Christ and St. Steven's Church on the Upper West Side of Manhattan. But Penney's rehabilitation does not seem to have always gone smoothly. He dropped out of sight at times. He resisted therapy. It is not clear that he stopped using drugs. He appeared and reappeared at the Harlem Men's Shelter, which was taken over by another program, Ready, Willing and Able, in 1996.

"From the time he came into the Hope Program, we did conduct the routine medical and psychological examinations," Bunge said. "We figured that jail really changed Richard. He really didn't want to open up at all and it was extremely hard to get any information out of him. We knew he had a son, and as I look back there is a part of me that wishes I could have spent more time looking for Richard, Jr., but my work to find jobs for everyone sometimes overwhelms any personal desires to do more than that."

Another social worker, Khimo Pereyra of the Grand Central Neighborhood Social Services Corporation, which provides food and shelter to the homeless, recalled that Penney was withdrawn. But he did talk about his family with Pereyra who believes that he wanted, sooner or later, to be back in touch with Valada, whom he had never divorced, and hoped to be reunited with his son.

"He was thin, around one hundred thirty-five pounds," Pereyra said, recalling her first meeting with Penney. "He had a backpack and a book or a magazine in his hand. He sat down and we talked. I asked him questions, where he was from and stuff like that. He told me New York. I asked him if he had a family and he said yes, that he was married and had a son. I later found out he never told stories about his wife and son to any social workers, only me. He said he hadn't seen his family in a long time and that he was trying his best to recuperate.

"Penney was a man with a lot of respect for himself, his wife, his son, and friends," Pereyra said. "He often told me he was saving money so he could go down to see his son, with money. Basically I think he was ashamed of going down there with nothing. He felt he couldn't go down there empty-handed."

In 1999, Penney made a major step forward. He got a job with Project Renewal, a social services agency that held the recycling contract for the entire World Trade Center and gave jobs to about twenty people who circulated through the towers collecting paper, plastic, and cans. Penney got $6 an hour, enough for him to get a room in a rooming house in Brooklyn, paying $235 a month. The house was shabby by any standard, its parlors crammed with bunk beds. It was also very close to Green Street, where Penney had grown up under far better circumstances, and nobody knows exactly how he felt about that, whether he felt good to be on familiar turf, or whether it reminded him of how far down his life had slid. But at least he was living independently, saving a bit of money, and going regularly to work where he soon got a reputation for reliability, for being the first to show up at the Trade Center every morning.

And maybe that's why Richard didn't make it through September 11. If he had been less conscientious, if he had only shown up a little bit later for his job at Project Renewal, maybe he would still be alive. And in this sense it was his very determination to turn his life around that cost him everything. In fact, nobody who survived September 11 actually saw him that morning, but everybody knew that he was never later to work than 8:00 A.M., which would have meant leaving his rooming house in the Bedford Stuyvesant section of Brooklyn at about 7:00 or earlier.

He had a routine. He always started on the 105th floor of the north tower, on the top floor of the several floors of offices occupied by the bond trading company Cantor Fitzgerald, and he worked his way down through the offices of Marsh & McLennen, dumping recyclable paper into a big wheeled cart. Around noon, he would go down to the basement to dump the paper, which was loaded onto trucks from New Jersey, but because he tended to work from the top floor down, at 8:46 he would have to have been near the beginning of his daily round, someplace above the 100th floor, which was a very bad place to be.

FOURTEEN

The Commandos in America

One of the reasons for supposing that Mohammed Atta was the mastermind of the September 11 operation is that soon after arriving in the United States, he and al-Shehhi began receiving substantial sums of money in bank transfers, which he must have parceled out to his co-conspirators so they could pay for their expenses. Between June 29 and September 18, 2000, a total of $114,230 was wired to Atta and al-Shehhi in five separate transfers, all of them from a bank in the United Arab Republic to the Sun Trust Bank, where Atta and al-Shehhi had an account.

But Atta had other things to do as well. Most important, he and the other plot leaders had to learn how to fly the airplanes they would commandeer. To do so, they enrolled at American flight schools, in Florida, Arizona, California, and Oklahoma. In May 2000, al-Midhar and Alhamzi—the two who had arrived on the West Coast from Bangkok in January—were settling into life in southern California. Indeed they alone among the hijackers integrated themselves into a local community. They went to the San Diego Islamic Center, the region's biggest mosque, and there Alhamzi met Abdusattar Shaikh, a retired English professor from San Diego State University and a member of the local police commission. Shaikh rented Alhamzi a room in his house in San Diego's Lemon Grove neighborhood. He observed that his tenant was devout, spending his spare time reading books on Islam and visiting Islamic web-sites on the

Internet, including, it would seem, an electronic marriage bureau. One of Alhamzi's messages read: "Saudi businessman looking for a bride who would like to live in this country and Saudi Arabia."[1] This seems like a strange thing to do for a man who was part of a martyrdom operation. Maybe Alhamzi just needed to cling to a sense of normal life; maybe he didn't know at the time that his mission was one in which he would be expected to lose his life. A less likely possibility is that he didn't yet know that there was going to be a mission. According to Shaikh, Alhamzi got responses from two Egyptian women. It is not known if he answered them.

Soon after they arrived in San Diego, al-Midhar and Alhamzi showed up at a place called Sorbi's Flying Club near San Diego, saying that they had never flown before and they wanted to learn how to fly Boeings. Their instructor, Fereidoun "Fred" Sorbi, later recounted how he told them that, no, you don't jump right into Boeings. Instead, he gave them an initial lesson on a single-engine Cessna or Piper Cub, and he remembers that when one of the men was at the controls to effect a landing, the other man prayed loudly.[2] They didn't last long at that school though. Another instructor, Rick Garza, asked them to leave after giving them a few ground lessons and two practice flights.

"They had no idea what they were doing," he said, adding that the two offered him extra money if he would teach them to fly multiengine planes.[3] He didn't, and there is no record that they received flight training elsewhere.

Hani Hanjour, on the other hand, who was on the same hijacked plane as al-Midhar and Alhamzi, American Airlines flight 77, got a pilot's license in 1999 after several years of lackadaisical study at several flight schools in Arizona. At the CRM Airline Training Center in Scottsdale he often cut class and never showed much passion, said Paul V. Blair, the center's controller. Only a month before September 11, he went to a private airport in Maryland to rent a plane there, but he failed his test flight and the rental request was denied. Still, in April 1999 he did get a Federal Aviation Administration license for multiengine planes, and in June 2001 he seemed to be brushing up when he spent time on a simulator at the Sawyer School of Aviation in Phoenix. Most likely, shaky as he was, Hanjour was the pilot-hijacker of flight 77.

Meanwhile, Ziad Jarrah, one of the men who came from Hamburg,

was living in a seedy, palm-fringed complex of single-story adobe apartments in Hollywood, Florida. He drove a red Mitsubishi Eclipse, which,
according to one neighbor, "stood out." He told his landlord that he was
taking flying lessons, and indeed he was, taking six months of lessons at
the Florida Flight Training Center in Venice, Florida, and in July 2001 he
earned a certification for single-engine planes.

As for Atta and al-Shehhi, they visited the Airman Flight School in
Norman, Oklahoma, soon after they arrived in the United States, but they
decided not to study there, going instead to Florida. They trained first at
Huffman Aviation, also in Venice, and they lived in a little pink house in
Nokomis, a nearby town. They drove a red Pontiac, wore polo shirts and
khaki pants, and paid their instructor $10,000 in cash each for four
months. Like Jarrah, they got certified in single-engine planes.

"They spoke quite good English," their instructor, Rudi Dekkers,
said. "They were by themselves, not hanging out with other students.
Most of our students from other countries go to bars and take their times.
They were strange birds."

They were strange enough, not doing some of the elementary things
that you'd think people on a mission like theirs would do, and that created
some temporary problems for them. At one flight school, Jones Aviation
in Sarasota, their instructor asked them to leave after just three weeks
because of what he described as their poor attitudes. Their initial landlord
and landlady in Nokomis, Charles and Dru Voss, kicked them out in less
time than that, only one week. The complaint was that they left their beds
unmade and a lot of water in the bathroom after showering. Mrs. Voss's
annoyance is reminiscent of the complaint of one of Atta's German
roommates, that he was inconsiderate and slovenly. He dirtied the dishes
but never washed them. And then there was the weird incident in which
Atta and al-Shehhi stalled their rented Piper Warrior on a runway at
Miami International Airport. Rather than radio for help and wait for the
plane to be towed away, they simply turned off the lights and walked
away, leaving the plane where it was.

Flying a single-engine plane is a prerequisite for flying commercial
jetliners, but it is not training to do so. To get more advanced training,
Atta and al-Shehhi moved in December 2000 to southeast Florida and
trained on the jet airline simulator at SimCenter Aviation in Opa-Locka,

paying $1,500 apiece and, according to their instructor, Henry George, spending most of their time practicing maneuvers and turns (though they practiced take offs and landings as well). During this time, Atta and al-Shehhi, inseparable as always, lived in several rental apartments in several places, Delray Beach, Coral Springs, and Hollywood. Atta carried a briefcase, Nancy Adams, a neighbor at his Delray Beach home, the Hamlet Country Club, said.

Given what happened on September 11, it seems safe to assume that during their time in Florida and California, all of the leaders of the September 11 plot knew exactly what they were training for, that the plot was already fully formed when they took their aviation lessons. But maybe it wasn't. There are strange inconsistencies in the trajectory of Atta in particular, events that are difficult to explain—unless, in fact, the exact plot carried out was formed only in the late months of their American sojourn. There are certainly signs that when the men arrived in 2000, they knew they were going to carry out a terrorist assault on the United States, but they might not have known until much later exactly what kind of assault.

In January, Atta went on the first of two trips he made to Spain, spending about four days there and leaving almost no known trace. Presumably he did not go out of an interest to visit the Alhambra before he died; he went because he needed to see somebody in Spain who could help him with his plans to launch an attack in the United States. Spain, as we will see later, was an important European center for Muslim extremists from Egypt and Algeria. In addition, it was a country where considerable fund-raising was done for Al Qaeda by Arab businessmen with European connections, and it is very likely that Atta's trip to Spain is related to them. In any case, when he came back to Florida, he began making inquiries about crop-dusting planes. In February he asked about crop dusters at the Municipal Airport in Belle Glade, Florida, home of the South Florida Crop Care Company's hangar. According to James Lester, who cleans and loads crop dusters, Atta asked him how much fuel and chemicals the planes could hold, even asking if he could sit in the cockpit of one of the planes. Later he made at least two inquiries about getting government loans to buy a crop duster.

One such inquiry showed him at his most belligerent and strange. He went to a Department of Agriculture loan officer in Florida named

Johnell Bryant and demanded a $650,000 loan to buy a twin-engine crop duster with a very large tank. When Bryant turned him down, she later said on ABC News, he asked her what kept him from slitting her throat and stealing the money out of the safe behind her desk. Then he threw a wad of money on the table, trying to buy an aerial picture of Washington, D.C., that hung in her office. According to Bryant, he even spoke glowingly about Osama bin Laden.

This interest in crop dusters was not short-lived and it was not confined to Atta. In June, Zacarias Moussaoui, a Moroccan-born French citizen living in the United States, downloaded crop-duster information on his computer and asked about starting a crop-dusting company in Oklahoma. Moussaoui, who was arrested in August when the flight school he was attending became suspicious of his interest in flying Boeing jetliners, is believed by prosecutors to have been intended as a substitute hijacker, the missing twentieth man. It will be remembered that a friend of Atta's in Germany, Ramzi bin al-Shibh, applied several times for visas to the United States but was turned down. Presumably, al-Shibh was part of the original hijacker team and Moussaoui, who took pilot training in Oklahoma, was designated as his replacement. Now he, like Atta, was asking about crop dusters. Could it be that two of the intended hijackers were asking questions about crop dusters out of a casual and unimportant interest? According to J. D. Lee, general manager of Florida Crop Care, Atta was asking about crop dusting until just a few days before September 11.

It is possible that Lee got the date of his last inquiries wrong, since it would seem that Atta would have been far too busy with the final details of the September 11 plan to be looking into crop dusting that late. Still, these inquiries about crops dusters suggest that as of March 2001 or so, Atta was still not sure what sort of attack he would carry out, and one plan he was considering involved the use of crop dusters to spray deadly chemical or biological agents over a densely populated district—perhaps several crop dusters piloted by several terrorists on the same day. He might have killed more than a few thousand people that way.

Atta made at least two, possibly three, trips to Europe after his crop-dusting inquiries, and, given his single-mindedness and the importance of his mission in America, it is difficult to believe that any of these trips was unrelated to the September 11 plot. There are reports that in March 2001, he was in Hamburg with al-Shehhi, and that together they moved out of the Marienstrasse apartment. It is also around that time, after his trip to Florida in any case, that he made his crop-dusting inquiries. And then, on April 8, according to Stanislav Gross, the Czech interior minister, Atta met with the Iraqi intelligence agent, Ahmed Khalil Ibrahim Samir al-Ani, the same man who Czech officials said he did not meet with on his trip to Prague the year before.

Atta, as we have seen, was also in Prague on his way to the United States in June 2000, and there has never been any information to explain that itinerary. And even the announcement, made in a press conference at highest levels of the Czech government, that Atta met with al-Ani on his second trip to Prague has been disputed by some. After Gross's announcement that a meeting definitely took place, Czech president Vaclav Havel said that there was a 70 percent chance that the two men met during Atta's April 2001 stay in Prague. Havel did not say how that 70 percent figure was calculated, but there were reports in Prague that al-Ani had a used-car business and met with a dealer from Germany who bore a striking resemblance to Atta, so perhaps Czech intelligence confused the two men. Other Czech officials said that the Mohammed Atta who came to Prague was actually a Pakistani businessman who just happened to have the same name as the Mohammed Atta who was an international terrorist. On the other hand, responding to these doubts about his initial declaration, Czech interior minister Gross issued a statement saying: "BIS guarantees the information, so we stick by that information."

Probably, in other words, the terrorist Atta was in Prague on April 8, and, if he was, it would be a rather extraordinary coincidence that al-Ani just on that day was meeting with somebody who looked like him, or somebody else with the same name. Atta himself would have been of little interest to Czech intelligence either in June 2000 or April 2001, but al-Ani clearly would have been. Edward Jay Epstein, author of the book *Deception* and other works on intelligence and espionage, has pointed out that al-Ani's predecessor in the Iraqi embassy in Prague, a man named Jabir Salim, was entrusted by Iraqi president Saddam Hussein with a mission to blow up the offices of Radio Free Europe in Prague in 1998. Salim was ensnared in a homosexual sex scandal and defected to Britain, where he told intelligence agents of the Radio Free Europe plot, including the salient detail that Saddam had spent $150,000 to further it. Salim's story of a planned attack on Radio Free Europe in Prague gave the Czech intelligence agency a good reason for maintaining close surveillance of Salim's successor, al-Ani, and that, presumably, is how the BIS observed his meeting with Atta in April 2001.[4]

What, if such a meeting did take place, fourteen weeks before September 11, would it have meant? One possibility is that Atta and al-Ani talked about Atta's investigation into using crop dusters to mount a terrorist attack on the United States. Certainly all the evidence indicates that Iraq possesses the chemical or biological agents that Atta would have needed had the crop-duster plan been carried out. Osama bin Laden most likely did not have those agents. But Atta might have been a kind of independent contractor working two angles at the same time. He would have been in touch with Al Qaeda for one type of operation even while asking Iraq for the wherewithal to murder thousands of Americans in a chemical or biological attack. If Atta did make such a proposal, it seems that al-Ani turned him down, and it would have been then that Atta embarked definitively on his other plan, to hijack airplanes and use them to hit American targets.

There is another possibility: that Iraq provided some services to Atta and Al Qaeda in connection with September 11, even as the attack remained mainly under Al Qaeda's supervision. Senior Iraqi defectors—in reports confirmed both by American intelligence officials and by United Nations weapons inspectors—have spoken of the existence of a training camp southeast of Baghdad called Salmon Pak where, among other things, terrorists from countries like Saudi Arabia, Yemen, Algeria, Egypt, and Morocco have trained in the techniques of airplane hijackings. One former captain in the Iraqi army, Sabah Khodada, who now lives in Texas, said on a *Frontline* television documentary that he worked for eight years at Salmon Pak, describing it as a highly secret installation that brought Arabs from Persian Gulf countries, including Saudi Arabia, and trained them "on assassinations, kidnapping, hijacking of airplanes, hijacking of buses, hijacking of trains, and all other kinds of operations related to terrorism." James Woolsey, a former director of Central Intelligence in the Clinton administration, has said that satellite photographs show a Soviet-built passenger jet on the ground at Salmon Pak that could be used in

Moments before United Airlines flight 175 strikes the south tower of the World Trade Center (NAKA NATHANIEL/*THE NEW YORK TIMES*)

AMERICAN
AIRLINES #11

Satam al-Suqami

Waleed Alshehri

Wail Alshehri

Abdulaziz Alomari

Mohammed Atta

AMERICAN
AIRLINES #77

Majed Moqed

Khalid al-Midhar

Nawaq Alhamzi

Salem Alhamzi

Hani Hanjour

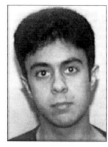 Saeed Alghamdi

 Marwan al-Shehhi

 Ahmed Alhaznawi

 Ahmed Alghamdi

 Ahmed Alnami

 Fayez Ahmed

 Ziad Jarrah

 Hamza Alghamdi

 Mohand Alshehri

(SOURCE: U.S. DEPARTMENT OF JUSTICE)

Rick Rescorla advancing through the underbrush of the Ia Drang Valley in November 1965 during the Vietnam War (AP/WIDE WORLD PHOTOS)

Rick and Susan Rescorla

Yeneneh Betru

Khamladai and Roshan Singh

Mohammed Atef
(*THE NEW YORK TIMES*)

Osama bin Laden
(AP/WIDE WORLD PHOTOS)

Ayman Zawahiri
(AP/WIDE WORLD PHOTOS)

Omar Abdel Rahman
(FRED R. CONRAD/*THE NEW YORK TIMES*)

el-Sayyid A. Nosair
(AP/WIDE WORLD PHOTOS)

Abu Zubaydah
(*THE NEW YORK TIMES*)

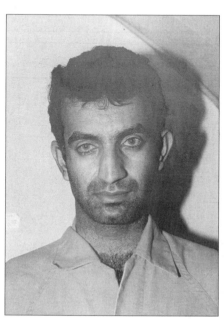

Ramzi Ahmed Yousef (FRANCES ROBERTS
FOR *THE NEW YORK TIMES*)

Ramzi Mohammed Abdullah bin
al-Shibh (AFP)

Evacuation of the north tower (SHANNON STAPLETON/REUTERS)

Jeremy Glick at his wedding to Lyzbeth Makely in 1996

John Ogonowski and daughter Caroline in 1992

Harry Ramos

Peter Ganci and family (*left to right*): son Peter Jr., daughter Danielle, Peter Ganci, wife Kathleen, and son Chris at Ganci's promotion to Chief of Department, October 7, 1999

A worker stands at the ruins of the World Trade Center's Building 7, Thursday, September 13, 2001. (JAMES ESTRIN/ *THE NEW YORK TIMES*)

Rev. Mychal Judge, a New York City Fire
Department chaplain (ASSOCIATED PRESS)

Victor Wald and family: Victor and wife
Rebecca, daughters Daniella (*left*) and
Alexandra (*right*) in 1999

Sylvia and John Resta on their wedding day in August 2000

Rescue workers amid the debris that was the World Trade Center (EDWARD KEATING/ *THE NEW YORK TIMES*)

such training. Could it be that the September 11 hijackers may have been dispatched to Iraq to carry out dress rehearsals for the seizure of American passenger planes?

There is no proof that such was the case, but one of the pieces missing in the reconstruction of the September 11 plot is the training in hijackings that would need at some point to have taken place. There has been no information in the wake of September 11 that the men practiced hijackings while they were in the United States, no indication that they had at their disposal mock-ups of passenger aircraft interiors where they could have gone through dress rehearsals. It is possible, of course, that they dispensed with such rehearsals, and simply made their plans on the basis of what they knew of the interiors of Boeing 767s from having been passengers on them. But it would seem more likely that the hijackers would have preferred to do some serious practice. We know that the curriculum at Al Qaeda terrorist training camps included hijackings, and perhaps most, or even all, of the nineteen hijackers received training at one of Osama bin Laden's lairs in Afghanistan. It is also possible that the men who carried out the hijackings of September 11 were trained at Salmon Pak. Atta's two trips to Prague could have been taken to arrange such training with al-Ani, who, it should be noted, was expelled from the Czech Republic two weeks after his supposed meeting with Atta for activities incompatible with his status as a diplomat—in other words, for spying.

While the reasons for Atta's trip to Prague cannot be known for certain, there is no doubt that after his return to the United States in April, the planning for September 11 reached a new stage. Most important, it was during the late spring and summer of 2001 that the second wave of hijackers, the foot soldiers from Saudi Arabia, began arriving in the United States, and Atta and al-Shehhi got busy helping them to settle in. They flew in from different destinations, Hong Kong, Zurich, and London, but the commonest point of origin was London on flights that originated in Dubai, which would be a normal transit point if the men had originated their journeys in Afghanistan. The normal route would first have taken them across the border to Peshawar and then, most likely, to Karachi, where they could have gotten flights to London, via Dubai. Most of them flew straight to Miami International Airport, where they were absorbed into the polyglot, multicultural, transient culture of South

Florida. In April and May of 2001, nine bank accounts later associated with hijackers were opened at Sun Trust branches in Florida. Seven hijackers got Florida driver's licenses within a fifteen-day period in early summer.[5] They shared apartments in Delray Beach, Hollywood, and Boynton Beach. In May, al-Shehhi's cell phone records show that he made a large number of calls to rental agents, motels, apartments, and the Palm Beach driver's license office. In June, a Florida rental agent, Gloria Irish, remembered she helped Marwan al-Shehhi and Hamza Alghamdi find apartments. She recalled that al-Shehhi, who was smiling and friendly, did the talking while Alghamdi stared sullenly at her. Al-Shehhi told Irish that he was doing pilot training and wanted a three-month lease. In July and August, Atta made numerous visits to a small mailing business in Punta Gorda, Florida, where he bought many $100 and $200 money orders.

Then, on July 18, Atta left the United States again, flying to Spain. He stayed about ten days, putting twelve hundred miles on a car he rented in Madrid, possibly driving to Salou, where, possibly, he met with members of the groups Anathema and Exile or the Group for Preaching and Combat, both of which are gathering points, respectively, for Egyptians and Algerians in exile in Europe. After September 11, European police made arrests in England, Belgium, and Spain of members of these groups. In one case, several men picked up by French police are believed to have been in the advanced stages of a plot to conduct a suicide bombing against the American embassy in Paris; one of the bombers was a well-known Tunisian, Nizar Trabelsi, who played soccer for a German team. In Spain after September 11, the police rounded up six Algerian members of the Group for Preaching and Combat who, the police said, were linked to Trabelsi. The Egyptian group Anathema and Exile is also known to its members as Vanguards of the Conquest or the New Jihad Group, and its leader is believed to be Ayman Zawahiri, the powerful Egyptian in bin Laden's organization. The Algerian Group for Preaching and Combat is believed to have its own organization and leadership but to have close ties with Al Qaeda.

It is unlikely that Atta would have traveled to Spain less than two months before September 11 unless there was something connected with the plot that needed to be taken care of there. One strong possibility is that Atta went to Spain to get money. American investigators, as we have seen, have traced something over $100,000 wired to Atta and al-Shehhi in the United States from a bank in the United Arab Emirates. But Atta would surely have needed much more than that—indeed, investigators have estimated the total cost of his operation at between $200,000 and $500,000. Several months after September 11, Spanish police arrested a Syrian-born real-estate entrepreneur in Madrid named Mohammed Galeb Kalaje Zouaydi and charged him with channeling funds to several terrorist organizations, including the Hamburg cell of Al Qaeda.

One of the people, the Spanish police said, who received funds from Zouaydi was Mamoun Darkazanli, the Syrian businessman in Hamburg who was close to Atta's roommates in the Marienstrasse apartment in Frankfurt.[6] Subsequently, the Spanish police traced Ramzi bin al-Shibh, the Atta roommate who was turned down several times for visas to the United States, in Salou at the time that Atta visited there. Again, and as is so often the case in this shadowy affair, we have no proof that Atta was in Spain to meet either Zouaydi or al-Shibh. Still, the presence of all of these men in the same country, each with his connections to Al Qaeda or to the September 11 plot, is enormously suggestive. And if, as the Spanish police said, Zouaydi was a terrorist financier, what more promising person for Atta to see than him?

And then, there is the possibility that Atta went to Spain to get a kind of final go-ahead for September 11, an approval passed along indirectly from Al Qaeda itself. We know from a later videotape of bin Laden procured by American intelligence during the war in Afghanistan that bin Laden knew details of the September 11 plan, including the choice of the World Trade Center as the main target. Bin Laden's patient construction of a truly global network, a kind of terrorist multinational conglomerate with branches and associates from Malaysia to Spain seems to come into play here. Was it during Atta's trips to Europe, and especially his two trips to Spain, that he made his connections with the conglomerate? Was it in Spain that bin Laden, or perhaps Zawahiri, used intermediaries to pass a message on to Atta that Al Qaeda sanctioned the September 11 plan? Could the approval and the money have come as part of the same package?

Again, we may never know the answers to these questions for certain, but that reconstruction of events seems to account for the known facts and for the timing of key events—Atta's meetings both in Prague and in

Spain, the crop-duster inquiries, the arrival of the second wave of hijackers, and bin Laden's foreknowledge of the nature of the attacks. This reconstruction also fits another key ingredient in the Al Qaeda modus operandus, which is that, following the cruise-missile attacks on its camps in Afghanistan in 1998, it avoided telephonic and electronic communication, preferring to do its business in person or via couriers. Atta would surely have wanted to avoid ruining his plan by having some crucial message intercepted by American or European intelligence—just as the members of the Nairobi cell, suspecting, correctly, that American intelligence was tapping their telephones, still managed to pull off their bombing of the African embassies without being detected beforehand.

In any event, it seems close to a certainty that when Atta returned from Spain to Florida in the middle of July, there was no longer any doubt about what he was going to do. The plan, approved and financed and furnished with a team of trusted commandos, was now fully operational.

FIFTEEN

Peter J. Ganci:
Born to Fight Fires

O n the sparkling Sunday of September 9, 2001, just two days before September 11, Peter J. Ganci, who was the Fire Department's highest-ranking uniformed officer, and his oldest friend, Dan Nickola, did what they often did on weekends. They went clamming not far from Ganci's house in North Massapequa on Long Island Sound. The two men, who met forty-nine years earlier when they went to St. Kilian's Elementary School in Farmingdale, got to talking about the things men in their late middle age talk about—their grown kids, their fathers, retirement, mortality—especially mortality. Ganci's father had died of emphysema in 1989, and Pete, as his friends called him, remembered how terrible it was—his father's unshaven face burned under his oxygen mask. Pete was a smoker too, a heavy one—pack after pack of Winston's, Marlboro Lights, the occasional cigar—and though he'd tried to give it up many times, he had never succeeded for very long. Maybe that was what was on his mind when he turned to Nickola and repeated one of his favorite phrases:

"I'm gonna die right here, clamming and not collecting moss on the north side," he said.

Ganci didn't die clamming, but he didn't collect any moss either. He died fighting a fire among the men he commanded, which is what had made him one of the most honored—and certainly one of the most decorated—firefighters in the history of the department—the highest-ranking officer in a department of eleven thousand men. And he died because he didn't leave the scene of the most devastating fire in the city's history. He told other men, including the city's mayor, to clear out of the area, and, as chief of the department, he could easily have done the same thing. But he didn't, and that was not a surprise to the fraternity of fire-fighters in whose company he spent his entire adult life. To them Ganci was the complete fireman; his bravery was laced with an almost reckless competitiveness, the desire that all fireman have to be able to say later, "I opened up the door first" or "I got to the fire first." Or, to put this another way, he was known for his instinct to be in front in a fire, to embody the New York Fire Department's sobriquet—the bravest.

"Firefighters, the good ones anyway, live to do a good job at the right places—that's all you want to do," said Angelo Catalano, a firefighter who served in the same company as Ganci when both of them were young. "And Pete hated guys who were skaters."

Ganci was the kind of guy who seemed to fit into his life like a glove. He moved up but he never moved away. He lived all his life in the town, North Massapequa, New York, where he was born—in 1946. Aside from being a fireman, he was the part owner of a bar and restaurant called Pot-ter's Pub, which was the kind of local Irish hangout where everybody who comes in seems to know everybody else, and that is emblematic of Ganci himself, the man standing immovably inside his place. It's not that his life was easy or that he didn't have other choices, but that he felt natu-rally rooted, even though he did have his share of early hardship.

His mother died young; a brother, Michael, shot himself by accident; and a cousin was shot while managing a club and bar. Ganci went to St. Kilian's, where he was in the boys' choir, and then Farmingdale High School, and from there he worked his way up in life, getting no help from social or political connections. He was an eighteen-year-old driving a turquoise '57 Chevy when he became a volunteer at the local Farmingdale fire station, where he remained a volunteer firefighter even as he rose through the ranks in the New York City Fire Department. When he was twenty, at a time when a lot of other young men like him were smoking marijuana and protesting the war in Vietnam, he became a paratrooper with the 82nd Airborne at Fort Bragg, North Carolina. And when he got out of the service in 1968, he became a firefighter with Engine Company 92 in the Bronx.

He still saw some bad luck in those years, some family anguish. After he got out of the air force, he bought a house in Gilbertsville, in Upstate New York, where he invited his father, whose business making redwood bird feeders had gone bankrupt, to start anew by turning a barn on the property into a workshop. The day that the first batch of new bird feeders was to be picked up for distribution to stores in New York and New Jersey, it snowed so hard that the pickup was canceled. That night, a fire broke out and the barn burned down.

Still, Ganci had certain gifts and he was going to do well. "His biggest attribute was that he maintained his composure," said Rick Kopitsch, another childhood friend. Ganci was naturally gregarious and naturally generous. Kopitsch remembers once casually mentioning to Pete that he needed to put up a partition in his living room at home, and, a few hours later, without telling him anything, Ganci turned up at his house and put up the wall. "I was careful saying things I needed to do in fear that he would do them before me," Kopitsch said. He had a knack of making people feel comfortable, without being so chummy that, as his responsibilities grew, he lost his authority. His old firefighting buddies talk about how they called him "Pete" when their wives were around but when the boys were drinking alone they called him Chief. It was a sign of respect but also of a certain unspoken distance.

"Some officers who rise in the ranks have never paid their dues," Catalano said. "You see guys running the show who really don't understand and don't belong. But Pete paid his dues."

Ganci had a steady rise in the Fire Department. It was a rise that made him as much as any fireman in the city an emblem of the firefighter's culture. "We like to go to fires because we are action-oriented people," he said once. And although at the time he was talking of the need to learn how to prevent fires from happening as much as putting them out, he did love to go to fires. The fireman's calling is to save people, whoever and however they can, and the chief's duty is to save people while losing none of his own. Firemen run into burning buildings and up smoky staircases with air tanks and masks and fifty pounds of hose over their shoulders because that's the honor and the glory. There is a code.

You do everything you can to save people. You never leave another fire-fighter alone in a burning building. If you're not willing to take the chances firefighters have to take, you should have gone into another pro-fession. A newcomer has to fit in and prove himself, or he will find the rest of the company or squad putting him in for a transfer—to some company or squad where there aren't very many fires. Pete was in this sense the fireman's fireman. He backed you up if you were a tried member of the club; but he'd sign the transfer request if he thought you weren't up to the job. He was the kind of chief who would never send men into places where he wouldn't go himself.

"He had a knack for making you feel comfortable," Catalano said. "He never got angry. No, wait, the only time he would get angry was if a young rookie didn't show any respect for the job. You know, the know-it-all that has no experience. That would get you immediately trans-ferred."

Just two weeks before September 11, the Gancis and Kopitsches and two other couples went canoeing on the Nissequogue River at King's Point on Long Island. After a day on the water, on the way to a restaurant at night, Kopitsch noticed that Ganci's Fire Department uniform was in a plastic bag on the backseat, and there were so many medals for bravery on it that he quipped he would have to start pinning them on the back. A lot of those medals were for pulling people out of burning buildings.

A firefighter, Peter McCarthy, who served with Ganci at Ladder Com-pany 124 in Brooklyn when Ganci was a young lieutenant, remembered a fire thirty years ago that illustrated Ganci's stuff. It was a time in early 1972 when, for some reason, there were a lot of fires in New York, and a fire-man could show up for duty in the morning expecting to be called to sev-eral fires, maybe even six or seven of them in a day.

"One night we got a call about a fire on the second story of a three-story building," McCarthy said. "Pete tells me to go check the basement just in case. I go to the basement and everything was okay, so I came back up to the first floor and I hear yelling. I couldn't tell who it was or what they were saying but it was yelling. So I got to the second floor and see that Ganci isn't there. That's when I knew the yelling was from Pete. He was already up on the third floor without any backup."

Any fireman knows that the worse place to be is the third floor of a building where the fire is on the second floor. A fireman doesn't want to get caught where the heat and fire are likely to rise.

"So I went up there and you couldn't see one damn thing with all the smoke," McCarthy said. "I hear Pete yelling and we were both on our hands and knees on the floor looking for each other and we eventually slammed our helmets right into each other. He said, 'We better find a window,' so it took us a while but we found one. You see, Pete was up there by himself in a situation where it normally calls for four guys. Nobody was hurt, but I think all we rescued was a dog."

That was Ganci during his thirty-three years in the department, during which he went from ordinary firefighter, to lieutenant, to captain, to battalion chief, to deputy division chief, to deputy assistant chief in charge of fire investigations, to assistant chief of operations, to chief of the entire Fire Department, with an office at headquarters in Brooklyn. He was a man who always combined the love of the action with plain good sense, and a big part of his legacy was the stress he put on prevention, training, improved firefighting equipment, and technology. There were a lot of tough moments, but one that he remembered and talked about shows the kind of man he was. It was at a fire in 1979, also when Ganci was at Ladder Company 124.

"One of my people was trapped, with fire coming out over his head," Ganci told a reporter for an in-house fireman's newsletter. "I thought for sure he would come out the window. But the aerial ladder got to him in the nick of time. It may not sound that dramatic, but I'll never forget it. My heart still races when I think of it and it made me realize what an awesome responsibility an officer has on this job."

One of the things that other firefighters liked about Ganci was his utter lack of pretension, his regular guy–ness. No matter how high he rose in the Fire Department, he always told people who asked him what he did that he was, simply, a fireman. He liked to go to the fire stations and drink beer in the kitchen with the men, or share one of the meals they used to cook for each other. That might sound like a cliché, an effort to foment a legend—the chief who loves to hang out with his men—but it was true in Ganci's case. He put in eighty-hour weeks. Once a group of firefighters were eating wee-hour pizza at a place called Patti's under the Brooklyn Bridge when Ganci saw they had left their truck—their "rig" in

fireman's lingo—in the middle of a dead-end street, blocking everything.
Ganci got out of his car and saw that the keys were in the ignition, so he
fired up the rig, made a professional three-point turn, and began driving
away, just slowly enough for the men in the pizza joint to notice him and
to come out running after him in a panic that the truck was being stolen.

"Hey, anyone can drive one of these things," he shouted.

"He loved the young guys," his son Chris said. "He was never a
bureaucrat. He was more like an ambassador or a diplomat. All these
guys would crowd around my father, and would be so captivated by his
fire stories."

Ganci was the kind of guy that all the other guys wanted to be pho-
tographed with. His old colleagues at Ladder 124, where he first made his
reputation, had bragging rights because they had served with "the Chief"
when he was a mere lieutenant. When Ganci went to national fire chiefs'
conclaves in other cities, he was treated like a movie star. "It was as if God
himself walked in the door," Catalano said. The Fire Department is an epicenter of what it's common to call "male bonding." Firemen eat together;
they sleep in the same room; they spend long days and nights waiting
together; they play on the same sports teams together; they drink together after hours; above all, they face danger together and they all know
that they might die together. Firemen see their ladder and engine companies and their rescue squads as their families. "You're close when you fight
a fire," McCarthy said. "You'd rather see yourself hurt than the guy next
to you, honestly." And Pete, in this sense, was the perfect family man, the
one who wanted to be the best player on the best team. It's not too much
to say that the other men loved him. The story is told of the time he was
sitting at a bar frequented by firefighters, and somebody was speaking dis-
respectfully to him, picking a fight. Ganci didn't rise to the bait. He just
sat there and nodded. But another fireman, hearing what he thought were
insults to the chief, came over and rendered the offensive person uncon-
scious with a punch to the jaw.

Samples from a kind of "Quotations of Chairman Ganci" were
repeated around the department. One of them was "When you walk out
the door in the morning, don't let your wife see how happy you are to go
to work." And another: "Never tell your wife how good the station house
food is. If she asks, tell her you had hot dogs." At a medals ceremony in

2000, Ganci, who was giving awards this time, not receiving them, said, "Wherever needed, we go. While a dangerous and difficult job, firefighting is still the best profession of all."[1]

In 1972, Ganci married Kathleen Koster, a hometown girl whom he had known for a very long time, since she was fifteen and Ganci drove her to her junior prom with her date, who happened to be Ganci's younger brother. Years later, Ganci went into the bank in Farmingdale, New York, to cash some unused traveler's checks—he had been to the Octoberfest in Germany—and Kathleen was a secretary in that bank. "It was quite a whirlwind romance," Kathleen said. In a few years they had three children, Peter 3rd, who is also a firefighter, Chris, and Danielle, and that meant that Ganci himself had to supplement his income with other jobs.

The truth is that a fireman with a wife and three kids doesn't make enough money to live comfortably in Manhattan, even if he puts fires out there. Firemen live in Queens or Staten Island or, like Ganci, in Nassau County, "out on the island." For a while he moonlighted as a bartender at his friend Dan Nickola's restaurant in Farmingdale; then, in 1990, he, Nickola, and another partner opened Potter's Pub, an Irish bar and restaurant. He took carpentry jobs, built extensions on homes, even washed windows. He was also a very good Sunday golfer, an avid fisherman, a boat owner, the opposite of a homebody, and there was a cost to that.

"As a kid I hardly saw my dad," Chris said. "Because he worked so hard, he would also go out with the guys a lot for beers. My mom would be so mad, wondering why he hadn't called to tell her when he would be home after work. And he used to say, 'Why would I call, when I know I would be yelled at twice, once on the phone and once when I got back, for not coming straight home from work.' But I think we all became very independent because he was so busy. I like that, and we supported him."

Still, busy as he was, there were family vacations—at Lake George in Upstate New York and at Busch Gardens in Virginia. The Nickolas, with four children, and the Gancis with three took their families together to Niagara Falls. Ganci was the one who stayed with the children, taking them for rides on the roller coaster, or, back at home, he chaperoned trips to museums in New York City. He was a Little League coach, famous for not giving preference to members of the team who were his own two sons.

Looking forward to his retirement, Ganci and Kathleen bought a condominium in Florida and they expected to begin using it soon. Ganci planned to play a lot of golf at the nearby East Lake Woodlands Country Club. But up to September 11, Ganci, busy as always, had never once visited it. On that Sunday when he went clamming with Dan Nickola, he was debating with himself about the future, knowing that he wanted to keep going as a firefighter a bit longer, while his family wanted him to retire. But two days later, on September 11, he was up early, as always, and off to work.

SIXTEEN

The Terrorists Stay
One Step Ahead

Nine months after the terrorists' successful strike of September 11—
on May 28, 2002, to be exact—the new director of the FBI, Robert S. Mueller
III, held one of the more extraordinary press conferences in the bureau's
history. After denying for months that there would have been any way for
American law enforcement or intelligence to have detected the terrorist
plot beforehand, he admitted that important clues to the coming disaster
were ignored or neglected by the FBI. If those signs had been properly
analyzed in the weeks and months leading up to September 11, he said, it
is possible—though far from certain—that the FBI might have been able
to thwart the attacks altogether.

Mueller's startling disclosure was followed a week later, on June 6, by
a televised address to the nation by President Bush in which he announced
major reorganization of the government. Twenty-two federal agencies
would be combined into a new cabinet-level Department of Homeland
Security with a budget of $37.5 billion, whose task would be to prevent
future terrorist attacks against the United States.

These announcements amounted both to an extraordinary admission
and to a shift in national priorities. From now on it would be the war against
terrorism (rather than the war against drugs or white collar crime) that
would most occupy the FBI, the CIA, and other agencies (even though the
FBI and CIA were not included in the new department). Terrorism would

be treated as not only as the most immediate threat to the security of Americans but as a threat that extended indefinitely into the future. That was the reordering of priorities. The admission was the apparently reluctant response of the Bush administration to an embarrassing series of disclosures in the press that revealed that warnings about a possible looming terrorist attack issued by lower levels of the FBI were ignored by senior levels.

These missed signals, now admitted by Director Mueller, are part of the larger story of September 11, and, indeed, certain missed signals go back to the beginning. We have seen how as early as 1989 the FBI dropped its surveillance of the men who would later bomb the World Trade Center in 1993. More generally, for years American authorities had underestimated both the global reach of Al Qaeda and the growth of its ambitions. The connections that would have outlined the arc of Al Qaeda's anti-American enterprise, in which the 1993 bombing was the opening salvo in a lethal war of Islamic extremism against the United States, were not drawn.

But the lapses getting most attention at the time of Mueller's press conference were the ones that took place just before September 11, when the plan of Atta and his commandos was entering its final stages. It was in those final weeks and days that the United States bungled its last good chances of preventing the disaster before it happened, and the unhappy thriller of September 11, in which the evildoers stayed one step ahead of the law, reached its tragic climax.

On August 13, Atta, Hanjour, and Fayez Alhamzi were all in Las Vegas, Nevada, staying at the modest Econo Lodge on the edge of the casino strip where they no doubt discussed the final details of the plan. This way of meeting would fit the modus operandus of the terrorists, which required that they conduct their critically secret business in person and not take any chances with tapped telephones or e-mails. Las Vegas is a place of millions of visitors where nobody is particularly conspicuous. And yet, as with many of the movements of the hijackers, the trips to Las Vegas are also inexplicable, because, except for that one meeting on August 13, members of the September 11 commando team went there when no other members were present.

FBI agents have told reporters that Atta, al-Shehhi, Hanjour, Jarrah, and Alhamzi—all except Alhamzi alleged hijacker-pilots—were in Las Vegas at one time or another but mostly by themselves. Atta himself

stayed at the Econo Lodge from June 29 to July 1, and there is no indication that any of his confederates were there at the same time. On that
trip, he stayed in a room with one queen-sized bed; on his second trip in
mid-August, he specifically asked for a room with two beds. It's easy to
understand why the hijackers would have met in Las Vegas on August 13,
a place where people would find nothing strange in the sight of a few
Arab student pilots taking a breather. Hanjour and Alhamzi were officers
in the West Coast contingent of the September 11 plot and clearly they
had a good deal to talk about with Atta, the presumed operational commander of the East Coast contingent. By mid-August, they would have to
decide which flights would be hijacked and which team would hit which
target; they would have to assign the foot soldiers to the four hijack
teams, making sure that everybody had his identification documents in
order, coordinating signals in case some emergency, or maybe just bad
weather, required a last-minute postponement or cancellation of the plan,
moving the West Coast contingent into place in the East.

Why the solo trips? It could be that Atta went to Las Vegas to case out
possible terror targets there—maybe a bomb in one of the immense
casino-hotels that to a good Muslim fundamentalist would symbolize
Western decadence. But by the end of June, it was unlikely that he didn't
already know what the targets were—the World Trade Center, the Pentagon, and one more target in Washington. Some journalists have speculated
that various members of the team, the hijacker-pilots especially, went to
Las Vegas simply to rest from the ardors of planning a terrorist attack, but
that too is improbable. Atta and company were not thank-God-it's-Friday
types who worked hard and then played hard. Vacations were not part of
the routine. Since news of their visits to Las Vegas became public, the FBI
began receiving hundreds of calls from people there saying they had seen
one or more of the hijackers—buying incense at a local store, using a computer at a cyber café near the University of Nevada Las Vegas campus, even
attending strip clubs, perhaps for a firsthand look at the sexual decadence
of the West. One of their predecessors in Islamic fundamentalism, the
Islamic Brotherhood founder Sayyid Qutb, had found an American square
dance to be sexually immoral—how much more so the strip joint near the
Econo Lodge that advertised itself as "home of the $5 lap dance"! Only the
sighting of Mohammed Atta spending long hours at a computer at a cyber

café has been confirmed, by the fact that the FBI carted off the computer
hard drives to read any e-mail messages that might have been archived
there, or to see what websites Atta might have logged onto (the FBI has
released no information it has found in this way).

But nothing has explained the solo trips to Las Vegas. Perhaps they
were for the purpose of meeting with someone other than a known
member of the hijack team, a higher-up, an emissary from Al Qaeda. "I
don't know that we'll ever know," one FBI agent named Grant Ashley said
to the *Las Vegas Review-Journal*.[1]

It is worth noting here that much else of what the nineteen men did
during this final period, and in earlier periods, is simply unknown. Where
did they rehearse the hijackings? How, generally, did they communicate
with each other? How did the commanders choose—or have chosen for
them—the foot soldiers who arrived during the course of the early summer, and how did they receive information about them? Where did Atta—
assuming that he was indeed the operational leader of the plot—receive
his instructions and from whom? We know that much of the money came
to Atta and Al-Shehhi in the form of remittances from a man named
Mustapha Ahmed in the United Arab Emirates, but who is Mustapha
Ahmed and where did his money come from? Clearly American investigators believe that the man ultimately behind September 11 was Osama bin
Laden, and there is an enormous amount of circumstantial evidence to
support that conclusion. But what exactly was the relationship between
bin Laden and Atta and how did they communicate, if they did?

It's like that FBI agent said in Las Vegas—we don't know, and, given
that the nineteen hijackers are dead, we may never know. We do know,
however, that by the time the hijacking plot entered its final stages Atta
and the others had accomplished their objectives up to that point. They
had trained as pilots and assembled a team to carry out the worst attack
on the American mainland since the War of 1812 without being detected,
without even arousing any suspicions. And they did this despite a couple
of close calls, situations where a more in-depth investigation, or more
aggressive work by intelligence and law enforcement agencies, would
have had a good chance of uncovering the entire plot before it could be
implemented.

The first of these situations involved the Moroccan-born French citizen Zacarias Moussaoui, who briefly studied at the Pan Am International Flight Academy just outside of Minneapolis, Minnesota. In the middle of August 2001, the local FBI field office in Minneapolis received a call from a flight instructor at the school warning that Moussaoui might pose a danger to American security. The flight instructor, a former military pilot whose name has not been released, told the FBI that Moussaoui, who had come to the United States via London about a year before, was behaving very suspiciously. He was belligerent; he was evasive when questioned about his background; he seemed unnaturally interested in learning how to fly Boeing 747s even though he was clearly incompetent as a pilot of small single-engine planes. The flight instructor then gave the FBI one of those warnings that might have seemed just rhetorical at the time, but has a retrospectively chilling and prophetic quality to it now.

"Do you realize that a 747 loaded with fuel can be used as a bomb?" he said.

The school had become aware of Moussaoui some time before when he had written an e-mail to the Pan Am International Flight Academy's main office in Florida expressing, in his imperfect English, a desire to "pilot one of those Big Bird." The e-mail allowed that Moussaoui's qualifications "could be better," but it ended with a patriotic flourish. "I'm sure you can do something," he wrote. "After all we are in AMERICA, and everything is possible."

When, on August 13, Moussaoui showed up at the school's flight training center near Minneapolis, he attracted attention right away. He was in a hurry; he wanted to learn fast; he paid his tuition by pulling a wad of cash, about $6,800, out of a satchel. He asked lots of questions about communicating with the control tower, which is odd for a beginner pilot. It happened that Moussaoui's second day was the date of the school's monthly meeting of instructors and administrators, and some people at the meeting had the prescience to wonder aloud if Moussaoui might be a hijacker planning to seize an airliner full of passengers. One of the flight instructors said he had a friend at the local FBI office and would call him. He did, and the next day, August 15, the FBI turned up at the school and, in the course of questioning Moussaoui, discovered that he was technically in violation of his ninety-day visa, so they turned him over to the Immigration and Naturalization Service.

In fact, the immigration violation was just a handy excuse to take Moussaoui away. We know this from a lengthy, angry memo sent to FBI director Robert Mueller in May 2002 by Coleen Rowley, the legal counsel of the Minneapolis office, who detailed several ways in which FBI head-quarters in Washington obstructed an investigation of Moussaoui. According to Rowley, the agents who interviewed Moussaoui called her at home late that night to ask her advice about the next step to take. The real reason the agents took Moussaoui into custody, Rowley said, was to elim-inate the terrorist threat they already believed he posed. The agents "believed that Moussaoui signalled he had something to hide in the way he refused to allow them to search his computer."

But Moussaoui's computer never was searched, at least not until after September 11. FBI headquarters found several ways and several reasons to turn down the urgent, repeated requests made by the Minneapolis field office for a full investigation into Moussaoui, and it was because of this strange obstructionism that the FBI missed its main chance to get infor-mation about the September 11 plot before September 11. First, the Min-neapolis office requested that Washington open a special investigation of Moussaoui. Following that request, there were at least two secure confer-ence calls among FBI counter-terrorism experts and their counterparts in the CIA and the National Security Agency to discuss the Moussaoui case. Following Moussaoui's arrest, the FBI representative in Paris had for-warded a classified cable from the French intelligence service saying that Moussaoui was known to have "Islamic extremist beliefs." In the mid-1990s, according to French intelligence, he was known for urging Muslims in France to heed the call of jihad. He himself seems to have gone several times to Pakistan and Afghanistan and, clearly, the French thought he was dangerous. Confirming the French portrait of Moussaoui was one Hus-sein al-Attas, a friend who had driven Moussaoui from Oklahoma to Min-neapolis and was interviewed by agents in the FBI Minneapolis field office. Al-Attas described Moussaoui as the kind of man who believed it was acceptable to kill civilians who harm Muslims and that he approved of the "martyrs" who did just that.

In 2001, before going to Minnesota, Moussaoui had spent three months attending classes at the Airman Flight School in Norman, Okla-homa, and from there he had called Atta's friend Ramzi bin al-Shibh in

Hamburg. Like Atta's team members, he signed up at health clubs and kept himself in shape. Like Atta, he made inquiries about crop dusters. Early in August, while still in Oklahoma, he received a wire transfer of about $10,000 from Dusseldorf, Germany, which was presumably the roll of cash he pulled out to pay for his lessons in Minnesota.

All of this, except for the information provided by the French and by al-Attas, was known only later. In Washington, the FBI, unable to determine that Moussaoui represented a threat, declined to take the first step necessary to open a special terrorism investigation, which would have been to ask for a go-ahead from the Justice Department. What the Minneapolis field office wanted was a special warrant to be issued under the Foreign Intelligence Surveillance Act of 1978. But the lawyers at bureau headquarters determined that an essential criterion for approving such a warrant was missing—namely evidence that Moussaoui was operating at the behest of an overseas terror group. This led the FBI in Minnesota to try a different line of approach. They asked permission to open an ordinary grand jury criminal investigation, rather than a special terrorist investigation, which would have allowed them to get search warrants to look at the computer and the phone records. This request too was turned down.

Perhaps it should have been, especially if the case of Zacarias Moussaoui was considered by itself, separate from everything else that was available to the FBI. After all, the only information that the FBI field office had on Moussaoui was that he had some extremist beliefs and he seemed a bit strange to instructors at the Pan Am International Flight Academy. He had committed no crimes other than his minor visa offense. There were news reports after September 11 that Moussaoui had aroused suspicion because he only wanted to learn how to maneuver a big plane in flight and showed no interest in landing or taking off, but these reports proved to be untrue; he did seem unduly interested in in-flight procedures, but he also said he wanted to learn to take off and land as well. So while in the wake of September 11 Moussaoui's behavior seems criminally suspicious, before September 11 it might, taken by itself, quite properly have seemed a slender reed on which to build a full terror investigation.

But the fact is that three weeks before Moussaoui's arrest in August 2001, the FBI had received a memorandum from an agent in its Phoenix office warning that some of the Middle Easterners attending American flight schools might be terrorists. The agent, Kenneth Williams, was conducting an investigation of several men from the Middle East who were training as pilots in Arizona, and he specifically mentioned Osama bin Laden as one known terrorist who might want to get pilot training for his operatives as a first step in placing them with airlines around the world. The odd thing is that Agent Williams was right, though for the wrong reason—none of the men he was investigating turned out to have anything to do either with terrorism or with bin Laden. But he had the right ideas. He specifically recommended that the FBI examine the visa applications of all the Middle Easterners studying at American flight schools to try to ferret out any terrorists among them.

Williams did not learn three weeks later of the arrest of Moussaoui and the Minneapolis FBI office did not know of Williams's memo. But here was one agent warning that terrorists might be training at American flight schools and there was Moussaoui who was deemed almost immediately by the FBI agents on the scene to be a likely terrorist. "It is obvious from my firsthand knowledge of the events and the detailed documentation that exists," Rowley wrote in her memorandum nine months later, "that the agents in Minneapolis who were closest to the action and in the best position to gauge the situation locally did fully appreciate the terrorist risk/danger posed by Moussaoui and his possible coconspirators even prior to September 11th." Still, the FBI did not conduct the visa examinations suggested by Williams and it put up a series of legalistic roadblocks to a full investigation of Moussaoui. This, of course, is the same FBI that failed to maintain its watch on the men of Al Kifah in Brooklyn way back in 1989. It is the FBI that had years earlier created a special Osama bin Laden and Al Qaeda task force to collect and coordinate information on what was deemed to be the most dangerous terrorist organization in the world. But nobody at the FBI, not even the terrorism task force, made the connection between the Phoenix memorandum and the arrest of Moussaoui.

Would it have stopped the attacks of September 11 had the connection been made? Very likely it wouldn't have, and yet, the possibilities are intriguing. Had the FBI plunged into the Moussaoui matter, it might have found Moussaoui's calls to al-Shibh in Hamburg, and al-Shibh was well known enough to American intelligence to have been turned down for

American visas several times. The FBI might also have found that Moussaoui had downloaded considerable information on crop dusting into his computer. If the FBI had gone to the Airman Flight School in Oklahoma where Moussaoui had studied for three months, perhaps it would have learned about the two other Arab men, Atta and al-Shehhi, who had stopped off there a year earlier. Most intriguing perhaps, the FBI would probably have found out that in October 2000 Moussaoui got a letter from a Malaysian company called Infocus Tech, signed by one Yazid Sufaat, making him the company's sales representative in the United States and Europe. The letter was apparently intended to give Moussaoui a cover for his travels. If they had known about it, the FBI might also have uncovered evidence that Moussaoui had traveled to Malaysia in October 2000 where, according to the Malaysian police, he met Sufaat. And then, it might have found out that Sufaat was the very man who had hosted a meeting in early January at which Khalid al-Midhar and Nawaf Alhamzi had met with an Al Qaeda operative involved in the attack on the USS *Cole* in Yemen, which took place on October 12, 2000.

In other words, the FBI would probably have picked up evidence that Moussaoui was part of a larger network connected to Al Qaeda, which might have made the agency and the American government more alert to the possibility of a plot to attack the United States.

But none of this is certain. The only certain things are: 1) that one FBI agent warned that terrorists might be in training in the United States, and 2) that Moussaoui, who probably intended to participate in the September 11 hijackings, was in custody for a month prior to September 11, and no investigation of him was made. He is said to have cheered in his jail cell when he saw television images of the hijacked planes hitting their targets.

As we have seen, Moussaoui shared a Malaysian connection with Khalid al-Midhar and Fayez Alhamzi, and therein lies yet another missed chance to stop the plot before it could be carried out. It will be remembered that Malaysian intelligence had turned over to the United States information that both al-Midhar and Alhamzi, who had arrived in the United States in January on a flight from Bangkok, had been observed at a meeting of suspected terrorists in Kuala Lumpur in December 1999. The CIA learned of that meeting, and of al-Midhar's and Alhamzi's presence at it, sometime in 2000. It also learned that both men had made visits to the United States, al-Midhar several times. Then, after October 2000, the CIA learned that one of the men at the Malaysia meeting had been involved in the attack on the USS *Cole* that month, and that led it for the first time to appreciate the possible importance of al-Midhar and Alhamzi, who seemed likely Al Qaeda operatives, as terrorist threats. Still, for reasons that have not been made public, the CIA passed along no information about either man to the FBI, not even that the two might be in the United States, until August 23, 2001. At that point, the FBI mounted a search for them. An FBI official in San Diego told the *Wall Street Journal* that his office wasn't given al-Midhar's or Alhamzi's name until after September 11. But the FBI field offices in both Los Angeles and New York, where the two men were deemed most likely to have gone, did conduct searches, checking the registry of every hotel in the two cities in the weeks before September 11.

The strange thing is that al-Midhar and Alhamzi were the least undercover of the nineteen hijackers. They went regularly to the San Diego Islamic Center; al-Midhar used a credit card in his own name; Alhamzi was listed in the San Diego telephone directory. Still, even though they were the targets of a nationwide search, neither man was found. And even though they were suspected terrorists linked to the bombing of the *Cole*, both men were able to buy airline tickets in their own name, to board their flights, and to carry out their missions without the slightest interference from the law enforcement authorities of the United States.

Sometime in late July or early August, somebody drove the pale blue Toyota Corolla that al-Midhar and Alhamzi had used during their time in San Diego across the country. Eventually, the car was abandoned in the parking lot of Dulles Airport on September 11, but before that it seems to have served a group of the hijackers continuously as they got into their final staging areas. Some of them, including Atta, Al-Shehhi, Jarrah, and several of the foot soldiers, remained in Florida until just days before September 11. But a secondary staging area was Paterson, New Jersey, just over the Hudson River from New York. In this community of some seventy different nationalities and numerous new immigrants a group of

Arab men living together and not going to regular jobs would attract very little attention.

There, early in the spring of 2001, Hani Hanjour, who had been part of the California group, signed a lease for a one-bedroom apartment at 486 Union Avenue under the bodega where Ahmed Alghamdi made a daily trip for twenty-five-cent donuts. Hanjour paid $650 a month in what his landlord, Jimi Nouri, called "Franklins," $100 bills. The apartment was unfurnished and it seems to have remained unfurnished while Hanjour and company lived there. After September 11, neighbors identified a number of other hijackers from their photos as having spent time there, including Salem Alhamzi, Nawaq Alhamzi, Saeed Alghamdi, and Mohammed Atta—five hijackers in all, who were on three of the highjacked planes. The men rented cars in nearby Jersey City; they used Mail Boxes Etc. stores in Wayne and Fort Lee as their addresses. They spoke only to one another, never to their neighbors, who assumed they probably didn't speak much English. They used to have dinner at the nearby Wo Hop III Restaurant.

What were they doing there? It is noteworthy that of the hijackers recognized in Paterson, only Alghamdi was on flight 93, the plane that left from Newark, a short drive from Paterson, and that was probably piloted by Ziad Jarrah. Could they have been there to survey their main target, the World Trade Center, visible in southern Manhattan from just about any high point in that part of New Jersey? That is possible, but Hanjour, who rented the apartment, is assumed to have piloted the plane that crashed in Pennsylvania, when it was most likely on its way to a target in Washington, D.C., not New York, and the two Alhamzis were on flight 77, which hit the Pentagon. And, besides, casing the World Trade Center from the ground would not have been essential to a plan aimed at hitting the towers from the air. No clear purpose for the men being in Paterson has emerged, except that they all had to be someplace; they probably didn't want to take the chance of all being together; and polyglot, multicultural Paterson was as good a place as any. And since only one flight, United flight 93, left from a nearby airport, geographic proximity to the field of operations was not a factor.

Meanwhile, by the end of August, the five hijackers of American Airlines flight 77, which left Dulles International Airport bound for Los Angeles, were occupying a single one-bedroom efficiency apartment, room 343, at the Valencia Motel in Laurel, Maryland. Gail North, a fellow resident, remembered the time she was in her car in the parking lot being blocked by the Arab occupants of room 343, who were standing in the way and talking. When she honked her car horn to get by, they didn't even look up. A twenty-two-year-old unemployed man named Toris Proctor, who lived next door to the men at the Valencia, said that he saw them leave the motel every morning at ten and pile into a pale blue Toyota Corolla parked in the front. Two of them went to a nearby Pizza Time restaurant while three waited for them in the car, and then they would drive away for the day.

This group included al-Midhar, who is likely to have been the highest-ranking Al Qaeda operative among the nineteen hijackers, and, in fact, could be the link between them and Al Qaeda itself. It is even possible that he, rather than Atta, might have masterminded the plot in the United States, a possibility that makes it all the more poignant that the FBI's search for him in the weeks before September 11 was unsuccessful. After living for some time in San Diego, al-Midhar seems to have gone abroad around the end of October 2000. Then, after a few months away, he returned to the United States, arriving in New York on a flight from Saudi Arabia on July 4, 2001. Al-Midhar is one of several of the hijackers who got drivers' licenses through a black market in official government-issue identifications that operated out of a parking lot in Arlington, Virginia. By the end of August, he and the other hijackers of flight 77 were living in the Valencia Motel in Laurel, Maryland.

On August 25, al-Midhar became the first of the hijackers to buy his ticket—on American Airlines flight 77, from Dulles International outside of Washington, D.C., to Los Angeles. He made a reservation on American Airline's on-line site, on which he had registered the day before, getting a frequent flyer number in the process. He picked the ticket up at the Baltimore-Washington International Airport on September 5, and was assigned seat 12B. The next day, August 26, Waleed Alshehri and Wail Alshehri reserved seats on American Airlines flight 11, from Boston to Los Angeles, giving a Florida contact address and being assigned seats 2A and 2B. And the day after that, Fayez Ahmed and Mohand Alshehri, who also gave Florida contact addresses, made electronic ticket reservations for United Airlines flight 175, Boston to Los Angeles.

On August 28, Atta and Abdulaziz Alomari reserved their one-way tickets for flight 11. Atta used the American Airlines website and his mileage card, AAdvantage Profile #6H26L04, which he had created three days earlier, listing his address as 3389 Sheridan, Hollywood, Florida. He paid for his own ticket and for Alomari's on his Visa Card, number 40118008407778, expiration 7/02. He, Ahmed Alghamdi, and Hamza Alghamdi used a computer at the same Kinko's copy store in Hollywood to buy their tickets.

During these final weeks, the men stayed sharp and in shape and some of them brushed up on their piloting skills. On August 16, only three days after being sighted in Las Vegas, Atta rented a single-engine Piper Archer at the Palm Beach Country Park Airport in Lantana, Florida, presumably to brush up on his airmanship before the big day. An instructor went up with him to make sure he could handle the plane. Then, for three days, the 16th, the 17th, and the 19th, he and three others rented a single-engine plane from Palm Beach Flight Training in Lantana, paying $88 an hour. He told the school's operators that he wanted to increase his flying time, even though he had already logged three hundred hours and was a certified commercial pilot.

Meanwhile, Hani Hanjour, who seems to have moved back and forth from his base in Paterson to the Washington area, took flying lessons at Freeway Airport in Bowie, Maryland. At the end of August he moved out of the Paterson apartment, and on September 1 he rented room 343 at the Valencia Motel in Laurel, Maryland. The next day he bought a one-week membership at Gold's Gym on Greenbelt Road. Most of the flight 77 team took out identical one-week memberships, so, presumably, they were all interested in keeping fit for what was to come.

Of all the hijackers, Ziad Jarrah may have moved around the most in the final weeks. Early in July, he extended his membership in the U.S.-1 Fitness Club in Dania, Florida, telling an employee there that he was planning to go back to Germany after his flight training was over. He then did go to Germany for about a week, to visit Aysel Senguen, his Turkish girlfriend. His sister was getting married in Lebanon on August 2, but he didn't go to the wedding, returning instead to Florida to keep an appointment for his pilot's certification test, which he passed on July 30. A few weeks later, in Fort Lauderdale, he bought three maps of the northeastern

United States from a pilot supply store.[2] In the last week of August he was in Laurel, Maryland, renting a room at the Pin-Del Motel. On August 30, he was back in Florida trying to rent a room with Internet access at the Longshore Motel in Hollywood, but he quarreled with the owner about the use of the phone lines and left the same day.

On September 1, a Saturday, he asked his family in Lebanon to send $700, in addition to the allowance of $2,000 a month they sent him for his pilot training, so he could have some "fun."[3] And then, getting closer now, he and his roommate, Ahmed Alhaznawi, went to Passage Tours in Fort Lauderdale and each bought a one-way ticket to Newark for a flight on September 7.

Atta was busy with other things too. In August and early September, he rented cars three times, keeping them for as much as five weeks, from Warrick's Rent-a-Car in Pompano Beach, driving more than six thousand miles during that time. Months before, he had bought flight deck videos for the Boeing 747, 757, and 767 aircraft, as well as for the Airbus 320. On August 22, Jarrah bought an antenna for a Global Positioning System computer, the highly accurate satellite-connected portable navigation device used by millions in cars, planes, and boats. On August 30, Atta bought a utility tool that contained a knife (the Moussaoui indictment, which contains this information, does not specify what kind of knife it contained or where Atta bought it). Early in September he sent a package and some money to the United Arab Emirates, presumably returning the funds he didn't use in fomenting the plot.

Then, in the final days, an intricate, choreographed relocation involving all nineteen hijackers took place. As we've noted, Jarrah and Alhaznawi bought a ticket from Fort Lauderdale to Newark for September 7, and that indeed is when they and the two other hijackers of the plane that left from Newark arrived there. They seem to have split up, some of them staying at the Marriott Hotel—according to witnesses, they drove up there in a red Mitsubishi Galant, though it is unclear where this car came from—and some of them at a nearby Days Inn.

On September 10, the day before the attacks, one of the hijackers was seen at a go-go bar called Nardone's in Elizabeth, New Jersey, about two miles from the airport. The man had a beer, said the bar's owner, Pat Nardone, and then he paid $20 to watch a dancer in the private "VIP" room—

where Nardone says he watched him with a security camera. Hotel workers told journalists after September 11 that agents identified three of the hijackers captured on surveillance tapes from cameras at the parking lot and hotel entrance of the Marriott Hotel.

The hijackers of flight 77, including the three members of the California contingent, al-Midhar, Nawaq Alhamzi, and Hani Hanjour, were at the Valencia Motel by early September. Hanjour, though considered to be the hijacker-pilot of flight 77, went three times to a nearby flight center in Bowie, Maryland; each time he failed his test flights and wasn't allowed to rent a plane. Members of the other two teams, flight 175 and flight 11, both of which left from Boston, seem to have stayed in Florida until at least September 7. One eyewitness, a waitress named Patricia Idrissi at Shuckums Oyster Pub and Seafood Grill in Hollywood, Florida, says that she served drinks to Atta and al-Shehhi there on Friday night, September 7. Atta, she said, drank vodka and al-Shehhi drank rum, but Shuckums's manager, Anthony Amos, later said that Atta drank cranberry juice, not vodka, and that would be in keeping with his observance of Islam, which forbids alcoholic drinks. Idrissi said that the tab came to $48 and that there was an argument about it. When Amos came over to ask if the men could pay, one of them said, "Of course I can pay. I'm a pilot." It is possible that Idrissi's identification of both Atta and al-Shehhi is wrong and that neither man was at the bar that night, though they did have a history of going to bars. Months before, when living in Hamburg, Atta used to hang out at a pool hall called Sharkey's Billiard Bar, which advertised itself as "the Bar with Mega-Possibilities."

Meanwhile, the hijackers of flight 11 and flight 175, including Atta and al-Shehhi, were making their way to Boston. Like some of the others, al-Shehhi sent his leftover money to Mustafa Ahmed in the UAE—$5,400 in his case. He and two others checked out of the Panther Hotel in Deerfield Beach, Florida, tossing a flying school tote bag into a Dumpster as they left. Inside were a box cutter knife, aviation maps, martial arts books, a notebook, and a protractor used in navigation.[4] Brad Warrick, the owner of the car rental agency that Atta patronized, says that al-Shehhi returned the last car that Atta rented from him on September 9. By the 10th, al-Shehhi had arrived in Boston and was staying at the Milner Hotel downtown.

Atta too was in Boston, probably by September 9, because on the morning of the 10th, he and Alomari drove a rented Nissan Altima to Portland, Maine, about 110 miles to the north, where they checked into the Comfort Inn on Maine Mall Road late in the afternoon. Both men were caught on surveillance cameras at the Key Bank drive-up ATM, and then at a Fast Green ATM in the parking lot of Uno's Restaurant. They made a quick trip to the Wal-Mart in Scarborough, Maine, and then they seem to have gone to bed.

Why did they make this trip to Portland? There is no answer to that question, though it seems impossible that they would have added that trip to their itinerary without a very good reason. Did they want to begin their travel on September 11 from a city other than Boston, so that they wouldn't have to board American Airlines flight 11 together with the other three hijackers? But if Atta was concerned that five Arab men boarding the same flight might attract attention, why didn't he require any of the other hijack teams to take the same precaution? It is, of course, possible that it was Atta's job to smuggle the weapons to be used in the hijacking onto the flight, and that he had a confederate in Portland to help him get through the security check. Since he would be a transit passenger at Logan, he wouldn't have had to go through security there. But the hijackers boarded two planes at Logan within fifteen minutes of each other, and Atta had not had any of the hijackers on the other flight come to Portland with him. He was accompanied by Alomari, who was on the same flight as he was. Could he have passed the smuggled weapons on to the hijackers of United flight 175 in the transit lounge itself? Probably not, because the two airlines involved, American and United, do not use the same departure lounge at Logan Airport. The Portland trip remains inexplicable, one of the most puzzling details of the plot.

In any case, what is important is that by the night of September 10, all nineteen men were in their final staging areas—at hotels in Newark, in Maryland, in Boston, and in Portland, Maine. They had their equipment and their instructions. Each man knew what he had to do. This had all been worked out presumably by Atta, in Las Vegas, in Paterson, in Laurel, and in Florida as he put those six thousand miles on his rental car from Warrick's. The men had a final sheet of instructions provided by Atta that told them what they were supposed to do on their final night on earth.

They were to shave excess hair from their bodies. They were to read *Al Tawba* and *Anfal*, the traditional war chapters in the Koran, and to reflect on the things that God has promised the martyrs.

"Remind your soul to listen and obey," the instructions read, "and remember that you will face decisive situations that might prevent you from one hundred percent obedience, so tame your soul, purify, convince it, make it understand, and incite it. God said, 'Obey God and His messenger, and do not fight among yourselves or else you will fail. And be patient, for God is with the patient.'

"When the confrontation begins," the instructions continued, "strike like champions who do not want to go back to this world. Shout 'Allah'u Akbar' [God is great] because this strikes fear in the hearts of the nonbelievers. God said: 'Strike above the neck, and strike at all of their extremities.' Know that the gardens of paradise are waiting for you in all their beauty, and the women of paradise are waiting, calling out, 'Come hither, friend of God.' They have dressed in their most beautiful clothing."

We do not know for sure, but probably the men read those paragraphs and reflected on the magnificent deeds they would accomplish for the sake of God and His glory the next morning and for which they would be rewarded by dark-eyed virgins. It is a vision to fill the heart of a young Islamic extremist, a vision full of vengeance, power, and sex. One can imagine the hijackers' excitement as they bowed in the direction of Mecca on that last night, pressing their foreheads into the industrial carpeting of various motel rooms from Maine to Maryland in the traditional Muslim act of submission.

Still there was an almost poignant gesture by one of them, Ziad Jarrah, the young Lebanese who had asked his parents for $700 so he could have some fun. Early on the morning of September 11, during what must have been a night of restless sleep, he called his girlfriend in Germany. Later she told police that he sounded normal. He said that he loved her.

SEVENTEEN

Like a Knife into a
Gift-Wrapped Box

At 5:30 on the morning of September 11, Steve Mosiello and his neighbor and best friend, Peter J. Ganci, the chief of the New York City Fire Department, were sitting in the kitchen of Mosiello's house in North Massapequa, Long Island. Mosiello, who was Ganci's executive officer at the Fire Department—meaning that he was his driver, his chief adviser, his aide and protector—happened to live in the house across from Ganci's, so the two men started most days together, smoking cigarettes (though Ganci had given up smoking a few weeks before) and drinking coffee. At about 6 A.M. on September 11, they began their hour's drive to the Fire Department headquarters in Brooklyn, having no reason to expect that the day would be much different from any other.

Ganci and Mosiello were like thousands of others that morning, people who went to work early, or who got up to catch early flights from Boston, Newark, and Washington's Dulles Airport to Los Angeles and San Francisco. No doubt some of these thousands were thinking about what they had to do in the hours that stretched ahead of them, or they had in mind the events that were dominating the news, perhaps the Pete Sampras upset loss at the U.S. Open on Sunday, or the still-unresolved disappearance of Chandra Levy, the special friend of Congressman Gary Condit of California. There was a mayoral primary election scheduled for September 11 in New York, and some people were heading off to vote before they went to work. And surely some of the twenty-six hundred employees of Morgan Stanley who worked in the World Trade Center were buzzing about news of a sex bias suit that was being brought against the company by the Equal Employment Opportunity Commission.

It was like that insurance company ad playing on television in those days, showing a woman busily getting her kids ready for school in the morning. "She's not thinking about life insurance," went the tag line. The people who got up early to go to work or to catch long-distance flights on September 11 weren't thinking about dying.

Brian Clark, an executive vice-president of Euro Brokers, doesn't remember what he was thinking about, though he was already beginning to study the question of new quarters for his company, since the lease on the offices on the 84th floor of the south tower in the World Trade Center was going to expire in another couple of years. Clark left his house in Mahwah in suburban New Jersey as he always did, at 6:15. And, also as he always did, he went by car to the Radburn train station in Fairlawn, took the New Jersey Transit train to Hoboken, and transferred to the PATH train with direct service to downtown Manhattan. He went up to his office on the west side of the Trade Center, where he sat with his back to a glorious view of the Hudson River and beyond, and that's where he was at 8:46 when the universe canted and everything changed.

Rick Rescorla, as we have seen, was up at 4:30 that morning, and Richard A. Penney was on the job by 8 A.M. as always, and Victor Wald took his usual subway from the Upper West Side, and Harry Ramos the train from Newark. The tragedy of September 11 was a tragedy of early risers. Those who stayed in bed remained safe. Khamladai Singh, twenty-five, and her younger brother, Roshan Singh, twenty-one, left their home in Woodhaven, Queens, at 6:20 to take the "A" Train to the World Trade Center. Both worked at Windows on the World at the very top of the north tower, and that morning was going to be a busy one because there was a breakfast for the 135 attendees of the Risk Waters Financial Technology conference. So Roshan got busy right away with the arrangements for an audio-visual presentation that was to be a part of the program, while Khamladai, an assistant banquet manager, waited to greet the guests, who were due to arrive at 8:00. Every day at 8:30, either Khamladai or Roshan made a quick call to their mother, Toolsedai Seepersaud, an accountant who worked two blocks away, just to make sure she had gotten to Manhattan safely, but on this day, Mrs. Seepersaud arrived fifteen minutes late, so she wasn't at her desk when her children's call came.

Mychal Judge, known as Father Mike, the beloved chaplain of the New York City Fire Department, parked his car at Engine One, Ladder Company 24, on West Thirty-first Street, and went to his room in the Church of St. Francis of Assisi, just across from the fire station. That was his routine; he stayed there for a while reading, or thinking, or praying, and then, when something happened, a fire, an emergency, an injury, he rushed out to help. He was there when shortly after 8:46, Father Brian Carroll, O.F.M., went up to tell him that a plane had struck the World Trade Center. "I think they need you," Father Carroll said.

Lauren Manning, forty years old, director of market data sales at Cantor Fitzgerald, had a hectic morning mixing duty and love. She was late for work because she was on the phone with a friend trying to arrange for someone to pick up keys to the country house she and her husband went to on weekends. She was also late for work because she had a hard time that morning tearing herself away from Tyler, her seventeen-month-old son, in the hallway of their Greenwich Village home. Every time she was ready to leave, she couldn't resist giving him one more hug. Usually she was at her desk by 8:30; but this morning her taxi pulled up to the entrance of the north tower on West Street at about 8:45, maybe a few seconds later, and she was just at the lobby door of the building at 8:46.

Zhanetta Tsoy, the thirty-two-year-old immigrant from Kazakhstan, left her house in Jersey City without breakfast and earlier than she needed to because it was going to be her first day on her new job at Marsh & McLennan. Tsoy and her family, including Sasha Tsoy-Ligay, her four-year-old daughter, had arrived in the United States three weeks earlier, after Zhanetta won a green-card lottery in Kazakhstan that enabled them all to become new immigrants. "We could have gone to California, but she wanted to be in New York," her husband, Vyacheslav Ligay, twenty-eight, used to say. "She loved the idea of working on top of the world."[1] She didn't have to be at work until 9:00, but she was on the 93rd floor of the north tower by 8:46 on September 11. It was the first day of the rest of her life, and she wanted to get off to a good start.

Wendy Faulkner, a daughter of missionaries who grew up in Japan and Jamaica, lived in Mason, Ohio, with her husband, Lynn, but she had come to New York on September 10 for meetings at Aon Insurance, whose offices were near the top of the south tower. That night, she had dinner with her two sisters and then she went back to the Marriott Hotel, which was on the Trade Center plaza below and between the north and south towers, where she was staying. Before going to bed, she called her husband, who was also on a business trip. She told him she was looking forward to getting home after her meeting early the next morning.

John and Silvia San Pio Resta, a married couple who worked as traders for Carr Futures, on floor 92 of the north tower, usually took the bus to the train and then the train to the subway, to get to work in lower Manhattan. On this morning, because Sylvia had a doctor's appointment, they drove to the Bayside Station for the Long Island Railroad line trip to Pennsylvania Station in Manhattan. We don't know what they talked about as the train rolled through the flat commercial and industrial scenery of Queens. It could have been about recipes, since Silvia was so devoted to cookbooks that she used to read them from cover to cover as if they were novels. More than likely, since they had just been to the doctor, they were talking about the baby they were expecting, their first, and how Silvia felt in her seventh month of pregnancy.

They came from many places that morning and they were going to many places as well. Berinthia Berenson, known as "Berry," a fifty-three-year-old photographer, was another of the publicly known people caught in the snare of September 11. She was the granddaughter of the fashion designer Elsa Schiaparelli, a more distant descendant of the art critic and collector Bernard Berenson, the sister of the model and actress Marisa Berenson, and the widow of the actor Anthony Perkins. On the morning of September 11, she got up early to catch American Airlines flight 11 to Los Angeles, where she was returning home after spending time at her summer house on Cape Cod.

Mary Alice Wahlstrom, seventy-eight years old, had gone to help her daughter, Carolyn Beug, get her twin granddaughters, Lauren and Lindsey, installed at the Rhode Island School of Design. She and Ms. Beug, a successful music producer from Los Angeles, went to Logan Airport from their hotel in Providence, where they had spent the night, with plans to return together to Beug's home in Santa Monica.

Jeremy Glick went to Newark Airport, and Yeneneh Betru, just back from Addis Ababa, to Washington Dulles, going standby. Richard Guadagno, thirty-eight, the manager of the Humbolt Bay National Wildlife Refuge in Eureka, California, had spent a few days with his sister and her boyfriend in Vermont and then they all drove to Trenton, New Jersey, for the one hundredth birthday of his grandmother, held in the nursing home where she lived. On the 11th, Jerry Guadagno, Richard's father, drove him to Newark Airport and dropped him off at the curb, and on the drive out, Richard said he was worried about his father, now seventy-seven, driving back to Trenton by himself in the morning traffic. His father told him that he would be fine, and that he and his wife would come to California in a month to see the home that Richard had built by himself on the Pacific Coast.

Leslie Whittington, Charles Falkenberg, and their two young daughters, Zoe, eight, and Dana, three, had sold their house and were staying at a child-friendly motel near Dulles Airport. This is because they were planning, once they got back from their two-month adventure in Australia, to move into a new house they were buying in Chevy Chase, Maryland. While they were waiting to board American Airlines flight 77 to Los Angeles, on the first leg of their long journey to Australia, Whittington called her mother, Ruth Koch, at home in Athens, Georgia, to say good-bye. "I just told them, 'Have a wonderful adventure,'" Mrs. Koch said later. They wrote a few postcards to friends, like this one to Sara and Jay Guest, Leslie Whittington's sister and brother-in-law:

"Well, we're off to Australia. When we return we will have a new address (as of 11/30): 8034 Glendale Rd. Chevy Chase, MD 20815. We don't know our phone # yet. While we are in 'Oz,' email will work best for contacting us: whittin@georgetown.edu."

As we've seen, John Ogonowski was also up early that morning, driving his pickup from the White Gate Farm to Logan Airport, and so were Mohammed Atta and the other four hijackers of flight 11, for whom everything went without a hitch. Atta and Alomari checked out of the Comfort Inn in Portland, Maine, at 5:33 and drove their rented silver-gray Nissan Altima to Portland International Airport, arriving at 5:40. Three minutes later they checked in at the U.S. Airways counter for their 6 A.M. flight on Colgan Air to Boston. There they were joined by Satam al-Suqami,

Waleed Alshehri, and Wail Alshehri, who had all passed through security with no problems.

In the departure lounge they showed their boarding passes to the ticket agent at Gate 26 (who probably smiled at them and wished them a good flight), and walked through the ramp onto the plane, John Ogonowski's Boeing 767. Also on board were First Officer Thomas McGuinness, nine flight attendants, and seventy-six other passengers.

Flight 11 took off four minutes after schedule at 7:59.

One can imagine the two very different states of mind on that plane and on the other planes hijacked that morning. The passengers would have been reading the morning papers, or looking at the route maps to see which states they would fly over, or listening with half an ear to the announcement they had heard so often before about buckling seat belts and not disabling the smoke detector in the lavatories. It is fair to say that hurtling across the continent inside a winged metal tube at nearly six hundred miles an hour has become so ordinary that passengers don't think much about how technologically extraordinary it is, or how there are rarely small accidents involving wide-bodied jet planes, only big ones. For the most part, flying is safe. Accidents happen, but accidents can happen anyplace, and, except for moments of turbulence, passengers are far more inclined to a kind of cramped boredom on flights across the country than they are to alertness to danger.

And so, one can imagine the passengers on flight 11, a bit sleepy from their early wakeups gazing at the sky blazing in the east, looking forward perhaps to a snooze on the way to Los Angeles or maybe the new John Grisham novel or electronic solitaire on their laptop computers. And, of course, unknown to them, the five Arab men sitting in seats in the ninth and tenth rows were now face-to-face with the greatest, and the last, moments of their lives. If the five were heeding Atta's written final instructions, they were engaging in acts of mental discipline and prayer, steeling themselves for the task ahead. Atta understood after the months of preparation that a last-minute panic among his forces could ruin everything, and in anticipation of that possibility he had some psychological and religious reassurance programmed into the fateful day.

The final passages of his instructions focused on the very moment when the plane would take off, or as his written guidance put it, "the moment that both groups come together"—both groups being terrorists and their victims. You can see in these sentences the culmination of what must have been months, perhaps years, of indoctrination in the duties and glories of jihad, religious war.

"So remember, as He said in His book, 'O Lord, pour your patience upon us and make our feet steadfast and give us victory over infidels,' " the instructions continued. "Pray for yourself and all of your brothers that they may be victorious and hit their targets and ask God to grant you martyrdom facing the enemy, not running away from it, and for Him to grant you patience and the feeling that anything that happens to you is for Him."

The hijackers must have prayed and then they made their move on flight 11 after about fifteen minutes, as the Boeing 767 was nearing the border of Massachusetts and New York. At 8:13, everything was still normal. The Boston controller told Ogonowski to turn twenty degrees to the right, and Ogonowski acknowledged the instruction in the standard fashion, repeating it and the number of his flight.

"Twenty right AAL eleven," he said.

Those were the last words heard from the captain of flight 11.

"AAL eleven now climb, maintain FL350," the Boston controller ordered next. FL350 means thirty-five thousand feet.

Flight 11 did not reply.

"AAL eleven climb, maintain FL350," the controller said again, looking for a reply and not getting one. The time was now 8:14 and 33 seconds, a minute and a half after the routine instruction of 8:13, but it was in that tiny sliver of time that the hijackers seized control of the airplane and transformed it into a guided missile. Boston control tried one more time to get an answer from Captain Ogonowski.

"AAL eleven, ah, the American on the frequency, how do you hear me?" he asked.

This time a controller in Athens, New York, who would have picked up the next segment of the flight, came on the line and identified himself to the controller in Boston.

"I turned American twenty left and I was going to climb him; he will not respond to me now at all," the Boston controller complained, apparently disconcerted because he said "left" when he should have said "right."

"Looks like he's turning right," the Athens controller said.

"Yeah, I turned him right," Boston said, acknowledging his mistake.

"I'm not talking to him," Boston complained again.

"He won't answer you," Athens replied. "He's nordo," controller's slang for no radio, not in contact.

At about that time as well, flight 11's transponder, which emits a signal giving ground control a plane's coordinates and altitude, was turned off. Not only was the plane "nordo," but its whereabouts could now only be tracked when the plane came into range of ground radar.

A few minutes later, the controllers discovered what had happened. At 8:24, nine minutes after the plane had been commandeered, AA 11's radio became active and controllers heard a voice, not Captain Ogonowski's, probably Mohammed Atta's, making what sounded like an announcement to the passengers.

"We have some planes," they heard. "Just stay quiet and you will be OK. We are returning to the airport. Nobody move, everything will be OK. If you try to make any moves, you'll endanger yourself and the airplane. Just stay quiet."

Just as Atta had anticipated the psychological needs of the hijackers, he thought of a bit of deception for the passengers, aimed at keeping them in their seats. But in carrying out that part of the plan, he apparently keyed the radio switch rather than the public address system. In any case, hearing his message, Boston flight control now understood what had happened, and it notified other control centers that a hijacking was taking place.

What Boston was soon to learn was that more than one plane was going to suffer the same fate, beginning with United Airlines flight 175, another Boeing 767-200 that took off from Logan Airport at 8:15 bound for Los Angeles. Flight 175 carried fifty-eight passengers and nine crew, including the pilot, Victor J. Saracini, a former navy flyer. Among those on board were Garnet Bailey, fifty-three, the director of scouting for the Los Angeles Kings professional hockey team; Mark Bavis, thirty-one, a Kings scout; Christopher Carstanjen, thirty-three, a computer research specialist at the University of Massachusetts, heading off for a motorcycle trip up

the Pacific Coast; Heinrich Kimmig, forty-three, chairman of BCT Tech-
nology of Germany; and William Weems, a commercial producer from
Marblehead, Massachusetts. Also on board were Marwan al-Shehhi, Fayez
Ahmed, Ahmed Alghamdi, Hamza Alghamdi, and Mohand Alshehri.

Flight 175 followed the same flight path that flight 11 had followed
fourteen minutes before, heading out of Logan and over Massachusetts
just a few degrees south of due west. And, it was probably because of the
similarity in their flight paths that, at 8:37, the Boston controller asked
Captain Saracini of flight 175 if he could see American Airlines flight 11,
now both silent and lost someplace up there in the sky.

"Do you have traffic?" Boston asked. "Look at, uh, your twelve to one
o'clock at about, uh, ten miles southbound to see if you can see an American seventy sixty seven out there please."

"Affirmative," UA 175 replied. "We have him, uh, he looks, uh, about
twenty yeah, about twenty-nine, twenty-eight thousand."

Boston control told flight 175 to turn thirty degrees to the right, in
order to steer clear of what now appeared to be a runaway plane. And
then, four minutes later, at 8:41:32, UA 175 reported evidence of what was
to be the biggest news of many years:

"We heard a suspicious transmission on our departure out of Boston.
Someone keyed the mike and said, 'Everyone stay in your seats.'"

Just to make sure, UA 175 asked: "Did you copy that?" and the Boston
controller indicated that he had heard.

And then flight 175 went silent too. Its transponder was turned off at
8:46:18.

It all happened so quickly. By the time flight 175 was commandeered, the
Federal Aviation Administration had notified the North East Air Defense
Sector of the North American Aerospace Defense Command, or Norad,
of the hijacking of flight 11, and at 8:46, six minutes after the alert, two
1977-vintage F-15 fighter planes, equipped with heat-seeking and radar-
guided missiles, were scrambled at the Otis Air National Guard Base at
Falmouth, Massachusetts, on Cape Cod, and ordered to fly toward New
York. But, as the world knows, 8:46 was also the moment that the ninety-
two passengers, crew, and hijackers on American Airlines flight 11 were

already playing out the terrible last instants of their lives—in their different ways.

For the hijackers, and especially for Mohammed Atta, it was now that the months of pilot training—and the $1,500 for the use of that flight simulator at SimCenter in Florida—paid off. Whether Atta simply programmed the automatic pilot by feeding in the coordinates of the World Trade Center or whether he piloted the plane by hand, we don't know. Either would have been pretty easy in that bell-clear weather, even for somebody who had never actually flown a Boeing 767 before. From the New York–Massachusetts border, the plane flew south over the Hudson River Valley, following it all the way down to Manhattan Island, descending to about one thousand feet so as to be at about four-fifths of the way up the target, the north tower of the World Trade Center.

The last instants of the hijackers, or, at least, the last instants of the hijacker-pilot, would have consisted of watching the tower appear to catapult toward them. Inside the cockpit, there would have been tremendous noise, coming from the abnormal degree of wind resistance generated by a plane traveling far faster than a plane should be traveling at such a low altitude. Alarms would have been shrieking too, alarms that go off automatically to alert a pilot that he is going much too fast.

Still, despite all that racket, which might have distracted a less single-minded man, Mohammed Atta experienced no temptation to pull up or to the side and not to become a martyr on that day—or, if he did experience any such temptation, he resisted it. But then Mohammed Atta was not the kind of guy to lose faith at the last minute, and he kept his eyes on the approaching target, banking slightly near the end to stay on course. If he followed the written instructions he distributed to the others, he would have been shouting "Allah'u Akbar," God Is Great, as that silver, miragelike obelisk hurtled toward him, until, suddenly, he passed—or so he was taught to believe—into paradise, where the promised dark-eyed virgins, seventy of them, were waiting.

On flight 11—and perhaps on all the other flights as well—the attempt had been made by the hijackers to lull the passengers and crew into a false sense of hope, into believing that the plane would land someplace safely and the hijackers would use them as hostages in exchange for the satisfaction of demands—money, or the release of Palestinian prisoners by Israel, or something. They had all read of other hijackings, which often came to more or less happy endings when the hijackers' demands were met, or when the hijackers gave up, or when commandos stormed the plane. It's easy to imagine people on the hijacked planes not comprehending that the hijackers were on a suicide mission, spending their last few seconds contemplating their chances, nurturing the hope that somehow it would turn out all right.

Perhaps that is what David Angell of Pasadena, California, executive producer of the TV sitcom *Frasier,* told his wife, Lynn, as they sat on flight 11. Maybe that was the hope being nourished by the other three married couples on flight 11, Jude and Natalie Larson of Los Angeles, Robert and Jacqueline Norton of Lubec, Maine, and James and Mary Trentini of Everett, Massachusetts, or by Berry Berenson, or Carolyn Beug and her mother, Mary Alice Wahlstrom, traveling together. We're not sure if the passengers on flight 175 were also reassured by an announcement over the public address system, so we have less to go on in trying to imagine what the computer expert, motorcycle enthusiast, Morris dance–loving Chris Carstanjen was thinking in his last minutes, or William Weems, or the three members of the Hanson family, Peter, Susan, and two-year-old Christine. We do know that Peter called his parents on his cell phone and told them he thought they were going down, so there's no reason to think that he was fooled. And another passenger on flight 175, Brian Sweeney, thirty-eight, of Barnstable, Massachusetts, left a message for his wife, Julie, just before 9:00 that demonstrated great presence of mind and spiritual generosity, but revealed no illusions:

"Hey Jules, it's Brian. I'm on a plane and it's hijacked and it doesn't look good. I just wanted to let you know that I love you and I hope to see you again. If I don't, please have fun in life and live your life the best you can. Know that I love you and no matter what, I'll see you again."[2]

And, most dramatically, there was flight attendant Madeline Sweeney's telephone call to United Airlines ground control at Logan Airport. Cool and collected, she had described what had happened, where the hijackers had been seated, and that they had slashed a passenger and two stewardesses, and then, at the end, suddenly she lost it, screaming: "I see water and buildings. Oh my God! Oh my God!"

Near the end, in other words, when passengers could see that the plane was very low and that New York Harbor and New York City were just below them, it would have been hard for them not to have realized that they were about to die.

Did they experience anything at all as the plane plowed into its target, a monumental physical shock, an instant of searing fiery pain followed by nothingness? Or was death instantaneous and painless? There is no answer to that question.

At 8:50, ground traffic controllers heard an unidentified pilot ask, "Anybody know what that smoke is in lower Manhattan?" And just after that, at about 8:53, with flight 175 already streaking toward the south tower and the control tower's desperate calls to that flight getting an awful silence, the reality was settling in that a second plane had been taken out of Boston. "We may have a hijack," a flight controller said. "We have some problems over here right now."

And, just a couple of minutes after that, it became clear that a third plane had been grabbed. American Airlines flight 77, a Boeing 757 bound for Los Angeles under the command of Captain Charles Burlingame, with First Officer David Charlebois, left Dulles Airport outside of Washington, D.C., at 8:20 and climbed routinely to thirty-five thousand feet. There were four additional crew and fifty-eight passengers on the flight, including three eleven-year-old schoolchildren and teachers on a National Geographic Marine Sanctuary Program field trip to Santa Cruz Island off the coast of southern California. One of the children was Bernard Curtis Brown II, a handsome African-American boy who loved school and was wearing a pair of Air Jordan basketball shoes he had bought for the trip. In addition, Leslie Whittingon and Charles Falkenberg, along with their children, Zoe and Dana, were on board, as was Barbara K. Olson, a television commentator on Fox News, and Yeneneh Betru, going back to his collection of dialysis machines.

At about 8:50, flight 77 became the third plane that morning to stop replying to radio calls. The transponder was turned off six minutes later, after which a controller in Indianapolis repeatedly asked, "American Seventy-seven, Indy radio check, how do you read?" At 9:06, a controller despairingly informed another controller that even American Airlines ground control had no idea where the plane was. "They can't even get a hold of him," the controller said. "So there's no, no radar, uh, no radio communications and no radar."

Three minutes before that, at 9:03, Marwan al-Shehhi, he of the round, friendly face and spectacles who was the inseparable companion of Mohammed Atta, brought flight 175, traveling at more than five hundred miles an hour, into the south face of the south tower of the World Trade Center. Al-Shehhi had steered his plane southwest across Atta's vapor trail. He crossed into New Jersey and then made a big turn over the New Jersey–Pennsylvania border so that when he headed toward Manhattan, he was approaching from the southeast. The silver Boeing 767 roared over the Verrazano-Narrows Bridge and the Statue of Liberty; it banked to the left at the very last minute and then disappeared into the south tower between the 78th and 84th floors like a knife hurled into a gift-wrapped box. Immediately afterward a tremendous spume of debris followed by a giant billowing fireball erupted from the tower, just as it had from the north tower seventeen minutes before.

When flight 175 hit its target, the two F-15s flying out of Cape Cod were still seventy-one miles and eight minutes away from Manhattan. It is not clear whether the pilots of those planes had been given orders to shoot down any hijacked passenger planes, but the point is moot. They were too late to stop anything. They were the fighter jets that pedestrians in New York noticed flying over Manhattan in the wake of the crashes, their pilots among the first to get aerial views of the devastation.

EIGHTEEN

"Protect the White House at All Cost"

Shortly after 9:00, President Bush was sitting in S. Kay Daniel's second-grade classroom in Sarasota, Florida, where she was giving a reading lesson to sixteen seven-year-olds at the Emma E. Booker Elementary School. The president was carrying out the sort of duty that presidents carried out in those innocent days, publicizing his ideas for education, being on hand for one of the more conventional routines of American life. And then, at 9:05, the president's chief of staff, Andrew Card, walked into the room and whispered in his ear. Reporters on the scene remember seeing the color drain out of Bush's face, and then he looked at the children, at the television cameras that follow every public presidential appearance, and at the textbook he was holding in his hands.

"Really good readers," the president said. "Whew! This must be sixth grade."

Then, at 9:12, he got up abruptly and left the room to confer with advisers. At 9:30 he went to the school library, where reporters had gathered together with children, parents, and teachers who had been waiting for an hour. Normally, the president, who stood in front of a suddenly irrelevant "Read to Succeed" banner, would have made a little speech about the importance of improving American education. Instead he announced what millions already knew, that both towers of the World Trade Center had been struck, and he made his first statement about the new American era: "Terrorism against our nation will not stand," he said.[1]

What followed was one of the strangest days in the history of the American presidency. At that point, two planes were known to have been hijacked and to have struck targets in New York, killing who knew how many thousands of people. A third plane, American Airlines flight 77, had also been commandeered, and its whereabouts were unknown. Later declarations from the White House had it that Bush wanted to return to Washington right away, but the Secret Service demurred. The situation was far too dangerous. The president himself might be a target. And so, the president left the Emma E. Booker Elementary School and was whisked back to Air Force One at the Sarasota Airport.

At about 9:25, something without precedent in the history of American aviation took place. The administrator of the FAA, Jane Garvey, ordered all aircraft in the United States out of the sky, and for no planes to take off. At about the same time, while most of the world's eyes were on the twin towers burning but still standing in New York, air traffic control radar picked up flight 77 moving toward the restricted air space over Washington, D.C. At 9:30, while the president was making his terrorism-will-not-stand statement in Sarasota, three F-16s belonging to the Air National Guard's 119th Fighter Wing, nicknamed the Happy Hooligans, were scrambled from Langley Air Force Base in Virginia and, for reasons that are not clear, ordered to head toward New York. Three minutes after that, at 9:33, a controller informed an operational supervisor that flight 77 had been detected moving toward Washington. The Secret Service was informed. While President Bush was not in the White House, Vice President Cheney was, and the Secret Service grabbed him and hustled him to an underground bunker.

At 9:36, controllers at National Airport, just across the Potomac from Washington, told a C-130 military cargo plane that had just taken off from nearby Andrews Air Force Base to identify the renegade plane. The C-130 reported that it was a Boeing 757 moving low and very fast.

In fact, flight 77 was in the final stages of a 360-degree turn just south of the Pentagon, which it had nearly overflown, at about eight thousand feet, a few minutes earlier. Now it descended as it banked right in an enormous circle over northern Virginia, and then headed northeast with the Pentagon directly in its path and the three F-16s not yet in the vicinity.

"I happened to look up and I saw this airplane not more than fifty feet coming right at us," said Alan Wallace, a Defense Department firefighter who was badly burned in the attack. "I yelled to my partner, and we dove underneath a van for protection."[2]

The Pentagon, as its name indicates, is an immense five-sided structure, with five concentric rings that together provide more floor space than the Empire State Building and have room for twenty-four thousand employees. It is an eerie fact that even as flight 77 got into position overhead to crash into them, many of the employees in the building at the time, fully aware that the United States was under attack, were, like people all over the world, watching the news of the World Trade Center disaster unfold on television. One person at least, Mike Slater, a former marine, even muttered "We're next" to those around him. But even though the entire Defense Department was aware of the Trade Center attacks, and even though flight controllers knew that flight 77 was heading toward Washington, there was no order to evacuate the Pentagon.

Defense Secretary Donald Rumsfeld had met that morning with some congressmen in a conference room and, coincidentally, had urged them to support greater defense spending, warning them specifically that every ten years or so the country is hit by a surprise, and that such a surprise would come again. Then he went to his office in the outer ring of the third floor and was receiving a briefing from the CIA. Though he had been told of the attacks on the World Trade Center, he wasn't watching the television accounts of the disaster in New York.

The pilot of flight 77 is assumed by the FBI to have been Hani Hanjour, even though he had been so inept on check-out flights he'd taken in the previous few weeks that no flight center had been willing to rent him a single-engine plane. Still, aviation experts say that a maneuver such as the one performed by flight 77 as it darted toward the Pentagon could be programmed into the automatic pilot. Or, perhaps it was not Hani Hanjour at the controls; perhaps Khalid al-Midhar, who had spent several months before the summer away from the United States, had gotten pilot training someplace else, and was the man flying the plane that day. In any case, flight 77 finished its turn, and, at 9:38, now oriented toward the northeast, it was barely skimming the ground and traveling at five hundred miles per hour. It slammed into the Pentagon, penetrating three of

the five rings on the southwest side of the building, killing 125 people
inside the building and all 59 on the plane (not including the hijackers).

After being ordered toward New York, the three F-16s from Langley,
traveling at subsonic speeds at an altitude of 25,000 feet, were ordered to
vector west and then south toward Washington. As they reached their
new destination, they got this message:

"Hooligan flight, can you confirm that the Pentagon is on fire?"

The lead F-16 pilot looked down and confirmed that, indeed, such
was the case.

The next message the F-16s received came from somebody who said
he was with the Secret Service.

"I want you to protect the White House at all costs," it said.

⸺

At 9:55, Air Force One with the president aboard took off from Sarasota,
escorted by a squadron of fighter planes, going on a zigzag, high-altitude
course—east to the Atlantic, then north, then south—that eventually
took the president to Barksdale Air Force Base in Shreveport, Louisiana,
a destination chosen at random. As reporters had scrambled up the rear
stairway of the plane, word had come of the strike at the Pentagon, and
during the flight, the unbelievable news kept coming in over the television screens on board—the White House, the Executive Office Building,
the State Department, the Treasury Department, and the Congress had
all been evacuated. The government had in essence gone into hiding and
the president was in the air heading for an undisclosed location that was
not the national capital. Reporters on the plane were not told where they
were going, and they spent time looking out their windows trying to figure out where they were. They were prohibited from using their cell
phones for fear that terrorists would be able to use the signals to trace
the location of Air Force One. There were reports, false as it turned out,
that there had been explosions at the State Department and at the Capi-
tol. Then, a bit after 10:00 came word that the south tower of the Trade
Center had collapsed and that there was still one hijacked plane unaccounted for.[3]

That plane was United Airlines flight 93, which had been scheduled
to leave Newark at 8:01 on a flight to San Francisco, but had been held on

the ground. One can imagine that the delay worried the hijackers on board—four on this flight, as opposed to five on the other three—because they knew that, eventually, when the first planes hit their targets, all flights would quickly be grounded, which is why they had chosen to hijack planes scheduled to leave within a few minutes of each other.

But flight 93 did take off, at 8:42, four minutes before flight 11 hit the north tower. It headed west across Virginia into Pennsylvania and then over northern Ohio. On board were Jeremy Glick, Lauren Grandcolas from San Rafael, California, on her way home from her grandmother's funeral, and Mark Bingham, thirty-one, heading a day later than expected to San Francisco for a meeting that afternoon with a client. (Like Glick, he was supposed to have flown on Monday but he delayed because he wasn't feeling well.)

Shortly after 8:53, seven minutes after flight 11 crashed into the north tower of the World Trade Center, the pilot of flight 93, Jason Dahl, and the first officer, LeRoy Homer, would have heard a kind of ping, a signal that a message was arriving on the cockpit computer, and then they would have read, in green letters against a black background, a three-word warning, "Beware, cockpit intrusion," which was sent out to all United flights in the wake of the crash of flight 11. Dahl and Homer replied by pushing a button confirming the receipt of the message, but there is no indication that they took any measures to prevent a hijacking of their flight. Probably, as one aviation official put it afterward, they thought, "It's already happened; it's probably not going to happen again."

But it did happen. At almost exactly the moment when flight 77 was observed heading toward Washington, flight 93 experienced the very "cockpit intrusion" that pilot Dahl and First Officer Homer had been warned about. It happened as the plane was over northern Ohio heading toward Lake Erie. At about 9:20 passengers in first class would have seen four Middle Eastern men—Ziad Jarrah, in seat 1B, and three others, Ahmed Alhaznawi, Ahmed Alnami, and Saeed Alghamdi, in seats 3C, 3D, and 6B—get up and put red bandannas around their heads. We know about the bandannas because a bit later, after 9:30, Jeremy Glick called his wife, Lyzbeth, on his cell phone and told her that three "Arab-looking men" wearing red headbands and saying they had a bomb had taken control of the plane.

In the wake of the disaster, the FBI seized the tape of the communications between flight 93 and air traffic control, and it has released no transcript of those communications. The FBI, which took over the investigation from the National Transportation Safety Board, which usually investigates plane crashes, has also declined to release the contents of the cockpit voice recorder that was recovered at the crash site—though, in April, it did allow families of passengers to hear that tape, on condition that they not disclose its contents. But reporters for several news organizations interviewed investigators who listened to both the cockpit voice recorder and the ground control tapes, which together gave a rough outline of what happened on that flight.

At 9:25, Dahl contacted Cleveland air traffic control and said "good morning." After that, at 9:28:19, or almost exactly the moment when flight 77 was slamming into the Pentagon, Cleveland air traffic control began to hear the sounds of a scuffle in the background. There were no calls of mayday from the crew, just the sounds of a fight and after a few seconds, a voice, probably Dahl's or Homer's saying, "Hey, get out of here." A foreign language was also heard being spoken on the frequency, and ground controllers thought it was Arabic. Ground control also heard a man speaking in a heavy accent saying, "This is your captain speaking. Remain in your seats. There is a bomb on board. Stay quiet. We are meeting with their demands. We are returning to the airport." Again, the hijackers seem inadvertently to have been speaking over the radio to ground control when they were trying to use the public address system. In one case, flight 11, the man making the announcement identified himself as a hijacker; on flight 93, he pretended, not very convincingly, to be the pilot. In both cases, and very likely on the other two flights as well, a part of the plan was to make some sort of announcement aimed at keeping the passengers from taking action.

On flight 93, and, it seems, only on flight 93, that stratagem didn't work. The rebellion organized by passengers and that probably prevented the plane from hitting a target in Washington—very likely the White House or the Congress or possibly the CIA—has already entered into American legend. The first step seems to have been a cell phone call that Tom Burnett made to his wife, Deena, in San Ramon, California, to tell her that his flight had been hijacked. Deena informed Tom of the news that two other hijacked planes had already hit the World Trade Center. There were several other calls. Jeremy Glick spoke to Lyz in Windham, New York, and, after describing the Arab-looking men with red bandannas, he asked her if the stories about the World Trade Center were true, and she told him they were. A flight attendant, Sandy Bradshaw, called her husband, Phil, in Greensboro, North Carolina, and told him that several of the flight attendants were filling coffee pots with hot water to throw at the hijackers. At about 9:45, Tom Burnett called Deena again and she told him the latest, that flight 77 had hit the Pentagon. Tom, according to Deena, replied: "My God. They seem to be taking planes and driving them into designated landmarks all over the East Coast. It's as if hell has been unleashed."

On board flight 93, as it happens, were a number of passengers capable of taking action. Besides Glick, the judo champion, there was Mark Bingham, a six-foot-five former college rugby player. One flight attendant, CeeCee Lyles, was once a detective on a Florida police force; William Cashman, sixty, was a former paratrooper with the 101st airborne; Alan Beaven, six-three, was a former Scotland Yard prosecutor. Rich Guadagno had been trained in hand-to-hand combat; Tom Burnett had played football in college and Todd Beamer had played basketball. Burnett told his wife in his last call to her, "We're going to do something." Glick told Lyz that several of the passengers were thinking of rushing the hijackers; Todd Beamer was talking on his cell phone to a GTE customer center supervisor named Lisa Jefferson in Oakbrook, Illinois, and Mrs. Jefferson says the last words she heard him say were, "Are you guys ready: Let's roll."

It is not clear exactly what happened. In the public address announcement accidentally relayed to ground control, the hijackers told passengers to remain in their seats. But the passenger cell-phone calls to relatives and others indicate that they were grouped in the back of the plane, guarded by a single hijacker who claimed to have a bomb strapped to his waist. Perhaps, the hijackers never did succeed in making an announcement to the passengers over the P.A. system, or perhaps they changed their minds and, after that announcement, told the passengers to go to the back of the plane, away from the cockpit. In any case, according to *Newsweek* magazine, which obtained a detailed account of the contents of the cockpit voice recorder, there were sounds of a death struggle in the cockpit beginning around 9:57. A lot of screaming could be heard and the crashing of galley dishes and the sound of a passenger calling, "Let's get them." One of the hijackers called out "Allah'u Akbar," God Is Great.[4]

On the ground in Shanksville, Pennsylvania, Paula Pluta, who lives about a mile from where the plane crashed, said that she heard a rumbling sound that made her house vibrate. Going to her porch, she saw the plane dip down at a sixty or seventy degree angle before disappearing behind a line of trees. When it crashed it sent a fireball a hundred feet into the air above the tree line, she said. Another witness, Terry Butler, working at a salvage yard a half mile from the crash site, said he saw a jetliner flying just above the treetops. The plane, he said, lifted slightly, turned sharply to the right, and nose-dived into an open field. The time was 10:10, exactly two hours and eleven minutes since AA flight 11 had taken off from Boston.

That was the end of the hijackings, though it took some time for government authorities to assure themselves that there were no more airplanes unaccounted for. Throughout the rest of the day, the federal government remained, essentially, closed down. President Bush made a short statement in Louisiana, saying, "Freedom itself was attacked this morning by a faceless coward, and freedom will be defended." Then he reboarded Air Force One and flew to Offutt Air Force Base near Omaha, Nebraska, the command center of the country's nuclear forces and one of the world's most secure military installations. He spoke by phone with Vice President Cheney and with his national security adviser Condoleeza Rice. He also spoke to his wife, Laura, and their twin daughters, who had been taken to an undisclosed location by the Secret Service.

It wasn't until about 7:00 P.M. that the president returned to the White House. All flights over American territory were grounded at that point, and cities like Washington and New York were being guarded by airborne fighter planes. Flights from overseas had either returned to their destinations or been diverted, mostly to Canada. The United States was effectively sealed off from the rest of the world. The name bin Laden was already being mentioned by senior government officials as the likely terrorist commander in chief. The president went on national television at 8:30, looking grim, his eyes a bit red.

"The pictures of airplanes flying into buildings, fires burning, huge structures collapsing, have filled us with disbelief, terrible sadness and a quiet, unyielding anger," he said. "These acts of mass murder were intended to frighten our nation into chaos and retreat. But they have failed; our country is strong."

What happened on the hijacked planes? How did Atta on flight 11 and the hijackers of flights 175, 77, and 93 manage to take over their planes without any apparent resistance from the pilots or crew?

In the wake of September 11, senior government officials, including Attorney General John Ashcroft and Secretary of Defense Donald Rumsfeld, said that the hijackers had used box cutters and plastic knives as their weapons. "It was beyond one's imagination that plastic knives and our own commercial aircraft with our own people would be used as the implement of war," Rumsfeld said on the *Lehrer NewsHour* on November 7. One newspaper report said that the hijackers "worked with legal instruments: box cutters and homemade knives fashioned with blades shorter than the FAA limit of 4 inches."[5]

That claim is credible, in part because boarding with box cutters and short knives, which were allowed on passenger planes before September 11, would have enabled the hijackers to avoid any risk of detention as they passed through security checks—though it is not clear what led the newspaper to conclude that some of the knives were homemade. On American Airlines flight 77, which hit the Pentagon, Barbara Olson, a lawyer and television commentator, used a cell phone to call her husband, Theodore Olson, who is the United States solicitor-general. According to Mr. Olson, his wife described the weapons as "knives and box cutters." Olson also said that she and the other passengers had been herded into the back of the plane, so it would seem that she could only know what the men guarding the passengers had in the way of weapons. She couldn't have known anything about the weapons used by the men who killed or disabled the pilots and took over the controls in the front of the plane.

In addition to Olson's testimony about box cutters, the FBI found at least one box cutter at the Pennyslvania crash site of flight 93, and a box cutter was inside the flying school tote bag thrown into a Dumpster by three of the hijackers in Florida. So, box cutters would seem a likely weapon, though the fact is that Barbara Olson's remark, as conveyed later by her husband, is the only mention of box cutters in any of the calls made from the four hijacked planes. And, in truth, it is simply not known exactly what weapons the hijackers were able to get on board with them. Certainly plastic knives had nothing to do with the hijackings. It was Jeremy Glick on flight 93 who, talking about what weapons the passengers would use to storm the hijackers, had joked about the butter knife on his tray left over from breakfast, but no passenger on any flight said anything about plastic knives in the hijackers' hands.

Several callers talked about knives, including Barbara Olson. On flight 11, two flight attendants made calls; one of them, Betty Ong, told American Airlines ground control that four men had come from first-class seats. They killed one passenger, and they used, she said, "some sort of spray" that burned her eyes and made it difficult to breathe. Ong did not identify the weapons the hijackers used other than the chemical spray. Another attendant, Madeline Amy Sweeney, called ground control from the economy-class section. Her call was not recorded and it is not clear exactly what she said. One report, issued by the FAA, quoted her as saying that a passenger had been "shot," but a subsequent report changed "shot" to "stabbed."[6] According to the indictment of Zacarias Moussaoui, Mohammed Atta bought a knife on or about July 8 at the airport in Zurich, Switzerland. Presumably, the prosecutors put this knife into the indictment because they feel it was used in the hijack operation. However, it is unlikely that you could buy a hardware store item like a box cutter at the Zurich airport duty-free shop, though Swiss airports usually have good collections of Swiss Army knives for sale.

Could they have had guns? It seems unlikely that they would have taken the chance of smuggling guns or bombs through security, even though they might have had a good chance of succeeding. In 1998, special FAA "red teams" that test airport security by trying to smuggle what are called "major weapons"—meaning guns and bombs—past security checkpoints succeeded 85 percent of the time in American domestic airports. Still, the hijackers themselves wouldn't have known that, and, even if the FAA teams succeed most of the time, they don't succeed all of the time, and there was not a single report of any person caught with a gun at any airport on September 11. Not a single one of the nineteen hijackers was stopped at any of the four different security checkpoints that they went through. Probably they didn't have either guns or bombs.

Most likely, in other words, the weapons used by the hijackers were box cutters and other knives, augmented possibly by mace or some other disabling spray.

Whatever the weapons used, it is clear that the seizures of the airplanes happened very quickly. The recordings of communications between the planes and ground control indicate that, with the exception of flight 93, they happened so quickly there wasn't even a struggle. No pilot on any of the flights issued a mayday or had time to tell ground control what was happening, and no passengers reported actually seeing a struggle in or near the cockpit. By the time the passengers realized that anything had happened, the planes had already been commandeered.

Entry into the cockpits, whose doors are normally kept closed on commercial flights, was critical to the hijackings. Some have speculated that the hijackers were able to seize keys from flight attendants, but according to airline spokesmen, the cockpit doors on most American commercial airliners don't have locks. Possibly, the cockpit crews opened their doors when hijackers threatened to kill passengers or flight attendants. It is a little bit strange, if that were the case, that no pilot took a few seconds to notify ground control that passengers were making such threats before opening the doors. It is also possible that the hijackers were simply able to break open the cockpit doors—which are built to withstand only about 150 pounds of pressure—and move in quickly with knives to stab the pilots or cut their throats while they were still sitting in their seats. In his cell phone call to Lisa Jefferson of GTE, Todd Beamer said that a flight attendant had told him that two people, presumably Captain Dahl and First Officer Homer, were lying dead or gravely wounded on the floor in first class.[7] It would certainly make sense, given that the hijackers didn't need or want the pilots, that they would have killed them and pulled their bodies out of the cockpits as they took over the planes' controls themselves.

We will never know for sure, but probably what happened on the hijacked planes was something like this:

The hijackers, responding to a signal from their leader, got up from their seats, which were in first or business class, and at least two of them went to the cockpit doors, which they broke open by force. They slit the throats of the pilots, or they stabbed them to death, as they sat in their seats. While two or three of the hijackers returned to the passenger cabins, the designated hijacker-pilot began to fly the plane, probably by programming the automatic pilot. He turned off the transponder, which is controlled by a simple on-off switch, and made a public address announcement to the effect that everybody would be all right as long as nobody tried to interfere with the hijacking. It is peculiar that passengers who described what was happening on their planes on their cell phones seem to have reduced the number of hijackers by one. Betty Ong on flight 11 said there were four hijackers, when, in fact, there were five, and Jeremy Glick said there were three on flight 93, rather than four. It is possible that as part of the plan, one of the hijackers remained concealed among passengers, continuing to sit in his seat, possibly to serve as a kind of surprise backup should anything go wrong. Because most hijackings in the past involved flying planes safely to some destination, where the hijackers then announced demands, passengers would not have suspected that this was a suicide mission on which everybody, including the hijackers, was going to die—except for flight 93, which had been delayed on the ground for forty-five minutes and therefore got under way late enough for passengers to learn about the events at the World Trade Center and the Pentagon. If flight 93 had left Newark Airport on time, at 8:01, it is more than likely that there would never have been a passenger rebellion and that the flight would have struck its intended target, maybe the White House itself.

The foot soldiers on each flight—four of them on flights 11, 175, and 77; three on flight 93—stayed in the main cabin to keep the passengers in line, killing one or two people. Betty Ong and Madeline Sweeney, flight attendants on flight 11, both said that at least one passenger and one attendant were killed by the hijackers. Possibly these victims disobeyed some order by the hijackers, or perhaps they were killed simply to intimidate the others. Again, with the important exception of flight 93, the hijackers met with no resistance, no opposition, no trouble at all, as they mounted the most costly surprise attack on the United States since Japan struck Pearl Harbor sixty years before.

And they didn't need battleships or carrier-based aircraft to do it. All they needed were knives, plane tickets, our own Boeing jets, and a willingness to die for their cause.

NINETEEN

"We Had a Lot of Dying and Fire Up There"

One of the first witnesses was Juan Suarez, a fifty-four-year-old iron-worker who was on top of a twenty-five-story building going up on Madison Avenue and Forty-fifth Street. At 8:45 on the morning of September 11, he was at work when his buddy Artie looked west and said, "Hey, that plane's flying kind of low." It was so low that it seemed almost as if it was going to clip the Empire State Building on Fifth Avenue and Thirty-fourth Street, but it was well west of there, and Suarez lost sight of it as it headed south. Jim Farmer, a film composer, didn't see it but he heard it. He was having breakfast at a small restaurant in Soho about twenty blocks north of the World Trade Center when he heard the sound of a jet—too loud and low to seem normal. Nature itself at that instant gave a sign of impending disaster:

"All the pigeons in the street flew up," he noted.

At 8:45, David Blackford was walking toward work in lower Manhattan when he too heard the jet overhead and looked up in time to see it slam into the north face of the north tower.

"You could see the concussion move up the building," he said.

"It was a large plane flying low," Robert Pachino, another witness, said hours after the impact. "There was no engine trouble. He didn't try to maneuver. This plane was on a mission."

"We were walking down the block to vote," said Barry Meier, a reporter for the *New York Times* who lives in downtown Manhattan. "We were walking down Greenwich Street with our daughter in the stroller. All of a sudden I heard a very high-pitched jet whine. We hear jets in this neighborhood a lot, but this was louder than I had ever heard it. It was closer to the ground than I had ever heard. I looked up and I saw a huge silver jet—I couldn't tell the markings on it—flying closer to the ground than I had ever seen. It was surreal because it was a beautiful silver jet against a bright blue sky, a crystal clear sky. I thought, that plane is flying so low it may hit the tower. The plane was banking slightly. It continued to bank, and it just smashed right into the tower. There was a huge fireball. It was the sound of an explosion, and the fireball."

In Brooklyn, in Fire Department headquarters, Pete Ganci was doing what he does every morning in his office, drinking coffee and talking with his chiefs about the previous day's events. Ganci's office faced west and gave him a view of lower Manhattan, including the skyline-dominating World Trade Center, and he happened to be looking that way when the plane hit the north tower. He yelled out at Danny Nigro, his chief of operations, to tell him what had happened, and Nigro and several others, including Ganci's executive assistant, Fire Marshal Steve Mosiello, rushed into his office.

"For a few minutes, we just stood in awe of the sight," Mosiello remembered later, "but we snapped out of that pretty quickly and we got into Pete's car and drove toward the WTC. By the time we got to the Brooklyn Bridge, we knew this wasn't just any ordinary fire and we went into high alert. So we got there pretty fast."

Inside the north tower, Joe Disorbo, an engineer who worked on the 72nd floor, sat near a north-facing window, and that is why, at an instant before 8:46 and 26 seconds, he heard the whine of a jet and simultaneously saw a shadow, and then he felt the building shake. He had no way of knowing what had happened. Tim Lingenfelder, thirty-six, an office manager at a small investment banking firm, was sitting in his office on the 52nd floor of the north tower when the entire building shook and he saw chunks of rubble falling outside his window.

"That can't be from here," he said to himself.

Anne Prosser, twenty-nine, a banker, rode the elevator to the 90th floor and as the doors opened, she heard what seemed like an explosion.

"I got thrown to the ground before I got to our suite," she said. "I crawled inside. Not everybody was at work." She said she tried to leave but, until she got some help, she wasn't able to because she couldn't breathe with all the debris and dust choking the air.

The American Bureau of Shipping was on the north side of the 91st floor of the north tower, one floor below where the plane hit and on the same side of the building. Eleven people were in the office at the time, and all of them survived by walking down the stairs to safety. Several of them later said that their window shades were closed against the morning glare, or they were looking at their computer screens, so they heard but didn't see the plane, and then felt the shock wave caused by the impact above them. Strangely, for the first few instants, nothing much happened, only a few books fell off shelves, and even knickknacks stayed where they were. But then the building started to sway back and forth as the impact wave radiated up and down the tower. George Sleigh, manager of the technical consistency department, was on the phone. He heard a roar and then he did see the plane—or, more accurately, the underbelly of the plane—when it was two or three plane-lengths away. And then, "everything just crumbled," he said. "The plane came into the building and my office collapsed instantaneously."

When Steve McIntyre pushed his way out of the ABS reception area toward the elevator banks and the building's core, he heard water cascading down the stairwells—from pipes that had been severed in the impact—and he saw that gypsum sheets, Sheetrock, had formed an impenetrable plug between his floor, 91, and the one above it. That plug was to mean the difference between life and death; it marked the divide in the north tower between those who survived—people on the 91st floor and below—and the sixteen hundred who didn't—on the 92nd floor and above.

Those outside knew immediately that a plane had hit the building—thinking either it was a terrible accident or an even more terrible act of terrorism—but most of those inside didn't know what had happened. Some people thought the big boom they heard had come from the Staten Island Ferry. Greg Shark, a marine engineer and naval architect at the ABS, remembered that some electrical work had been taking place nearby, and he thought a huge acetylene tank had blown up. "It did not seem that a plane hit and exploded," he said. "You felt this pressure go by you. It didn't push you in any direction." A cafeteria worker thought somebody had dropped a file cabinet—though she then told herself it would have to have been a very big file cabinet. Many people thought it was a bomb—1993 all over again. Susan Doyle of Kemper Insurance, on the 35th floor of the north tower, thought New York had been struck by an earthquake, but then she looked out the window and noticed that the rest of lower Manhattan seemed normal.

"Whatever had happened had happened just to us," she said.

Tom Tella, a representative of a Dallas consulting firm, was making a presentation to oil-industry analysts when the thunderous boom interrupted the proceedings. Like Susan Doyle, he thought that an earthquake had struck New York, but his colleague, Scott Rees, who had actually been through an earthquake, thought otherwise. It was a bomb, Rees said.[1]

Within minutes, as the sound of the impact rolled outward in waves, orange flames and white smoke began billowing from the north and east façades of the north tower, and the smoke was carried eastward toward Brooklyn by the wind. Debris arched outward and fell, small bits at first glinting in the morning light. Flames shot out of windows and then people could be seen waving things to attract attention, white shirts or T-shirts, from the windows above where the plane had hit. And then bodies could be seen falling, brown dots hard to pick out against the surrounding avalanche of things. People on the streets, crowded with rush-hour traffic, stopped and stared, pointing and gasping when they understood that among the falling objects were people preferring to jump and die outside than to be burned to death inside.

"You heard an explosion," said Clyde Ebanks, an executive of Aon, the insurance company, who was attending a meeting of representatives from around the country on the 103rd floor of the south tower. He was speaking of the impact of the plane at the tower next door. "Then you heard an explosion, I think it was from the east. It wasn't major or huge, or at least that's how I remember it. But there was smoke, black and gray, smoke everywhere and papers were flying, hundreds of them. We all huddled around the window and that's when I could feel the heat. That's when I knew that something major had happened, the heat. You could feel it through the glass. Then it started to smell like jet fuel."

Those in the south tower who stood at their windows also had the

best view of the grimmest spectacle of all, the people who held themselves over window ledges in a desperate effort to get air, and those who
jumped or fell out of the north tower altogether and hurtled downward
alongside the sheer gleaming face of the building. They watched transfixed in the south tower, or, as one of them later put it, they watched the
way one watches a horror film on late-night television, not wanting to
watch but unable to tear themselves away. They saw that some people
who tumbled out of the broken windows had their hands over their faces,
most likely because they were trying to protect their eyes from the
smoke, or because they were trying to use their hands to filter out smoke
and get some clean air. Videos show many people on the 103rd, 104th, and
105th floors, many shirtless in the heat, leaning out through broken windows. There were as many as four people at a window, piled on top of one
another. Observers in a police helicopter saw other people on high floors
who were unable to break windows, their faces pressed against the glass
as they tried to breathe. Some of the jumpers could be seen at the jagged
hole on the east side of the north tower, staggering there, apparently confused about where they were and what had happened. One of those who
watched for a time from the south tower and then made a run for the
stairs was Kelly Reyher, who worked for Aon, the insurance company.

"From what I could see it was sort of people were just trying to
breathe so they were hanging out with smoke filling," he said. "I think to
some extent they just let go because they couldn't hang on any longer, or
it was too difficult to breathe, or it looked like in some cases people just
chose their fate, and it was going to be one or the other."

There were several thousand different experiences of the hour after 8:46,
when flight 11 swept down the Hudson River going north to south and hit
the north tower, and after 9:02, when flight 175, coming from the eastern
tip of New Jersey and roaring over the Statue of Liberty, cut a diagonal
gash into the south face of the south tower. But those almost uncountable
experiences can be grouped into several basic kinds that together make
up that day.

There were two kinds of experience inside each of the stricken
towers—the experience of those above the floors where the planes hit

and the experience of those below those floors. Or, more properly, there were three experiences, if you add in those who were on the floors that received the direct impact of the strikes. A few people on the floors of immediate impact were not killed right away and spent a few seconds or a few minutes or even close to an hour clawing through the smoke and the debris struggling to get to safety. We know from survivors of the impact in the south tower that even on the floors directly struck by the plane there were areas of temporary safety, where, say, the wing of the plane sliced through the building on a floor just above or below where people were working, leaving their work cubicle or trading room or office sealed off from the areas where fires were raging. Some of the people in those areas might have survived for a while, but as the flames got hotter, they would have found themselves cut off from an escape route facing the terrible choice: to burn to death or to leap into the void.

One of the three stairways that ran the entire height of the building in the south tower remained intact and passable on every floor, and seventeen people who started above the point of impact are known to have used them to get to safety, but not a single person above that point in the north tower survived. In the south tower a large number of people died on the 78th floor, which was a Sky Lobby where express elevators coming directly from the downstairs lobby connected to the several sets of local elevators that went to higher floors.

At least several dozen, possibly several hundred people who had come down from higher floors after the first plane struck, were there waiting for express elevators when the wing of flight 175 sliced into the Sky Lobby. One second the floor was full of people milling about, wondering whether to go down immediately or to go back up and fetch a Palm Pilot or a purse, and the next it was a scene of flames, smoke, pulverized plaster, and the bodies of the dead and injured. Judy Wein, who worked at Aon Corporation on the 100th floor, suffered a broken arm, three cracked ribs, and a punctured lung, but she survived. She tried to move some chunks of marble lying on the broken legs of Richard Gabrielle, an Aon colleague, but he cried out in pain for her to stop. He died when the tower collapsed, waiting for help to arrive. Only a very few people whose offices were below the points of impact were killed—and among those who did not survive, many had failed to evacuate before the towers collapsed because they were injured and unable to move or because, like Abe Zelmanowitz, they stopped to help others.

The survival of those below and the deaths of those at and above where the planes hit points to the major division inside the buildings. For the vast majority of those below, the experience of September 11 was a long, smoky, harrowing escape down one of the three stairwells near the tower's core. Many of the same people who walked down and out of the towers on September 11 had done close to the same thing after the truck bombing of the Trade Center in 1993, though on September 11, many of the people in the towers knew from watching television that their buildings had not been bombed but hit by airplanes. Even so, as they descended the stairwells, they didn't think that the towers, which seemed at that point to have stood up to the attack, would collapse.

The people above the point of impact, with a very small number of exceptions in the south tower and none in the north tower, didn't or couldn't get down any more, their ways blocked by the planes' near amputation of the upper floors. At Aon Corporation, on the uppermost floors of the south tower, one man was thrown so hard against a wall by the impact of the second plane that he broke his back and couldn't move. Judging from the calls that many of them made to loved ones in their last minutes, many of them knew they were going to die, though they probably assumed it would be from fire or smoke inhalation, not because the towers would collapse altogether. And, until they did collapse, some of them stayed alive on the upper floors, perhaps hoping that if they could only continue to breathe and not succumb to smoke inhalation, they might make it if only the fires below them would burn out or be extinguished. The cell phone calls made from participants in the Risk Waters Conference at Windows on the World indicate that everybody on the 107th floor was ordered down to the 106th floor, and there they waited for the help that never arrived. But the smoke from fires on the lower floors rushed up the elevator shafts, which operated like chimneys, and within minutes the smoke was so thick on the 106th floor that visibility was reduced to ten feet. Some of the staff of the restaurant were on the phone to the Fire Command Center in the lobby, and they got the advice for everybody to wet towels and keep them over their faces. But the water pipes were broken and there was no water. In a phone call to his wife, a waiter, Jan Maciejweski, said he was looking for water in the flower vases.

In the south tower, while a few people went down the single open stairway, many more went up, trying to get to the roof, only to find that access was blocked. We know this from a cell phone call that Roko Camaj, a window washer who was on the 105th floor, made to his wife. This is one of the most poignant of many poignant aspects of the September 11 disaster. After the 1993 bombing, the Fire Department had decided against rooftop rescues by helicopter, largely for safety reasons, and ever since then the heavy doors leading from the floors to the building's sole roof exit were kept locked. And so, even though on September 11 a police helicopter hovered near the roof for a while looking for survivors, there were none to be found.[3] Inside the building, Camaj had a key, but the key had to be used in conjunction with a buzzer controlled by a technician at a command post on the 22nd floor, where a video screen displayed the faces of anybody wanting to go on the roof, and nobody was at the command post.

This, of course, was unknown to those who tried to make their way to the roof in the south tower, some of whom had come up from lower floors rather than attempt to evacuate by going down. And once they learned that the doors to the roof were closed, it was too late, or they never found stairway A, the only safe route to the lobby.

"The belief that they had a rooftop option cost them their lives," said Beverly Eckert, whose husband, Sean Rooney, died in the south tower.

And then there were those outside the buildings, either because they were just on the streets nearby when the planes hit and were showered by burning fuel or struck by debris, or because they were among the thousands of firefighters, police, Emergency Medical Service, Port Authority security, and other rescue workers who rushed toward the towers while everybody else was rushing away. Inside the tower staircases there was a grim two-way traffic, civilians coming down, firemen and others, but especially firemen, going up. Obviously, when the towers came down, all of those who were going up were crushed to death, in many cases their bodies never recovered. Of the total dead of 2,666 in the towers, 479 of them, which is 18 percent, were those who rushed in to save lives. Their tragedy is highlighted by the testimony of one Fire Department chief who said, weeks after the disaster, that in one of the two towers, every civilian below the point of impact had been evacuated and at the time of the collapse, only firefighters remained in the stairwells.

In the first few minutes after 8:46, a strange silence enveloped lower Manhattan, almost as though the urban organism was stunned, reeling from the knockout punch of a boxer when for a short time a temporary and welcome deafness prevails. And then, the sounds of disaster filled the air, first in the sounds of the sirens that began to shriek—ambulances, police cars, emergency services vans, fire trucks pouring into the area. Heavier debris began falling out of the gash in the tower. When a fire command station was set up in the lobby of the north tower, the people who leapt from the towers could be heard as they crashed onto the esplanade outside, making a shockingly loud sound, the sound of bodies breaking as they hit the ground.

At the instant the first plane struck the first tower, Lauren Manning was approaching the entrance on West Street. A sheet of flaming aviation fuel fell along the sheer face of the tower and Manning was burned on 90 percent of her body. Nearby, Jennieann Maffeo, a programmer at UBS Paine Webber who did not work at the World Trade Center, was waiting for a bus in the shadow of the towers, and she too was doused with flaming aviation fuel. Manning, miraculously, defying all medical prognoses, lived, though she had a long struggle, which is not yet over. Maffeo survived for forty-one days in a burn unit and then succumbed.

Chunks of debris were propelled outward and dropped, so that pedestrians and motorists experienced that nightmare come true—some lethally large object coming out of a clear blue sky and landing on or near them. One chunk flew a few blocks northward and hit the sixth-floor window of the fourteen-story office building at 75 Park Place, breaking the glass and then slamming to the street where two women lay amid broken glass and shredded pieces of insulation. Mike Diaz Piedra, forty-nine, who works at the Bank of New York, lay in the garage of 75 Park, unable to move his leg after getting run down by a crowd of people stampeding away from the Trade Center. People tripped but were pulled up by strong hands before they were crushed. One woman lost her bag and shoes but was pulled to a sidewalk and her belongings were returned to her.

"All of a sudden people went crazy," Piedra said. "And then a man built like a refrigerator ran over me."

Some people were lucky. Kathleen Dendy, fifty, had gotten her hair cut that morning, and that made her late for work, just late enough.

"I work on the ninety-ninth floor," she said. "There are hundreds of people in my office. We start at eight-thirty in the morning."

Rajesh V. Trivendi, forty, a computer programmer who was working on the 80th floor of the north tower, had to take his son to school.

"My scheduled time of arriving is seven," he said. "Today I am late. I am fortunate, very fortunate."

Joe Kosinski of Marsh & McLennan stayed home because his wife had given birth to a baby two days before. Otherwise he would have been at work on the 98th floor of the north tower, and he would be dead.

But 2,666 people were not lucky. Or, they didn't appreciate the danger because it didn't occur to them that the towers would come down, so they stopped to help other people and were killed when they did. On the 105th floor of the north tower, Stuart Meltzer, thirty-two, had begun his job as West Coast operations manager for Cantor Fitzgerald just a month before, called his wife, Lisa, and told her "Honey, something terrible is happening. I don't think I am going to make it. I love you. Take care of the children."[4]

Lorie Van Auken wasn't home when her husband, Kenneth Van Auken, called from the 102nd floor of the north tower, where he worked for the bond trading firm Cantor Fitzgerald. But later she got the message he left for her: "I love you. I'm in the World Trade Center, and the building was hit by something. I don't know if I'm going to get out, but I love you very much. I hope I'll see you later." Sadly, he didn't.[5]

Some employees of Cantor Fitzgerald in Los Angeles called their office in New York to ask what had happened, and, when they got through to somebody, they put the conversation on the in-house public address system. "Somebody's got to help us," is what they heard in Los Angeles. "We can't get out. . . . The place is filling with smoke." And then the line went dead.[6]

Dan Lopez, who worked for Carr Futures, a few floors below where the plane hit the north tower, called his wife on his cell phone and left this message: "Liz, it's me, Dan. My building has been hit. I made it to the seventy-eighth floor. I'm OK, but will remain here to help evacuate people. See you soon."[7] Liz didn't see Dan soon. She never saw him again.

At that same moment, Susan Rescorla, at home in Morristown, New Jersey, got a call from one of her daughters telling her about the plane crashing into the north tower. Susan turned on her television and saw the second plane hit the south tower where her husband, Rick Rescorla, security chief at Morgan Stanley, was on the 42nd floor. She burst into tears.

"Within half an hour Rick was calling me on my cell phone and it was the last call he ever made," Mrs. Rescorla said later. "He said, 'Stop crying. I have to get my people out of here. If something happens to me I want you to know that you made my life.' "

Within a few minutes of the first crash, most of the Fire Department's highest-ranking and most experienced officials were rushing from Brooklyn headquarters to the scene, and they knew as they did so that this was going to be the fire of their lives. Surveying the damage from the distance of the Brooklyn Bridge, Albert Turi, the deputy assistant chief of fire safety, realized that the problem was going to be beyond solving.

"I knew right from the start that there was no way this Fire Department could extinguish six or eight floors of fire, fully involved, in a highrise building," he said later. That expression, "fully involved," is Fire Department jargon for a well-established fire, not a fire that is just getting started. "It's just not possible, because we don't have the means to do it." Not long after that, he also understood that this was an extremely dangerous fire and that bad things were going to happen, and he told that to Ganci.

"Pete," he said, "we're going to lose some people here. It's inevitable. It's too tremendous. We're probably going to lose some people."

Turi knew that the problem was an especially difficult case of a highrise fire, a kind of fire that has generated its own lore and literature among firefighters. A high-rise fire is one that can only be extinguished from inside the building where it is raging, since no ladder truck and no stream of water can reach the affected floors from the outside. High-rise fires require firefighters equipped with masks and thirty-pound compressed-air tanks (with about thirty minutes of breathing time) to walk up smoke-filled stairways carrying hose that can be attached to interior standpipes to provide water. If conditions are favorable, and if there is an interior sprinkler system to help, such fires can be put out. If not, as Vincent Dunn, a retired deputy chief in the FDNY, has written, "there is no alter-nate plan." Then the only hope is that the building will stand and not too many people will die as the fire burns itself out.

"The best-kept secret in America's fire service is that firefighters can-not extinguish a fire in a 20–30,000-square-foot open floor area in a high-rise building," Dunn has written. "A fire company advancing a 2½-inch hose line with a 1¼-inch nozzle discharges only 300 gallons per minute and can extinguish only about 2,500 square feet of fire. The reach of the streams is only 50 feet. . . . A fully involved, free burning 20,000-square-foot floor area cannot be extinguished by a couple of firefighters spraying a hose stream from a stairway."[8]

The first alarm to be sounded on September 11 came at 8:47 from a firebox inside the south tower—reporting on the crash of the plane into the north tower. Within minutes, Joseph Pfeifer, who had been at Church and Lispenard Streets only a few blocks away, became the first fire captain to arrive on the scene. On his way, he had called dispatchers to sound a major alarm, which means that engine companies, ladder companies, and rescue squads are dispatched from all over the city, and he set up a staging area at West and Vesey Streets, almost directly below the Trade Center. Pfeifer realized quickly that the main task was not to attempt to put out the fires but to evacuate the buildings and he sent the first firefighters arriving on the scene to begin rescue work. Half the firefighters who began climbing up carried hose and half didn't. The first group would attempt to put out fires, or at least to keep them from spreading to unaf-fected areas; the second would try to rescue trapped people.

Fire Commissioner Thomas Von Essen and his two top deputies, William Feehan and Thomas Fitzpatrick, arrived at the Trade Center a few minutes later. What they saw was grisly and astonishing. Debris was raining down on the esplanade and so were the bodies of those who had jumped from the upper floors of the towers. Chunks of plaster were

"WE HAD A LOT OF DYING AND FIRE UP THERE" 211

falling from the lobby ceiling and the glass in the twenty-foot-high lobby windows was shattering, a sign that the building itself was torquing. There were cries of astonishment, screams of profanity from the fire chiefs themselves as they saw what few, if any, of them had ever seen before; that, as one fire marshall, Richard McCahey, put it, "those little black figures that were in the corner of my eye were actually bodies." When the firemen inside the lobby heard them hitting the ground outside, there were cries of "Oh my God, another one," until McCahey ordered them to compose themselves.

"Relax, don't be screaming that out," he said. "We got a job to do, OK."

Walter Kowalczyk, the senior Emergency Medical Service officer on duty that day, had seen and managed many disasters, including train wrecks and airplane crashes, but as he came into Manhattan through the Brooklyn-Battery Tunnel that morning, he knew immediately that this was something different.

"As you're driving down West Street and you have to maneuver the vehicle to avoid driving over what appeared to be body parts as well as debris, my mouth went dry," he said. "I had the sensation that I had a job to do. I had to ensure the safety of the E.M.S. workforce. But how do I do this if I can't talk?"

Then the second plane hit the south tower, and a second command post was set up in the lobby of that building, along with a coordinating command post outside on West Street. More firefighters arrived and went into the stairwells as civilians came down, many to the mezzanine level where they were directed to the pedestrian bridge that crossed West Street toward the World Financial Center. Several firemen died after being hit by debris or, in at least one case, by a falling body.

It was all happening so quickly. It became difficult for the chiefs in the lobbies to keep track of the numbers and identities of the firemen who were heading for the stairs. When the second tower was hit, the chiefs began talking among themselves about the possibility that the towers might collapse, and about the need, if there really was a strong possibility of that, of ordering the men out of the stairwells.

"The potential and the reality of a collapse was discussed early on," Peter Hayden, deputy chief of Divison 1 and therefore the official with authority for downtown Manhattan, said later. "But we were at a level of commitment. We also received numerous distress calls. We realized we had a lot of dying and fire up there."

Among those in the north tower who never had a chance were Kham-ladai and Roshan Singh, who, like the several hundred guests and work-ers that morning at Windows on the World, all perished. How quickly and how painfully we don't exactly know. We don't know if they were among those who leaped, or if they were together or apart when they died. We don't know anything about the last minutes of Zhanetta Tsoy either, whose employer, Marsh & McLennan, occupied the 94th to the 101st floors of the north tower, or about John and Silvia San Pio Resta, who worked on the 92nd floor of that tower. But more than fourteen hundred people died in the north tower, and it is clear from the calls that some of them made to loved ones that many of them, though choking on smoke, struggling to breathe, remained alive until the tower collapsed. Beverly Eckert was actually on the phone with Sean Rooney, her husband, when she heard the sound of an explosion and what she called "a sudden exhalation of breath," and she believes that that was the instant the floor fell out from under him. Jill Rosenblum happened to be talking to her husband, Andrew Rosenblum, who worked for Cantor Fitzgerald on the 104th floor of the north tower, when the plane hit.

"All of a sudden, he said to me, 'Did you hear that?'" she said. "I said 'Did I hear what?' and he goes, 'It was a really loud bang.' I said, 'I didn't hear anything,' and he goes, 'I'll call you right back.'"

Rosenblum worked in a large, open trading area with long rows of desks and chairs, and as it filled up with smoke, which happened quickly, he and another fifty or so people went to the northwest corner of their floor. He managed to get through to Jill on his cell phone and when he did she could hear people, including her husband, coughing and gasping for breath. That last call from her husband has given her knowledge of at least a few facts about the last minutes of his life. She knows, for example, that at one point they were able to break a window by throwing a com-puter against it, and they got some fresh air into their room that way.

"You heard a couple of people saying, 'Oh my God,'" she said, but they weren't panicking. There was no screaming, no audible hysteria.

She and Andrew lost their connection and then, two minutes later, the south tower collapsed, a possibility that had not until then occurred to any of them, but, now that it had happened, she realized that the same thing could happen to the tower where Andrew and his fellow employees of Cantor Fitzgerald were gathered. She kept on dialing his number in a desperate effort to tell him that—since, very likely, from where he was, he didn't know—and to tell him that he had nothing to lose by making an effort to get to a stairway and out of the building. She was unable to get through. Then, about four minutes before the north tower collapsed, her phone rang. She spent a long time saying "hello, hello, hello," but there was nobody on the other end of the line. She dialed *69—"you know, where they give you the phone number"—and Andrew's number played back, which means to Jill that he was alive and still on the 104th floor until the tower came down beneath and around and on top of them.

In all, 658 employees at Cantor Fitzgerald died on September 11.

A few floors lower down from Cantor Fitzgerald, on 87, John Paul DeVito and Harry Ramos were at work in the May Davis group, a small minority-owned investment bank that was recovering from some difficult times. The firm had been through some complicated litigation; shortly before, it had also paid a fine, without admitting wrongdoing, to settle a charge of illegal trading. Early in the morning of September 11, in fact, DeVito called the National Association of Securities Dealers to announce that May Davis was resuming normal operations. A new day beckoned. Things were looking up. And then American Airlines flight 11 hit the tower above them.

DeVito almost fell off his chair. Ramos braced himself in a doorway. Glass and debris and a storm of paper scraps filled the air, light fixtures crashed from the ceiling making holes that thick, white smoke began to pour through, and there was a sound, a kind of electrical snapping. Like many people, DeVito and Ramos thought a bomb had gone off. So did Adam Mayblum.

"I believe that there were 13 of us," Mayblum wrote later in an e-mail he sent to friends. "I can only assume that we thought the worst was over."

When Mayblum, DeVito, and Ramos went to the windows and looked down, they could see a crowd gathering at Battery Park City below and staring up. Still not sure what had happened, DeVito went out the doors of the May Davis office suite and into the elevator hall, and there he confronted the unimaginable.

"The floor was missing," he said. "You could see a void with steel girders and fire and you looked at this void and you realized that what was a robust building a minute before was actually missing."

DeVito, forty-five, the father of two daughters, was the chief operating officer of May Davis; Ramos, also forty-five and the father of two sons, was the firm's head trader; Mayblum, thirty-five, was managing director. When DeVito returned to the May Davis office from the wrecked elevator lobby, he began screaming at the top of his lungs that everybody had to get out of there.

Few people have faced life-threatening emergencies, when the right action leads to survival and the wrong one to death, so few people know how they would react if the building they are in is hit by a jet plane. In the case of the employees of May Davis, some actually tried to pack up their desktop computers and take them with them. It's an understandable, all-too-human reflex. People's lives are in their computers, their e-mail correspondence, their on-line banking, their address books and business files. Some people went for the elevators, others to the stairs. One employee, a Chinese immigrant named Hong Zhu, an investment banker, was powerfully shaken and wanted to stay where he was, preferring the safety of the building to the uncertainties of the way out. DeVito found a half-gallon jug of water and he used it to help people wet bandannas they made from ripped-up shirts. Mayblum ripped his T-shirt into three strips, gave two to colleagues, and kept one for himself.

DeVito began to lead the way down stairway A, while Ramos stayed behind to urge stragglers to the stairs, among them Zhu. The group formed a human chain, with each person's hand on the shoulder of the person in front, and they descended through the smoke. DeVito thought about going back up to ensure that everybody was evacuating the building, but he was dissuaded by a trainee, Jason Braunstein, who shouted at him, "John, what about your family?" But Ramos stayed upstairs, directing traffic, which now consisted of people he didn't know, to the stairwell.

For the first ten flights or so, from 87 to 78, the stairwell was smoky but uncrowded and the May Davis group moved quickly. Past 78, the stairwell got more crowded, but even at the time, DeVito was impressed by how the evacuees made way so that burn victims and other injured people could be brought out ahead of them. By the 50s, DeVito said later, the traffic became two-way, office workers heading down, firemen, wearing their signature black fireproof coats and carrying air tanks, masks, and other equipment, going up.

"Do you want some water?" DeVito said, offering his jug.

"I don't need no water," a fireman answered, and kept climbing.

Above DeVito on the 53rd floor, Mayblum came across a man he later described as "very heavyset" sitting on the stairs and unable to move.

"I asked if he needed help or was just resting," Mayblum wrote later. The man needed help, but Mayblum, who has a bad back, knew he would be unable to carry him down. The man, in any case, told Mayblum to go down and send help back up for him, and that is what Mayblum did.

A little later, Harry Ramos came upon the same man, and he stopped to talk to him. A minute later Hong Zhu, now walking briskly down the stairs, arrived also and stopped to help. The man was Victor Wald, who was walking down from his office at Avalon Partners on the 84th floor. Together, Ramos and Zhu helped Victor up and, with one of them on each side of him, carried him down a flight of stairs. It was hard and there was a long way to go, so Ramos and Zhu decided to try the elevators, even though a security guard had screamed at them to use the stairs. Zhu dropped a magazine onto the floor of a car and pushed the "down" button, thinking that if the car went down and then came back up and the magazine was still there, the elevator would be safe. But the doors didn't close, so Zhu got in the elevator himself and went down to the 44th floor with it. Then he went back up to 52 to pick up Ramos and Victor. Back on 44, a Sky Lobby, their local elevator stopped and the express elevators weren't moving. They knew they would have to walk.

While DeVito, Mayblum, and the others continued down, Ramos and Zhu struggled with Victor, getting down to the 39th floor where they went into the office of a credit union to rest a bit, and then one of those little events that highlight the absurdity of things took place. The phone rang; Zhu answered it and found himself talking to a customer of the credit union where Zhu did not work, insisting on knowing whether his accounts were safe.

"What do you mean accounts?" Zhu shouted back. "We need help."

The customer insisted on knowing if his money was safe. Zhu hung up on him.

The building began to shake—the south tower next door was coming down, though they didn't know it at the time. The three men, Ramos, Zhu, and Wald, got down to the 36th floor and there Victor said he couldn't move anymore. Zhu yelled at him to sit down and slide on his behind, but Wald was simply unable to do that. While the men were struggling, a fireman came shouting that he would take charge of Victor and that the rest should get the hell out of there. Zhu did leave, but Harry Ramos stayed behind and Zhu could hear him saying, "Victor, don't worry. I'm with you."

Later DeVito thought a lot about his friend Harry Ramos and his refusal to leave Victor, a stranger.

"Harry was a beautiful person, a real pro," he said. "Your word is your bond in our industry, and I think you have to see Harry saying, 'I'm not leaving you,' and that was his bond, his contract for life."

When DeVito and the people got down to the plaza level, they ran into a cordon of police and firefighters directing them downstairs to the shopping level, telling them to keeping moving, and not to look outside. The plaza level was at the level of the main elevator banks, where thousands would normally have been coming to and fro, or sitting at the fountain with a cup of coffee from Starbucks, reading their newspaper or chatting with friends.

"What they said was, 'Don't look out, keep moving, don't look out to the plaza,' and the first thing you did was look, and you saw hell," DeVito said. "It wasn't littered with bodies, but you saw something that resembled human parts. It's not like what you've seen in the movies, a field covered with bodies, but there was definitely a human element to it and masses and masses of debris."

DeVito and the others went downstairs and came out the exit of Building Four onto Liberty Street and, as he remembered it, ten seconds later, the south tower began to come down.

Getting out of the north tower was easier in its way because it stayed up for an hour and a half after it was hit, a margin of time that was critical for some: the difference between living and dying. Shortly before the plane struck the north tower, six men, most of them employees of the Port Authority, got into an elevator at the 44th floor Sky Lobby, the elevator going to floors 67 to 74. As their car rode up, they heard a muted thud and felt the building shudder. The elevator swayed back and forth, stopped, and plunged downward. One of the men had the wits to push an emergency button, and, in a sense, he didn't push it an instant too late. If he had pushed it earlier, all six of the men would now be dead.

When the men, who included a window washer named Jan Demczur, pried open the doors, they found themselves facing a wall with the number "50" stenciled on it. Because their elevator was an express to higher floors, there was no exit at the floor where they had happened to stop.

The men inside had no idea what had happened, but smoke was seeping into the elevator car and they knew that they had to get out, but they were unable to push out through the ceiling, and, in any case, they would only have succeeded in getting to where the smoke was coming from if they had. But Demczur, who had worked in construction in his native Poland, saw that the wall they were facing was ordinary drywall, Sheetrock, and he began scratching at it with the metal edge of his window-washer's squeegee, the only tool available. Atta and company had used knives to kill people, but the men in car 69-A didn't have knives to use to save themselves. When Demczur, his arm aching, dropped the squeegee down the shaft, he used the one tool he had left, a short squeegee handle.

They cut a hole through three layers of Sheetrock and then punched through a wall of tiles, which they came to on the other side, and then one by one they squeezed through the hole they had made, finding themselves inside a 50th-floor bathroom. It was about 9:30, and by then the floor was empty except for some firefighters, astonished to see the six men emerge.

On their way down the staircases, one of the men, Shivam Iyer, an engineer with the Port Authority, said, "We heard a thunderous, metallic roar." It was the sound of the south tower crumbling. "I thought our lives had surely ended then," Iyer said.

The men finally emerged into the dust and paper on the street at 10:23, and they headed north. Five minutes later, the north tower came down.

"If the elevator had stopped at the sixtieth floor instead of the fiftieth," Iyer observed, "we would have been five minutes too late."

Many people in the south tower, including those on upper floors, began
to evacuate their offices as soon as they got news that the first had been
hit. Some of them took elevators or stairways as far as the ground floor
lobby or to the Sky Lobbies on the 78th and 44th floors, where express
and local elevators met. When they got there, however, they heard
announcements being made by security personnel that the south tower
was safe, and they returned upstairs to their offices. Witnesses said that in
the elevator lobby on the 44th floor, a security official was shouting
through a megaphone and urging people not to evacuate, and the public
address system repeatedly broadcast a similar announcement throughout
the tower. Many people paid no attention to the security personnel and
they kept going to safety.

Surely those making the announcements did so for a reason that
seemed to make sense at the time, but they have a grim wrongness to them
in retrospect. One expert, Gary Lynch, a former fireman and now a consul-
tant on corporate security for Booz, Allen, Hamilton, said that urging people to stay in the towers might have been established as policy in order to
avoid the chaos that a simultaneous rush to the exits might cause. With
firemen coming into the building, Lynch said, a mass evacuation could
interfere with their ability to carry out rescue operations. In less dangerous
situations—for example, in the almost routine bomb scares that some cor-
porations receive—there is a general reluctance by management to encour-
age staff evacuations, which can cost a great deal of money in lost time and
business, especially in the stock and financial markets. It could be argued, in
the case of September 11, that security officials in the south tower couldn't
have been expected to anticipate that it too would be struck by a hijacked
airplane. But, Mr. Lynch said, given that an airplane had struck the north
tower and that chunks of debris along with thousands of gallons of aviation fuel were raining down on nearby buildings, that it was a staggering
mistake to order people not to evacuate. It was a mistake that cost lives.

"I know for a fact that announcement killed at least four people in
my company," said Steve Miller, who worked on the 80th floor at Mizuho

Capital Markets. "They were the senior Japanese management. When the announcement came on, they went back up. The rest of us kept going down."

Clyde Ebanks of Aon Corporation walked down from the 103rd to the 78th floor of the south tower, and there, he said, he heard the go-back-to-your-office announcement over the P.A. system. "The security guys were saying that there was an accident in Building One but there was no need to evacuate unless you were having trouble breathing due to smoke. I remember that last part clearly. These announcements were a double-edged sword. They kept people calm but they also made people think they had time. So people were on the phone calling their families or their wives or whomever. I heard later that there was another meeting of Aon workers on the 105th floor, and they all decided to continue on with their meeting. I mean, as a person in the insurance industry, I know that an explosion in one building can spread to another."

The announcement may have contributed to the death of Shimmy D. Biegeleisen, who worked in the offices of Fiduciary Trust International on the 97th floor of the south tower, though, in truth, no one will ever know with absolute certainty why he died. Biegeleisen was about to evacuate with fellow workers after getting news of the crash at the north tower, but, for some reason, he didn't leave, even though many of his colleagues were already heading down the stairs. Biegeleisen's wife, Miriam, who spoke with him on the phone, remembers with a kind of disturbing clarity hearing the announcement over the line—that the south tower was safe—and then in the months that have passed, she has continued to hear that same announcement as she has wondered if it explains her husband's loss.

Biegeleisen was a senior vice president at Fiduciary Trust, and the company's only Orthodox Jew; he was the man who wore the yarmulke and who left the office early on Fridays to be home in time for the Jewish Sabbath, which he spent with Miriam and their five children. Only the week before September 11, he had received a watch signifying twenty years of service. After the plane hit the north tower, he called home, and he stayed on the phone for the better part of an hour talking with Miriam and then with several family friends, who began arriving in the Biegeleisen home in the Flatbush section of Brooklyn. At first, he told Miriam just

that something had happened, but that he would be all right. Biegeleisen
was a veteran of the 1993 Trade Center bombing, when he had walked
down the ninety-seven flights of stairs from his office to the ground, and,
in the beginning, he seems to have assumed that that's what he would do
again. But his slowness in leaving—whether because of the announcement or for some other reason—meant that when flight 175 crashed into
his tower, he was still on the 97th floor, well above the plane's point of
impact, and it was too late.

It is not clear exactly when Biegeleisen realized September 11, 2001,
was not a repeat of February 26, 1993, but at some point it became clear to
those he was talking to on the phone that he knew he was going to die.
There was too much emotional chaos for family members to remember
exactly whom he was talking to, but Biegeleisen said to one friend, "I'm
not coming out of this," and he asked him to take care of Miriam and
their five children.

By this time, the Biegeleisen family and their friends were watching
the disaster unfold on television, and they could see what Biegeleisen
himself could not—the two towers burning side by side. The phone got
passed from one person to another after another as friends and family desperately tried to stay in touch with Shimmy, as if, somehow, keeping him
on the phone would keep him alive. At one point, in a three-way conference call, Biegeleisen complained to Gary Gelbfish, a vascular surgeon,
that he could no longer breathe, and Gelbfish advised him to hug the
ground and to put a wet towel over his mouth. Biegeleisen did go to the
water cooler and wet a towel there, and then he decided to go to the roof
along with the five colleagues who were trapped with him. But the heat
was so intense, he couldn't even get out into the hallway.

For a few minutes, it seems, Biegeleisen got off the phone and then,
at 9:45, as more friends arrived at the Biegeleisen home, he called again.
Miriam was too distraught to come to the phone so, again, he asked
a friend of his to take care of her. "Tell Miriam I love her," he said, and
he lay down on the floor near his desk beneath the family pictures he kept
in his office. Five days later, Biegeleisen was supposed to go to Jerusalem
with his nineteen-year-old son, Mordechai, to spend the Jewish New
Year with the Belzer Rebbe there, the leader of a two-hundred-year-old
Hasidic sect. Instead, he was trapped in the World Trade Center where he

began to recite a Hebrew psalm—"The Lord is the earth and its fullness." Another friend came to the phone and told Biegeleisen to break a window, and he heard Beigeleisen call out, "Let's go! Let's break the window." At 9:59, Biegeleisen told the friend that he was looking out the window; then he screamed "Oh God!" and the line went dead.[9]

After the first tower was struck, Felipe Oyola found his wife, Adianes, at the elevator bank of the 78th floor of the south tower. They had met seven years earlier when he was a cook and she was a cashier at a restaurant in Brooklyn. Now he was a supervisor of mail services at Fuji Bank where Adianes worked in the human resources and payroll departments. They were hugging when they heard the public address announcement that it was safe to return to their offices. Felipe went back to work first while Adianes stayed behind for a while talking with her boss and a coworker. Who was to think that there was any particular danger, that what had happened in the north tower would happen in the south tower? Felipe was on the 81st floor, which was above the point of impact of the second plane, but when it hit he managed, barely, to make it out to safety. Adianes worked on 82, one floor higher, above the point of impact, and she is missing.

On the 84th floor, three floors above where Felipe Oyola began his march down the stairs to safety, Brian Clark, the executive vice-president of Euro Brokers, heard a tremendous bang and out of the corner of his eye saw a flash of light outside his window. It was 8:46 A.M.

"The entire air space out my window was filled with flames," he said. "It was just a huge fireball."

He didn't know it, but flight 11 had just struck the north face of the north tower, on the opposite side from where Clark could see. His first thought was that there had been an explosion on the floor above his and since he was the fire marshal for his quadrant of the 84th floor, his instinct was to jump up, grab his flashlight and whistle, and start moving his coworkers out of the building. Clark was a veteran of the 1993 bombing, which led him to take his fire marshal duties seriously. He went into the large Euro Brokers trading room on the east wall of the south tower, where there was a television, and he saw from the news being broadcast what had happened. It was 8:50, and he realized that the damage wasn't in his building.

Clark called Dianne, his wife: "You won't believe this but a plane has hit Tower One," he told her. "Turn on TV. We're OK here but I'm sure there's a story developing that you'll want to watch."

So Dianne did start watching and a few minutes later she saw the plane hit the very building where her husband was and at a height that seemed to be near his floor.

Just at that moment, Clark was talking to two colleagues, Bobbie Coll and Kevin York, who had taken the elevator down a few minutes before, but then they heard the public address announcement that instructed people in the south tower to return to their offices, and they took the elevator back up. Given the inconceivability of a second plane hitting their tower and the dangers of falling debris outside, that announcement probably made sense to some of the Euro Brokers staff on the 84th floor, but it cost Coll and York their lives. Clark remembers word for word the announcement as it came repeatedly over the speakers:

"Building Two is secure; there is no need to evacuate Building Two; if you are in the midst of evacuating, you may use the reentry doors and the elevator to return to your office."

In the instant when the plane hit his tower, Clark later recalled, "there was a loud sort of *whompf*. It wasn't a huge explosion. It was something muffled, no flames, no smoke, but the room fell apart as the plane kind of torqued the building. Ceiling tiles fell from the ceiling; air conditioning ducts fell, door frames fell out of the wall."

Clark later figured that while the fuselage hit a couple of floors below where they were, the raised right wing of the plane probably hit at about the 84th floor. The south and east walls got blown out, where the large trading room was, and the sixty-one Euro Brokers employees who died were mostly there. But in the smaller trading room on the west side of the building, there was just a muffled thud.

"My only moment of terror was the next ten seconds," he said. "The tower swayed to the left, to the left, and to the left again. It seemed like it wasn't going to stop. But then it did stop and righted itself. In the eight years I'd been there I'd experienced some swaying in strong wind, but not like that. It felt like the tower moved maybe ten yards. That's when I thought it was all over."

That moment in the south tower, when the second plane hit, was experienced with similar terror both by those, like Clark, who had not evacuated, and those, like Clyde Ebanks, who were in the process of walking down the stairs. Ebanks remembers that he had left the stairwell at the 70th floor and was just about to go into an office to look out the window when, suddenly, he felt the whole building shake.

"We were running back to the stairwell when we heard these popping sounds," he said. "I think now, the popping sounds were coming out of the elevator shafts because of the fireball that was coming down. The popping sounds, I think, were the elevator doors opening up because of the fireball. I looked over to my colleagues and that's when we all knew we had to get out of there fast. Up until then, we were moving but at a calm pace. Now we started to run. We now knew the building was on fire. We hoofed it down the stairs but people were still calm. Nobody was yelling or screaming."

Brian Clark, who was on 84, had a longer way to go, and he started from a point above the floors where the plane hit. He ushered the seven people who were in the small trading room to the center core of the tower, where they usually went to get an elevator. He had several choices, to turn right to stairway C, to go straight to stairway B, or to turn left to stairway A. And he turned left to stairway A, probably because normally he turned left to go to the elevators, and even though he wasn't going to the elevators, force of habit made him turn in that direction. It was a reflex that saved his life, and it is a reminder of one of the signal facts of the disaster in the south tower—that people saved themselves or they failed to save themselves by deciding, with no information on which to base their decision, what to do. Some ran for the stairs after the plane hit, ignoring the public address announcement, and they survived. Some tried to go to the roof, and they died. Some, presumably, tried stairway B or stairway C, and they died. A few, as we will see, were on stairway A, but they walked up instead of down, and they died. And then there were several, like Brian Clark, who used stairway A to go down, and they lived. Few, if any, of the victims and survivors made their decisions on the basis of experience or knowledge. For the most part, it was just dumb luck, or the lack of it.

"I led our group down three floors to 81," Clark said. "The stairways go back and forth, a half landing in one direction and a half landing in another, and at one of the half landings, a very heavy woman who was walking up the stairs said, 'Stop, you can't go down.' She was adamant. 'You can't go down, the floors are in flames.' We stood there and argued. I was looking at her and saying to myself that her dress wasn't on fire or anything. It didn't make sense to me that we couldn't go down. At that point I heard a voice crying, 'Help, I can't breathe. Is anybody there?' I strained to hear it. When I was sure I could I grabbed Ronnie DiFrancesco, one of the colleagues who had accompanied me, and said, 'Come on, Ronnie, let's get this guy.'

"We were able to push the drywall aside in the stairwell and get onto the 81st floor. As I did, I had this distinct image of Bobbie Coll and Kevin York putting their hands under this heavy woman's arms and starting to ascend. My flashlight was like a high beam on a foggy road at night. All you could see was this black smoke and this single beam of light. But the guy who was calling for help could see the light and I heard him saying, 'Praise the Lord, I've been saved!' Then he asked me, 'Can you see my hand,' and I couldn't, but then I saw this hand sticking out of a hole waving to get attention, just the hand. The first thing he says is, 'One thing I've got to know. Do you know Jesus?' My reply was, 'I go to church every Sunday.'"

The man was Stanley Praimnath, who worked for Fuji Bank. Clark helped to pull him out of the closed space where he was trapped. It was as though he were in a cave, standing up but trapped. Clark doesn't know exactly how he did it, a burst of adrenaline probably, but he told Praimnath to jump, and Clark pulled as hard as he could and he made it out and the two of them fell into a heap on the floor.

"I'm Brian. Who are you?" Clark asked.

"I'm Stanley."

"Well, it's nice to meet you, Stanley. Now let's get out of here."

"All that time, I was fine," Clark remembers. "I was squinting a little in the smoke but I was breathing normally. I was in control, or something was in control of me. I wasn't in a panic.

"We started down. There wasn't a minute's hesitation. The first few floors were tricky. Drywall was blown over the stairs and there was a lot of water from the sprinkler system I suppose dribbling over the stairs, so they were kind of slippery. But that was just two or three floors. You could see through cracks in the drywall into the floors, and you could see fires, but they weren't very big. I don't know, maybe the fires were starved for oxygen, but they weren't shooting out at us. It was all very empty. The stairwell was dimly lit by emergency lighting, and I had my flashlight. There wasn't much noise, and there were no other people."

This is probably because, coming from the highest floors and having stopped to pull Stanley out of the rubble, Clark was one of the last people down and out of the south tower. Everybody else had already evacuated ahead of him, everybody but DiFrancesco who, bothered by the smoke and having heard the heavy woman warn of fires in the stairwell, walked up to the 91st floor. He sat there for a while, not knowing what to do, and then he thought of his wife and child at home and an intense desire to see them again came over him. He began walking down, several flights behind Clark and Praimnath. He was the last person to get out of the south tower to safety.

At around the 73rd floor Clark and Praimnath broke into fresh air. At 68, they ran into the only other person they would encounter in the stairwell. It was somebody Clark knew, a man named Jose Marreno, who also worked at Euro Brokers. Marreno, a fire marshal like Clark, had a walkie-talkie. He had been talking on it to another Euro Brokers executive named David Veirra, and he told Clark that Veirra needed help and he was going to walk back up the stairs to give it to him.

"I said, 'Come on Jose, come down with us,'" Clark said, "but he said, 'No, Dave Veirra needs my help,' and I said, 'Well, OK.' I didn't know the building was going to come down."

At the 44th floor, which is another express elevator stop, Clark and Praimnath found a Port Authority security guard and a badly injured man lying on the floor. The security guard told Clark to call for a medic and a stretcher. Clark and Praimnath got down to the 31st floor and went into a conference room where there was a telephone. It was now 9:40. Clark called home to tell his wife where he was and that he was OK. Then he called 911, and it was like a *Saturday Night Live* parody:

"I'm on the 31st floor of Tower Two and there's an injured man on 44 who can't move," Clark said to the 911 dispatcher. "They need a medic and a stretcher."

"Hold on a second," the supervisor said. "I'm going to have to have you talk to my supervisor."

Clark waited on the line for thirty or forty seconds, and when somebody else came to the phone, he described the situation again. Again he was put on hold. Another thirty or forty seconds passed and a third person came on the line.

"Listen, I'm only going to say this once, and then I've got to go," Clark said, and one more time he told them that they needed to send a medic and a stretcher to the 44th floor. Then he hung up and he and Praimnath continued down.

What's striking is that neither man had any sense that there was any particular danger anymore. The possibility that the tower might come down never occurred to either of them. At one point someplace between the 20th and the 30th floors, Clark even said, "Hey, let's slow down. We've come this far, there's no point in breaking an ankle."

When they arrived at the plaza level, which is usually thronged with people, they found what looked to Clark like an abandoned archaeological site, a moonscape, all white and gray. They stared at it for half a minute, disbelieving. From the plaza level they took the escalator down to the shopping concourse level.

"A woman was there who told us to go down the hall to where Victoria's Secret was, turn right, and go out by Sam Goody," Clark said. The underground passage took them to Building Four of the Trade Center and they exited there onto Liberty Street, which they crossed, dodging debris. They had made it. They were safe.

TWENTY

The Towers Come Down

Shortly after 9:00, after the second plane hit the south tower, the Fire Department under Ganci's orders had established three command centers, one in each of the lobbies of the afflicted towers and another on adjacent West Street where Ganci and several senior department officials were striving to gain mastery of the situation. A steady flow of people was coming down the stairs of the towers themselves, and firefighters and police were directing them out of the buildings, telling them, as they came into the lobby, to keep on moving, and not to look at the grisly spectacle on the plaza outside. Some people were directed to the escalator to the mezzanine levels above the lobby floors where they exited onto one of the pedestrian bridges that crossed West Street in the direction of the Hudson River. Others went downstairs to the shopping arcade and used the underground passage, past Borders Bookstore to Building Four and out onto Liberty Street south of the center. The evacuees certainly showed concern on their faces, but one is struck by the absence among them of a sense of grave danger, or of panic.

Many of these lawyers, stock brokers, insurance agents, bond traders, secretaries, computer programmers, and other office workers had been through something that seemed similar, when they evacuated the towers after the truck bombing of 1993. Since then, they had been through many evacuation drills, run by security chiefs like Rick Rescorla at Morgan Stanley every six months, and Rescorla didn't allow anybody

to sit at their desks when a drill was on but demanded that they participate. This alone was extraordinary in its way, since corporate executives,
especially at a time-is-money business like Morgan Stanley, have often
resisted serious fire and evacuation drills, which can cost millions of dollars in employee time and lost business. But following the 1993 bombing,
many companies in the World Trade Center were prepared. The evacuation was aided moreover by post-1993 improvements in the system, most
important perhaps the installation of battery-powered emergency lights
in the stairwells. In 1993, the staircases had gone dark; on September 11,
2001, they remained lit. Still, the one eventuality that doesn't seem to
have been on many minds was that the buildings would collapse altogether. Except for a few experts, few people had any reason to believe
that could happen.

Some did realize it, among them the old soldier Rescorla, he who,
with his friend Dan Hill, had pinpointed the spot where a terror bomb
could do the most damage, the man who used to predict to friends that
something more was going to happen. As soon as he found out about the
plane hitting the north tower—and even before he called Susan, his wife,
at home in New Jersey—he was on the phone to Hill in St. Augustine,
Florida, telling him that the worst was going to happen.

"Everything above where that plane hit is going to collapse, and it's
going to take the whole building with it," Rescorla told Hill, adding that
he was going to start evacuating the Morgan Stanley staff from the south
tower right away.[1]

Some of the Fire Department chiefs, especially those in the tower
lobbies, where chunks of ceiling tile were falling down and the lobby glass
was shattering, were coming to the same conclusion. About forty minutes after arriving on the scene, one ranking chief, Joseph Callan, made
the decision that the buildings were no longer safe, and he attempted, calling on the radio, to get the firefighters in the stairwells to regroup in the
lobby. But it is well known that the steel structure of a high-rise building
obstructs radio signals, with the obstruction increasing with each higher
floor. Above the 65th floor, Fire Department radios don't transmit at all. It
is therefore not at all clear how many of the firefighters in the stairwells
heard Callan's orders, though it is all too clear that more than three hundred of them were trapped there when the buildings fell.

"There were numerous discussions in the lobby," Deputy Chief

Hayden, who was in charge of the rescue effort in the north tower, later said. "The chief of safety came in. He discussed his concern about collapse. His advice to us was to let the buildings just burn, you know, get the people down and get out. We said that's exactly what we're planning to do."

But Hayden added that the chiefs on the ground had lost track of the number of companies on the scene and which companies were in which tower. In the major-catastrophe alarm put out by dispatchers, every company in Manhattan south of 125th Street had been ordered to the World Trade Center. The companies on the west side were ordered to go to the north tower and those on the east side to the south tower. Within an hour of the first alarm, all off-duty firefighters were ordered to come to the scene. But later, chiefs reported that the very large number of men and the chaos on the scene had gravely compromised the chiefs' ability to issue orders and assure that they were carried out.

"We were losing some control of the companies coming in," Hayden said. "There were also some communication problems later on with the companies coming in, units responding to the second alarm after the other plane hit. They weren't sure which was World Trade Center One and World Trade Center Two."

The fears that the towers couldn't stay up came from the reports of what one of the firefighters on the scene, John Peruggia, called an "engineer-type person" who was huddled with members of the rescue teams in the lobby. The engineer talked about "a near imminent collapse," which led Peruggia to try to get word to Ganci at the West Street command center. When he couldn't do that either by cell phone or radio, he dispatched Richard Zarrillo, an Emergency Medical Services technician, to run to the post.

"Ganci and I were both at the command post when the EMS guy came over to me first," Mosiello remembers of Zarrillo's arrival on the scene. "He said, 'Pete, where is the chief? I need to talk to him because I just got word that both buildings are in danger of collapse. I need to tell him this.' Ganci and I were only five to eight feet away from each other, so I took the EMS fellow over to Ganci to deliver the message. We really didn't have time to react to what he said, it was all so quick."

Ganci and Mosiello were working at the command post on the exit ramp of the parking garage underneath 2 World Financial Center, which is a fifty-one-story building on the opposite side of West Street about two hundred feet from the north tower of the Trade Center. Danny Nigro, the chief of operations for the Fire Department, had been there too, but he had gone to the east side of the tower to survey the damage. About seventy-five firefighters from different engine and ladder companies were there, in Mosiello's estimate, waiting for orders. The truth is that nobody really knows who they were or which companies they came from. The situation was too chaotic and it got worse. About a minute after Zarrillo delivered his report to Ganci, the south tower collapsed.

"We all bailed into the garage," Mosiello said later, meaning the garage of the World Financial Center. "I think it was like twenty-five feet or so from where we were to get inside. There was dust everywhere; everyone had trouble breathing. There was lots of debris. Someone found stairs that led us out of the building, so most of us took those stairs."

The men, including Ganci, Mosiello, and William M. Feehan, the first deputy fire commissioner, found themselves on West Street just above the pedestrian bridge that connected the World Trade Center with the World Financial Center, and they all walked north.

"Nobody said much," Mosiello remembered. "It was very, very quiet. Then we stopped walking and Pete decided he and Freehan should go south again to check out the damage." It was typical of Ganci. He told others to keep going north to safety and then he and a couple of others went back to the danger zone. "We set up a new command post there," Mosiello said, "and Pete asked me to get two ladder trucks, which had all the necessary equipment."

One has to remember the situation, that the inconceivable had occurred. One tower of 110 stories had just collapsed, and tons of dust, ash, and paper had rained down on West Street, causing a bewildering, shattering scene of devastation. Ganci and the other chiefs knew that many men must have been lost in the collapse and their effort now was to try to regain control of the situation so as to get the firefighters in the one remaining tower out of the building to safety. But there wasn't enough time.

"Then a rumbling started and there was an immense showering effect of debris," Mosiello said. "The second tower's collapse was much worse than the first one. There was no visibility of any kind. You never knew where you were. I think I ducked behind a parked fire truck and after I climbed out of the debris, I started to radio for Pete. But after thirty or forty seconds of no answer, I kinda knew he was in trouble at this point."

In fact, it was probably at that moment that Chief Ganci was killed. His body was recovered later that afternoon under four feet of the rubble of the north tower. The command center on West Street was literally buried under a rolling wave of concrete chunks. William Feehan, seventy-one years old, the first deputy fire commissioner who had risen through the ranks over a long and distinguished career, was killed on that spot too. He was the oldest and highest-ranking New York City firefighter ever to die in the line of duty.

Elsewhere, someplace nearer the towers, Father Mychal Judge who was reported to have given last rites to two victims, a woman who had leapt from the tower and the fireman who was killed when she fell on him, had taken off his helmet and was kneeling in prayer when a chunk of debris felled him as well. A group of firemen carried the body of their beloved chaplain to St. Peter's Church just a block away, and they laid it on the ground there, covering it with a sheet and with the dead priest's fireman's badge. They knelt in prayer for a time, and then all of them rushed back to the scene of the disaster.

The south tower fell at 9:59, fifty-seven minutes after being hit by flight 175, and twenty-nine minutes before the collapse of the north tower, which was hit by flight 11 fifteen minutes earlier. Afterward aviation experts said that the south tower was the first to go in large part because the plane that plowed into it was flying at up to 586 miles per hour—about a 100 miles per hour faster than the plane that hit the north tower. A plane flying that fast and at such a low altitude risks breaking up in midair, though that did not happen to flight 175. The FAA speed limit for any commercial plane below ten thousand feet is 287 miles per hour.

A faster speed translates into more kinetic energy, and kinetic energy varies exponentially with velocity, so a 25 percent difference in speed actually becomes a 50 percent difference in the kinetic energy released at impact. The Trade Center towers were held up by two sets of steel columns.

There was an outer palisade of relatively slender columns spaced about forty inches apart, fifty-nine of them on each of the four 209-foot façades, which was covered by an aluminum skin. The outer columns are held in place and supported laterally by a system of steel trusses, webs, angles, cross-sections, braces, and spandrels that ultimately depended on the millions of three-quarter-inch bolts that held these pieces to the main structural elements, the vertical columns.

A second set of thicker columns was installed at the building's core, forty-seven columns in all. Two experts at the Massachusetts Institute of Technology, Tomasz Wierzbicki and Liang Xue, calculated that at a speed of 500 miles per hour, a partly loaded Boeing 767 weighing 132 tons would have enough destructive energy to damage or break more than thirty of the exterior columns and twenty-three of the forty-seven columns in the building's core. At 586 miles per hour the damage would have been greater. And, as Jerome Connor, a professor of civil engineering at MIT, put it later, "If one building had more damage, it would take less for the heat to build up enough for it to come down. That would explain why the building that was hit second fell first."

When the Trade Center was constructed much was made of claims by the architect Minoura Yamasaki that it could withstand a collision with a Boeing 707, a statement that seemed to have been proved false by the collapses of September 11. Actually, Yamasaki was not so wrong as it seems. One of the reasons the outer steel columns were placed close together was to give the towers enough rigidity to withstand the collision Yamasaki talked about, though he and his engineers were actually more concerned about the towers being able to withstand hurricane-force winds than airplane crashes. The Boeing 767s that hit the towers on September 11 exerted the equivalent of 25 million pounds of sideways pressure, which, in structures less rigidly engineered, might have been enough to topple them over altogether, and there would have been no time at all for thousands who did escape to safety to get away. But the towers didn't topple over, nor did they collapse inward because of the impact of the planes themselves. This is because the undamaged steel columns instantly formed what engineers call a Vierendeel truss, creating a kind of arch, and that prevented an immediate downward disintegration.

Why then did the towers collapse? Different experts have different opinions about this, but a study commissioned by the federal government found three linked systemic failures that together explain the buildings' disintegration. First, and most important, the fires caused by burning aviation fuel reached temperatures high enough to soften the towers' steel; two, the planes' crash into the buildings dislodged the fire-proofing material that would otherwise have kept the steel structural elements from heating up so quickly and so much; and three, the pipes that supply water to the sprinkler systems were cut by the planes, destroying the towers' built-in firefighting systems.

As the federal report noted, after flight 175 hit the south tower, gigantic balls of orange fire, caused by the ignition of aviation fuel, erupted from three sides of the building. That, the experts say, would have consumed about one-third of the ten thousand gallons of fuel on the plane. The plane plowed with such force into the building that parts of it punctured the far wall and were hurled as far as six blocks to the north where they landed near the intersection of Murray and Church Streets. The aviation fuel not consumed in the initial explosion, or that didn't cascade down the sides of the towers, then burned intensely inside, spreading to the dozens of acres of offices with their thousands of pounds of plastic partitions, computer equipment, and rugs. The fire, fueled by oxygen sucked into the towers through the holes made by the planes' impact, was so hot that a stream of molten metal—probably aluminum from the planes' wings and fuselage—flowed out the northeast corner of the south tower's 80th floor.

Steel begins to lose its strength at 1,100 degrees Fahrenheit, and, according to Yogesh Jaluria, a professor of mechanical and aerospace engineering at Rutgers University, some areas inside the towers would have reached more than 2,000 degrees within seconds. The heat, according to this theory, caused the floors to sag between the interior and the exterior columns, and the pressure of the sagging floors caused the bolts holding the floor trusses to the columns to break. It was the floors themselves that gave the steel columns their lateral support, and once that support was gone, the columns bowed outward and buckled. The floors held up by the buckling columns fell onto the floor below, causing a chain reaction that built up energy and speed until the upper floors, by the time they reached the bottom, were plummeting at 120 miles an hour.

And when the towers did come down, they brought with them 400,000 tons of structural steel, 208 passenger elevators, 43,600 windows, 220 acres' worth of reinforced concrete flooring, 6 acres of marble, the stuff of 600 bathrooms, 49,000 tons of air-conditioning equipment, 12,000 miles of electrical cable, 23,000 fluorescent lightbulbs, 198 miles of heating ducts, 300 computer mainframes, and the accumulated materials of the banks, the stock brokerages with their parking-lot-size trading rooms, the insurance companies, the law offices, the investment houses, the real estate and employment agencies, the telecommunications companies, the wholesalers, the retailers, the engineering consultants, and the government tax and finance departments that were housed in the towers, with their tens of thousands of cubicle work stations, desks, filing cabinets, computers, chairs, coffee machines, telephones, copying machines, and bookshelves, as well as tens of millions of letters and documents, much of which, weirdly, did not burn, but floated down in a blizzard of singed sheets and scraps, some of it landing as far away as Brooklyn. And, of course, there were the 2,823 people who were on the planes when they crashed or in the buildings when they collapsed, most of whose bodies will never be identified or recovered. A few ten- to twelve-story segments of wall remained after the collapses, like relics of an ancient city sacked by barbarians. All the rest, all the persons and paraphernalia of American capitalism compacted into the sixteen-acre site of the Trade Center in an astounding three-dimensional Jackson Pollack–like dystopia of ash-covered wreckage that smoldered and burned literally for months.

To all but a few people like Rick Rescorla, the collapse of the south tower was completely unexpected, a bolt from the blue. Titus Davidson, fifty-five, a security guard at Morgan Stanley, where Rescorla also worked, was talking on the phone to his daughter, Tanya Dale, just before 10:00, and he seemed calm, she reported later. Davidson grew up in Jamaica, the second of sixteen children, and in a life that had not been easy, Tanya, twenty-five, was his greatest joy. He told her he had been guiding firemen upstairs and that he helped them evacuate a woman from a few floors up. He showed no fear of an impending collapse. After she had talked with her father for about two minutes, Dale heard a rumble in the background, then she heard her father shout her name. She looked at the television and saw the place where her father was helping to save people drop straight down on itself in a cloud of dust.

Rescorla, who had proved himself under fire forty-six years earlier in the Battle of Ia Drang, knew what he had to do. When the north tower got hit, he got a call from the 71st floor telling him what had happened, and, despite the public address announcement telling people to stay put, he ordered the evacuation of all the Morgan Stanley employees in the Trade Center complex, twenty-six hundred in the south tower and another one thousand in Building Seven nearby. Equally impressive, everybody else in Morgan Stanley knew what to do because Rescorla had insisted on all those evacuation drills in the years after 1993. Morgan Stanley, the Trade Center's biggest single tenant, occupied floors 43 to 74 of the south tower. One employee, Kathy Comerford, was in a meeting on the 70th floor when the north tower was struck. She heard a loud explosion, saw debris plummeting outside the window, and, while she didn't know what had happened, she and the others at the meeting headed for the stairwells, two by two just as Rescorla had ordered. When Comerford reached the Sky Lobby on the 44th floor she saw Rescorla—"larger than life," she said—directing traffic with a bullhorn and telling people to remain calm.

Then the south tower was hit.

"There were loud booms and the lights went out, the whole building did a shift," Comerford said later. "It bent over, and the floor was rolling like you were on a roller coaster."[2]

Rescorla called Dan Hill on his cell phone and asked if he'd seen what happened on television. Hill said, "Yeah, it's a bad one, much worse than the first one." Hill told Rescorla to get out. Rescorla replied:

"As soon as I get my people out, I'll go."

Morgan Stanley had twenty-six hundred employees in their thirty-one floors of office space, so getting "my people out" was clearly no simple or quick matter. Some of them—it's impossible to know how many—were already out by the time the south tower was hit at 9:02, but for those who were still evacuating, there were only fifty-six minutes left from that time, and while fifty-six minutes was enough for almost everybody else, it was not enough for Rescorla.

Comerford remembers that it was bedlam, panic, people thinking that it was the end, and she also remembers Rescorla's voice on the bullhorn saying, "Stay calm, keep moving down the stairs." Hill says that Rescorla resorted to the technique he was famous for in Vietnam, singing at the moment of maximum tension, and telling other people to sing with him. It was a way of collecting the mind, keeping hysteria at bay.

"'Stand ye now both straight and steady / Don't you see their spear-points gleaming,'" he sang, according to Hill. "And then he'd say stuff like, 'Today is a great day to be an American. Be proud you're Americans.'"

Rescorla was everywhere, as high as the 72nd floor escorting people down, according to at least one witness, clearing floors as he worked his way down, and it is not a small matter for a large sixty-two-year-old man to run up thirty or forty flights and then down fifty or sixty, speaking on his cell phone to somebody outside to get information on what was happening, shouting into his bullhorn, singing Cornish ballads to keep people's spirits up. Robert Sloss, one of the last Morgan Stanley people to leave his office, said later that he saw Rescorla on the 10th floor, telling people that they were almost finished.[3] Then, shortly before the towers collapsed, he called Morgan Stanley headquarters to say he was going up to make one last sweep, and that is when he died.

"I think he was getting everyone out," Susan Rescorla said, "and he decided to make the final sweep and to go up and make sure everyone was out, and I think he heard the ceiling coming down, and I'm just sure that he and his guards molded themselves to the stairwell and knew what was happening."

A few minutes before the fall of the south tower, Steven Turilli, a lieutenant with the elite Rescue 1 squad in Manhattan, had run into the lobby of the Marriott Hotel, which was situated between the two towers, to escape the debris and bodies falling on West Street. He saw the chief of Engine Company 58 there and was ordered to go with John Citarella, a firefighter from Squad 252 in Brooklyn and a friend of Turilli's, to the 90th floor of the south tower. But before he left the Marriott, he began to feel the whole building shake.

"I didn't know the building was coming down on us," he said later.

"It just felt like a giant rumbling. I felt like we had no time to react and I'm not sure what happened immediately after that. Basically, the deputy chief ran one way and John and I ran the other way, towards a wall. At first I just thought it was glass breaking or something. John and I dove for the walls and to this day I don't know why we went for the walls. Maybe it was some training we got or something, but it was a good move since the walls protected us. We both got completely flattened out by the debris. I remember as I dove to the wall, I could see through the windows that the building was coming down on us. I heard like five ba-booms in a row. Then I heard nothing."

Turilli remembers being under debris for about five to seven minutes before he managed to crawl out of it himself. He heard a cry for help from a doorman of the hotel, whose long black coat reminded Turilli of Dracula. He was coated in dust and was bleeding. Turilli walked around in what was left of the lobby looking for Citarella, who, it turns out, was trapped under debris and screaming for help. Turilli couldn't see him but he could hear him, though only faintly. He started to pull debris away and as he did, he could hear Citarella say to hurry because he couldn't breathe. When Citarella was able to stick a hand up through the rubble, Turilli pushed a gas mask toward him and managed that way to give him some air. It turned out that he was pinned down by a piece of plywood.

"When I finally got to John, his helmet was up against his nose, his knees were crunched up to his face, and he had a disconnected mask," Turilli said. "The plywood was still on John's leg. It was like a four-by-four or six-by-six sheet. I had lost one glove so while I was trying to pry off the plywood, I kept cutting my hands because of the protruding nails. Finally, the chief held on to my ankles and I dove in to grab John's ankles and pulled him out."

While Turilli was getting Citarella out of the rubble, other firefighters found a blown-out portion of wall that led to the street. While some men stayed behind to tend to a civilian too seriously injured to walk, the others were ordered out of the Marriott by the chief on the scene, Lawrence Stack. When he reached the street, Turilli saw Ganci and Feehan, who, after surviving the collapse of the south tower, had begun walking south, hoping apparently to set up a new command station on West Street. In Turilli's view, Ganci and Feehan both looked to be in a state of shock. Stack ordered him and Citarella to join Ganci, while other firemen stayed inside the Marriott to tend to the wounded civilian. Turilli believes that all of them were killed.

"What everyone noticed when we walked out of the Marriott," he said, "was that we saw sunlight. I felt the beams on my back and when I turned around, one of the towers wasn't there.

"I walked just south of the walkway and saw Joe Angelini, Sr.," Turilli said. "He had no gear with him and had this dazed look on him. He had dust all over him." Joe Angelini, Sr., another member of Rescue 1, was famous in the Fire Department both for having won three individual citations for valor and for being, at sixty-three, one of the longest-serving firefighters in the city. His son, Joe, Jr., was also a fireman and the winner of a citation for valor of his own. Both were killed on September 11. Turilli also had a family member in the department, his brother Tommy, and he was worried about him.

"I see Louie Torez from Squad Forty-one," Turilli said, "and he tells me he just saw my brother near the north walkway. Louie has no radio so I give him mine even though it wasn't working. Louie and Joey go towards the Marriott and I went in front of the north tower on West Street near the World Financial Center. I look up and the second tower is coming down.

"Because I had already been crushed, I heard that first 'Eeeeeer' and I took off running. John started to run first but I stood there like a bozo and saw the first ten floors come down, then I started to run. Then the wind just knocked me out, and I was underneath the walkway and there was dust everywhere. I saw on TV [later] that there was like a mushroom cloud. I dove behind a parked car and everything was in my ears, my nose, my throat. Then I heard some loud booming noises. My chest wasn't operating right at this point. I forced myself to throw up to clear a passageway. I took hits of oxygen from my mask and then the car started shaking, like it was being hit. This was worse than the first one since before I could see the floors collapsing from the windows. This one you were blindsided.

"I don't think the cloud lifted until like ten minutes later. Everything was dead silent. I crawled up the street in the dust and eventually I felt grass. I knew it was the divider of the highway so I tried to follow that north and I reached another parked car. I sidled up next to the car and stood up. The cloud was starting to lift. And you won't believe this. The first person, I mean the first person I saw when the dust all settled, was John."

Turilli said that he and Citarella walked north to Chambers Street where they were able to wash off with a hose. Turilli wanted to go back to look for Tommy, his brother, but Citarella dissuaded him, "There's nothing you can do," he said. "You almost got killed twice already." Turilli borrowed a cell phone from a civilian on the street and spoke to his mother-in-law, telling her that he was all right. As he continued walking north, he ran into another firefighter he knew, Kevin Rafter, who told him he had seen Tommy walking up on the east side of West Street. The brothers, in other words, were both on West Street but hadn't seen each other.

"We sat down for a bit to catch our breath," Turilli said, "and as I was talking to John and Kevin, my brother came walking back down West Street."

John Paul DeVito emerged onto the street from the exit of Building Four and took stock. Most of his employees were there, but Ramos, his head trader, was missing, and Adam Mayblum was somewhere behind him still in the stairwell. Should he go back and see what had happened to them? He didn't have long to think about that because only a few seconds after getting out onto the street, the south tower began to crumble. And then everybody began screaming and running at the same time.

"You came out and you looked up because inside you still weren't sure what had happened and you wanted to see and at the moment you look up it's tumbling down," DeVito said later. "You saw it before you heard it, and then, you can't imagine how quickly you are engulfed in blackness and suffocating. At that moment, everything passed by—Marilyn, the kids, my parents—and I said to myself, 'If you don't focus you're never going to survive this.' I felt that if I stopped I would suffocate because it was ripping into my lungs and I couldn't breathe.

"That day, I saw the face of Christ and I saw hell," DeVito said. "I was so petrified that if I stood still or if I walked south there'd be no way out. So I tried to feel north. What does north feel like? There was a sound to it, a sound of burning, crying, people saying, 'Help me,' and you couldn't open your eyes because if you opened your eyes it was blacker than if you had your eyes shut."

Mayblum was in the stairwell of the north tower when the south tower came down. He remembers that the lights went out and there was a rumbling that seemed to be coming from above as if the staircases were collapsing in on themselves. The people with him put their hands on each other's shoulders and kept walking. When they reached the bottom stairway, he saw a woman police officer soaking wet and covered in soot stay behind to help people on their way out, and afterward he feared that she might still have been in there when the north tower collapsed. Outside, he said, "there was at least five inches of this gray pasty dusty soot on the ground as well as a thickness of it in the air." He saw twisted steel and wires, and very few rescue workers.

"They must have been trapped under the debris when Tower Two fell," he said, and he was right. Ganci, Feehan, Judge, and hundreds of others were already dead. Mayblum also worried about Zhu, who was his trading partner and friend, and only found out later that he had gotten out, maybe ten minutes before the north tower collapsed. But Harry Ramos and Victor Wald, the stranger he stopped to help and wouldn't leave, had no chance. Mayblum figures that Ramos had about twenty-five minutes to move Victor down thirty-six floors. They were probably on around the 20th floor when they were crushed to death by dust and steel.

DeVito, ahead of Mayblum, walked north and east, bumping into parked cars, falling down, picking himself up and groping ahead, still not sure if he was moving away from the collapsing building or toward it. He had no idea how long he walked when, opening his eyes, he saw the light from a music store and he went in. It turned out to be J&R, a big electronics and music emporium on Broadway, a block east and a couple of blocks north of the Trade Center. Weirdly, somebody began taking his picture, maybe a news photographer, maybe an amateur who just had a camera.

"I must look like somebody from *The Twilight Zone*," DeVito thought to himself.

He wanted to call his family to let them know that he was safe, but no cell phones were working and there was a long line behind every pay phone. He found himself near an apartment complex and a security guard let him use the phone there. He couldn't get through to his wife, so he called his mother in Brooklyn and asked her to relay the news to Marilyn that he was alive. He walked farther north to the edge of Chinatown, where the owner of a restaurant let him use the phone there, and this time he got through to Marilyn, who told him to go to LeRoy Street in Greenwich Village, where some relatives of hers lived.

First he found a church near New York University, where he had been a student. He dropped to his knees and for the first time that day he let his emotions loose. He began to cry. He prayed. People in the church stared at him as though he were a visitor from outer space. A policeman tried to calm him.

"You need help," the policeman said. "Let me help you."

"I'm fine, officer," DeVito replied. "I don't need help. Other people need help."

"You're in a state of shock," the policeman said.

"I'm not in shock," DeVito replied, still weeping and covered in grime. "I like this state. I've never been more cognizant in my life."

Later he elaborated: "Can you imagine that you've faced hell and death and you walked away, and you're so in focus and so clear about the beauty of the day. Everything is so much more vivid. Everything tastes so sweet, every face is clearer, every moment."

The policeman asked DeVito if he could at least wash his eyes.

"I thought it was prudent to let him wash my eyes," DeVito said. "Then he wanted to clean me down, but I said no. I wanted everyone to see what I looked like, not because I wanted to be a poster boy, but I wanted everyone to see what they'd done to us, because at that point you knew we'd been attacked."

Brian Clark and Stanley Praimnath, having walked down eighty-four floors and gotten to the street from Building Four, the nine-story tower to the east of the twin towers, ran across Liberty Street and into a deli that they saw was open. The owner, who had seen everything, gave them a prepared breakfast platter, muttering a bit ruefully, "I guess nobody's going to come and pick this up." They walked to Rector Street, which slopes upward to the east as it runs alongside Trinity Church, where they encountered some ministers and, as Clark put it later, Praimnath broke down.

"This man saved my life," Praimnath said, pointing to Clark and weeping.

"Stanley, maybe you think so," Clark replied, "but maybe you saved mine." Clark was thinking that he had been arguing with the heavy woman on the 81st floor when he heard Praimnath's calls for help. If he hadn't, maybe he, like Coll and York, would have gone up instead of down.

One of the ministers suggested that the two men go into the church to pray and compose themselves, and as they walked up Rector Street, the World Trade Center came into view and they stopped to look at the smoke billowing out of the upper floors of both towers. They were next to Alexander Hamilton's grave, which is in the cemetery of Trinity Church, when Praimnath said, "You know, I think they could come down."

"I said, 'I don't think so,'" Clark recalled. "'That's a steel tower. It's just furniture and rugs and stuff like that that's burning.' And just as I was saying that, the south tower started to crumble. You could see the glass breaking, shimmering in the light like confetti. We stood there in awe. We didn't run away in panic, but stared at this cloud of dust. In fact, there was so much dust I didn't even know that the whole building had gone down. I thought it was just the upper floors, and all of a sudden this tsunami of dust came up over the church and we realized it was time to get out of there. We ran south to 42 Broadway when the front of the dust wave caught up with us, and we dove into a building to get some fresh air."

For some reason, Praimnath chose that moment to give Clark his card, and Clark put it in his shirt pocket, not thinking much about it. In fact, his mind was on two other matters, one small, one large. The first was that he was still carrying the breakfast tray the deli owner had given him on Liberty Street. He tore a piece of cantaloupe out of its plastic wrap and devoured it and then left the rest of the tray behind. Second, he thought of Dianne at home, and realized there was a good chance that she had seen the collapse on television and would be worried sick that he was dead.

In 1993, his office had been on a relatively low floor, the 31st floor of the north tower, and, by an odd coincidence, he and Praimnath had been on the 31st floor of the south tower when Clark had called Dianne. In

1993, because the stairways were so dark and crowded, it had taken two hours to walk out of the building, and this time Clark had called his wife about twenty minutes before the south tower collapsed, and he had told her he was on the 31st floor. He knew that not only was Dianne at home watching television but so were three of his children, Jeffrey, Kristen, and Tim, and Jeffrey's wife, Shannon, and their three children, and Tim's fiancée, Lisa, along with the minister from their church and several friends. It became a matter of great urgency to him to call her and let everyone know that he was safe.

But it was very hard to find a working phone. Clark and Praimnath walked out the back of 42 Broadway to New Street, then to Broad Street and to Water Street near the East River. It was now about 10:00, and suddenly the two men got separated. When he didn't see Praimnath beside him, Clark experienced a flood of emotion. He felt, it seems, the bond that you can only feel with someone who has accompanied you through great peril. He wandered up and down Water Street with his hands in the air yelling, "Stanley, Stanley." For a brief time he even had the impression that it had all been a kind of dream and that Stanley had been an angel and didn't really exist, until he remembered that he had Praimnath's business card, which was a source of stabilizing reassurance.

"I started to walk. I didn't know how I was going to get out of town, whether I should hitchhike or whatever," Clark said. "I walked up the FDR Drive, not the elevated part but down below. It was like a winter's day. There was ash over everything, like a fine snow. And through the haze of that gray day, I heard a bullhorn and an announcement, 'Next ferry for Jersey City.' Well I didn't know anything about ferries to Jersey City from there, but I walked down to the pier and there were these ferries that they had diverted from the west side to the east side. I walked down and got on the ferry, and just as I did, this very noticeable black cloud came down and enveloped the pier and the boat."

Clark didn't realize it at the time, but he was being pelted by the vaporized debris of the north tower, which came down at 10:28, killing Pete Ganci, Bill Feehan, and other firefighters on West Street.

"Everybody was yammering on the boat, yakety-yak," Clark said. "Nobody could believe what was going on and they didn't know what was going on. We hadn't heard about the Pentagon or hijacked planes. We gradually got farther north and alongside the World Financial Center, and we suddenly could see the areas the towers used to stand in, and everybody realized for the first time that the buildings were down. All of a sudden it was total silence on the ferry."

The ferry docked at Harborside in Jersey City, and Clark ran down the pier to the ticket booth, where he used the phone to call Dianne. He learned later that there were so many calls coming in to his home in New Jersey that Dianne, who had been pacing back and forth with several friends after they saw the tower come down, was outside and wasn't answering.

"Strangely when I called it was when she just came into the house, and not only was I able to get straight through, but she was the one to pick up the phone.

"Hi," Clark said. "I'm OK. It's me." There was silence on the other end of the line. "She dissolved in happiness," Clark said, "and somebody else came on the phone right away. She didn't even talk to me."

But for Gorday Aamoth, at the beginning of the alphabetical list, and for Igor Zukelman at the end of it, there would be no happy embraces at the end of the day. Aamoth was a wealthy investment banker with Sandler O'Neill & Partners, and Zukelman, a recent immigrant from the Ukraine, was a computer technician with Fiduciary Trust, another of the employees of that company who, like Shimmy Biegeleisen, failed to get out in time. Maybe the amazing thing is not that so many were killed in the disintegration of two 102-story towers, but that so many weren't. The evacuation of people below the points of impact was remarkably successful. Yes, it could have been worse. Nonetheless, for Aamoth and Zukelman and 2,821 others, there would be no going home.

Sasha Tsoy-Ligay will never see her mother again.

Once it has happened, it has happened forever.

TWENTY-ONE

A Nation Suspended

The immediate feeling was disbelief, and it was followed by a powerful and unprecedented sense of national vulnerability. Out of a clear blue sky, using our own engines against us, armed with nothing but knives, terrorists had struck simultaneously at the chief symbols of American commercial and military might. The inconceivable had happened, and it had happened even though we were supposedly protected by the world's biggest defense budget, by the greatest military power in world history, and by an at least creditable intelligence establishment that was supposed to find out about things like terrorist attacks before they happened. The phrases that were heard over and over again were "Everything has changed" and "Nothing will be the same again." People watched as the television news programs spent the afternoon of September 11 and all of September 12 playing their footage of the second plane hitting the south tower and of the tremendous fireball the crash caused and of the two towers collapsing in that billowing cloud of dust. If they could strike so devastatingly once, why couldn't they do it again?

Even in the two world wars, and in the Korean War and in the Vietnam War, there had been no real worry that our enemies could hit us where we lived. And now they had—not an enemy like Imperial Japan or Nazi Germany, world-class military powers, but a few men with knives inspired and manipulated by an ascetic Saudi Arabian fanatic who lived in a cave in Afghanistan. Previously unseen things were being seen—fighter jets patrolling the skies of Manhattan against the possibility of another aerial attack, national guardsmen in combat fatigues and masks over their faces marching in lower Manhattan. The entire island of Manhattan was sealed off to vehicular traffic. The stock markets were closed, and so were the bridges and tunnels. The baseball season was suspended for a week. There was no commercial air traffic at all on Wednesday, September 3, and very little of it on Thursday, when the first national grounding of planes in American history came to an end and the FAA allowed flights to resume. On a normal day there are about forty thousand flights. In that first week there was only a small fraction of that, and the planes were so empty that the airlines were asking for federal aid to enable them to survive. It was as though life as we knew it had stopped, to be replaced by an anxious emptiness, a national stillness, immobility.

In New York, the primary election that had been under way on September 11 was canceled. The Broadway theaters were closed, and if they had been open nobody would have gone to them. People did go to grocery stores to stock up on canned goods as if getting ready for nuclear war. Police arrested people all over the country—two men with box cutter knives on a train, ten men, one carrying a false pilot's identification, at La Guardia Airport in New York—and the country worried that there would be another attack in the days that followed. A spate of bomb scares emptied buildings, schools, and government offices across the country. In Manattan there were ninety such scares on September 13, causing evacuations of Grand Central Terminal, the MetLife Building, the Port Authority Bus Terminal, La Guardia Airport, Macy's department store, the Condé Nast Building in Times Square, and CNN's Manhattan bureau. For a week, people bearing snapshots of missing loved ones went to hospitals to see if they had been found, or they posted them at makeshift memorials, instant floral parks—in Washington Square, in the Times Square subway station, hoping that their husband or wife or son or mother was wandering around someplace, stunned, perhaps stricken with amnesia, but alive. None of them were. Even at the site in lower Manhattan itself, the mountain of wreckage that had once been the two tallest towers in Manhattan, only a very few people were pulled out alive.

Mayor Guiliani announced that the death toll would probably be close to five thousand and that, in the first two days of the rescue operation, only thirty-five of the dead had been identified. Was it the worst day ever on American soil? In Pearl Harbor, with which September 11 was immediately compared—another sneak attack by a determined foe— 2,390 Americans had died. During the long terrible day of the Battle of Antietam in the Civil War, 3,654 soldiers died on both sides. Eventually the estimates of the number of dead on September 11 would decline, to reach the final figure of 3,056, so it was the second most fatal day in the history of the United States, and yet the events, Antietam and September 11, weren't comparable. In one soldiers had killed soldiers, face-to-face and over the course of a day. In the other terrorists had killed civilians who had done nothing more than show up for work, and they had done their killing in a single explosive burst, lasting 102 minutes from the crash of the first plane to the fall of the second tower. It had been history's most devastating kamikaze attack. Unlike Antietam, it had been completely unexpected. People one instant had been drinking coffee from a paper cup and reading their e-mail and the next instant they were dead or dying. These facts and reflections, which were on everybody's mind, added to the shock and the incredulity. September 11 was the worst thing that had ever happened in so short a time. Perhaps the only comparable event in history was Hiroshima, but even Hiroshima had taken place in the context of a declared war. Hiroshima was a surprise attack but not a sneak attack. September 11 was both.

What to do? Most conspicuously, what people all over the country did was express their solidarity with the victims, and with the city of New York. Firefighters and rescue workers from many places came to the city to help at what was quickly termed Ground Zero. Indeed, a kaleidoscope of events showed the effects of the terror attacks. For several days in various places in the city—the Forty-second Street subway station and Washington Square Park, for example—people put up pictures of their missing relatives, asking other people to call them if they could give them any news. Wreathes and messages of thanks and condolences were placed by grateful citizens in front of every fire station in the city.

In Normal, Illinois, three local radio stations set up a tent in front of Schnucks Supermarket on Veterans' Parkway to collect donations in five-gallon water bottles—and the money came in at the rate of $5,000 per hour. Blood donor centers were jammed in Denver, Colorado, and at the nearby Silver Bullet Pistol Range in Wheat Ridge, customers who flocked to take September 11–induced target practice had bought out all the available ammunition by 10 A.M. Candlelight vigils were held in many cities, and people called friends whom they hadn't seen or spoken to in years to make sure they were all right.

New York's two baseball teams, the Yankees and the Mets, got special permission from Major League Baseball to wear police and firemen's and Emergency Medical Service hats to honor those who had died saving others. Muslim, Christian, and Jewish clergy joined each other in ecumenical services to condemn terror and to mourn the dead. On September 11 itself, Wal-Mart, the world's largest retailer, sold 116,000 American flags, nineteen times the number sold on the same day the previous year.

Vigilance was the word of the hour. When airline flights resumed two days after September 11, passengers heard unusual announcements from their captains, telling them, essentially, that if someone tries to hijack this plane, to fight back with whatever is at hand.

"Throw your shoes at him," the captain aboard a San Francisco to Charlotte flight said. "A couple of you get up and tackle him. Beat the snot out of him. I don't care." He said that he had an axe in the cockpit, sharp enough to shave with. "For anyone to try to break into the cockpit, it would be a very bad idea." And then: "Having said all this, I'd like you all to sit back, relax, and enjoy the trip."

And then there was this announcement, made by the pilot on United Airlines flight 564 from Denver to Washington, D.C.:

"If someone or several people stand up and say they are hijacking the plane, I want you to all stand up together, take whatever you have available with you, and throw it at them. Throw it at their faces and heads so they'll have to raise their hands to protect themselves. The very best protection you have against knives are pillows and blankets. Whoever is close to these people should try to get a blanket over their heads, pull them down to the floor, and I'll land the plane at the closest place, and then we'll take care of them. After all, there are usually only a few of them, and we are two hundred plus strong, and we'll not allow them to take over this plane."

Sometime later, an apparently deranged man, not a terrorist, tried to get into the cockpit on a flight from Los Angeles to Chicago. Several passengers, with flight 93 in their minds, jumped up and subdued him. There was the anthrax scare, when a man, probably someone living in the United States and unconnected with Islamic extremism, sent envelopes containing anthrax bacilli to newspapers and Senate offices—killing five people and infecting thirteen. As the United States went to war against Al Qaeda and the Taliban in Afghanistan, Muslim scholars held a press conference in Washington to announce a fatwa, making it a duty for Muslims to join in the fight against terrorism. The FBI arrested six hundred people, most of them foreign Muslims living in the United States, and began investigating them for possible connections with the September 11 attacks—though almost no such connections were found. Congress passed a law requiring airports to turn over the screening of baggage and passengers to a new federal bureaucracy, taking the job out of private hands. At Ground Zero itself one month after the attack, Mayor Giuliani led a memorial service against the background of the still-smoldering wreckage.

"The fire is still burning but from it has emerged a stronger spirit," he said.

And in Middletown, New Jersey, population sixty-six thousand, of whom thirty-six were killed on September 11, Barbara Minervo, whose husband was among them, woke up every morning to find gifts of food left at her door by strangers.

"The kindness of people is what is getting me through this," she said. "It's enlightening to know that I'm not entirely alone."

On the afternoon of September 11, the long north-south avenues of Manhattan were filled with pedestrians, people walking solemnly home from downtown because walking was the only way to get home. There were no subways or buses for most of the day. In the hours and days that followed, people went to blood-donor centers, thinking that that would be the way to help, but they were turned away after spending hours in line, because there were too many volunteers and, in a grim paradox, there weren't very many injured who needed the blood. People had either died or they had gotten away. Aside from several dozen people brought to the hospital with severe burns, many of whom did not survive, there seemed to be little middle ground. In front of the New York City Medical Examiner's office, trucks laden with body parts, which would be subjected to DNA tests as the long effort to identify victims got under way, were watched over through the night by Jewish volunteers who took turns chanting the psalms of David.

In Jewish law, the dead must not be left alone from the moment of death until their burial, and so a round-the-clock vigil outside the morgue on First Avenue and Thirtieth Street was organized by an Orthodox synagogue, Ohab Zedek, on the Upper West Side. On the Sabbath, when the men from Ohab Zedek were not allowed to ride to the site of the vigil, the relay was taken up by a group of Orthodox women from Stern College who camped out in tents and fulfilled the commandment to keep the dead company, singing the Hebrew psalms from midnight until sunrise.

The girls from Stern College symbolized a collective mourning, a shared sense of both tragedy and outrage. The victims had been so innocent, so many firemen and police and others among them who had bravely rushed to the scene to help, and that made the murderers seem to belong to a category of evil that was immeasurable even in a world that has seen so much evil. In this sense tragedy and outrage mixed with a sort of incredulity and wonderment: Why were we hated so much? Hadn't we been on the Muslim side in the war in Afghanistan? Didn't we help Muslims in Bosnia and Kosovo? Wasn't it the case that millions of Muslims, as President Bush pointed out in his speech before Congress, practiced their religion freely in the United States of America, to which they had come of their own free will? Clearly, we had something to learn about the unreasoning and unreasonable anti-American fury that existed in the Muslim world, where Osama bin Laden was being treated not as a villain but as a hero. There was a lesson there someplace, and it would be contemplated for a long time into the future. In the meantime, public support quickly built not just for a retaliatory strike, a few cruise missiles launched at a target, but for a long and complicated war against an only semivisible adversary. The Bush administration vowed to fight that war for a long time, against the terrorists themselves and against those who harbored terrorists, which in the first instance, meant Osama bin Laden and the Taliban of Afghanistan. The country would go to war and not since Pearl Harbor had the American people seemed so ready for it.

TWENTY-TWO

Aftermath

The funeral for Kazushige Ito, a thirty-five-year-old planning specialist at Fuji Bank, took place in that famously afflicted city, Hiroshima, Japan, on March 9, 2002, six months after Ito died in the south tower of the World Trade Center. Ito's father, Tsugio Ito, spoke at the ceremony, and there must have been an added measure of sadness for him, if it is possible for anything to add to the sadness of attending the funeral of a son without a body to put to rest. In the usual Buddhist ceremony of Japan, relatives meet in the crematorium and they use chopsticks to pick the cremated bones out of the ash and pass them from person to person. But this was the second time in Tsugio Ito's life when a funeral was held without the body being placed on an altar so that the sutras can be intoned by the priest, and without incense being sprinkled on the smoldering remains. The older Ito's older brother, the uncle that Kazushige never met, died many years ago at another ground zero. He was vaporized when the atomic bomb was dropped there on August 6, 1945. In both cases the grief of the Ito family was intensified by the deaths of young men in events so cataclysmic they left behind no trace of the deceased.

"What happened in Hiroshima and in the terrorism [in New York] is the same because there are many people who can't recover one tooth or one nail," Ito told a Japanese reporter.[1]

Kazushige Ito was a music lover who used to go to the Metropolitan

Opera House at Lincoln Center in New York twenty times in a season. He was also a marathoner who finished the New York City event in four hours eighteen minutes in 2000 and was jogging every day in Central Park to get ready for the Philadelphia Marathon, which he planned to run in November. His goal was to break the four-hour mark, and his wife, Yuko, said she believed he would have done it. He would have turned thirty-six the day after the Philadelphia Marathon, if he had lived. If he had lived, he would probably have settled permanently in New York, a city both he and Yuko loved.

But he didn't live. He was probably one of those killed when flight 175 plowed into the south tower at 9:02 on September 11, since Fuji Bank was one of the unfortunate companies whose offices were at the immediate point of impact. Maybe Kazushige Ito was one of those who heeded the public address announcements ordering people not to evacuate the south tower after the north tower was hit and that is why he was sitting at his desk when Marwan al-Shehhi slammed the hijacked Boeing 767 into his office on the 81st floor, killing sixty-two Fuji Bank employees altogether. Stanley Praimnath, who walked out of the south tower with Brian Clark, did survive the crash on the 81st floor. He also worked at Fuji Bank, and he may have been the only person who was on the 81st floor who survived.

In any case, Kazushige Ito is dead, though his body was never recovered. His remains are still there at Ground Zero in New York in what became a common mass grave. His father visited the site in October, and he remembers feeling for the members of the rescue and cleanup crews who, he felt, were freezing in the late autumn weather. He remembers also going to the bathroom to weep privately over his loss. Eventually he gave up on finding Kazushige's body, saying that everybody was doing the best they could. And in March, finally, a funeral service was held at which Ito addressed the spirit of his son directly:

"Please look after us from heaven," he said. "And don't worry. I'm thinking about making a new start today."

It is worth remembering one of the videotapes of Osama bin Laden in which he expressed his considered opinion about the United States getting what it deserved on September 11. "Here is America struck by

Almighty God in one of its vital organs so that its greatest buildings are destroyed," he said. "America has been filled with horror from north to south and east to west, and thanks be to God. . . . God has used a group of vanguard Muslims, the forefront of Islam, to destroy America. May God bless them and allot them a supreme place in heaven, for He is the only one capable and entitled to do so."

One wonders what bin Laden would say to Pauline del Carmen Cardona, four months pregnant, who was literally in her doctor's office having a sonogram when her husband, Jose, a clerk at Carr Futures, was killed in the south tower of the World Trade Center. The couple had tried three times to have a baby and had had three failed pregancies before this one that seemed likely to succeed.

"I feel him kicking and I feel happy and then I feel sad," Mrs. Cardona, who is thirty-three years old, said. "When I feel too sad, I pray to God, 'Make me strong like a rock so my baby is not affected.' But sometimes I can't help it. I cry a lot in the shower, while the water is running."

Nobody knows exactly how many wives were pregnant when their husbands were killed on September 11, but the number is high. At the bond-trading firm Cantor Fitzgerald, at least fifty pregnant women lost their husbands. The median age of the men killed in the attacks was thirty-five to thirty-nine, the main child-producing years, and many of their wives were pregnant.

Sonia Morron, forty-one, was three months pregnant when her husband, Jorge, a security guard, was killed. She said afterward that the baby inside of her was the only bright spot in her life and she was more than ever anxious to have it. But after September 11, she had panic attacks and nightmares that left her trembling and drenched in sweat.

"I would tell my baby, 'Daddy is not with us but you are. Don't go, you're the best thing I have.' "

On October 4, Mrs. Morron had a miscarriage.

"It felt like another tower fell on me," she said. She held a joint memorial service for her husband and the baby and she visits both of them at their tomb. "In that little piece of human being is my husband," she said.

Soon after September 11, a Twin Towers Orphan Fund was created to help children who lost a parent. As of April 2002, 746 such children were registered with the new charity, 446 of whom were ten years old or less. There were no reports of any children losing both of their parents, but there were forty to fifty who lived in single-parent households and have now been left with no parent at all.

———

Most of the dead were never found and never will be, which is one of the matters that makes the redevelopment of the Trade Center site in lower Manhattan so delicate a matter. It is hallowed ground and it is a commercial site. And, as always in matters of disaster, September 11 was followed by a debate about practical matters, legal disputes between the leaseholder and the consortium that insured the towers—for $3.5 billion or $7 billion, depending on whether the attack is considered a single event or two separate events. There were arguments about an appropriate memorial to the dead; there were demonstrations by firefighters who scuffled with police after Mayor Guiliani, one of the heroes of the day, decided in late October that the search for remains would have to end and the cleanup begin. An enormous outpouring of generosity followed the disaster, with donations pouring by the millions into the coffers of charities and relief organizations, but even that brought its dark side as quarrels erupted over when the money would be distributed, and how much. And then, of course, in the days right after the tragedy, the United States went on a war footing with President Bush warning the governments that had harbored terrorists, most notably the Taliban government of Afghanistan, that they would be treated as terrorists themselves.

———

In New York the mourning went on, and so did the many private struggles of the bereaved to come to accept the bitter fact, as Tsugio Ito was forced to do, that their missing loved ones were not going to turn up alive. By the first week of October, only 321 remains had been identified of the thousands who were missing. Mayor Giuliani himself went to the city morgue to identify the remains of Terence S. Hatton, a fire captain who was married to a longtime mayoral aide. A team of people, police officers, Fire Department battalion chiefs, clergymen, and others, were enlisted to go to the homes of the identified victims to give the news that a body had been found directly and in person. Members of some three thousand families gave DNA samples, toothbrushes, razors, even lip balm used by victims, and saliva swabs from the victim's relatives, to help in the work of identification, with DNA collection kits sent away to places like Germany and Guatemala where some of the bereaved families lived. And whenever a match was made—sometimes from nothing more than a fragment of bone found in the debris—there would be that visit to a family informing them that something had been found proving their loved one's decease, and at least the suspense and anguish of waiting would be over.

Inevitably this process entailed some heartbreaking bureaucratic formalities. Families were required to fill out forms in which they specified what they wanted to do if additional tissue samples of a loved one were found. There were two choices: they could be notified or they could have the sample disposed of by the authorities. Exactly how the disposal of what the printed form did not call body parts was to be done was not specified.

"When you get that knock on the door, it's the big one," said Michael Meehan, a New York City detective whose brother, Damian Meehan, a trader at Carr Futures, was among those whose bodies were identified in the wreckage.

After six months, a set of grisly statistics were announced in the cool language of bureaucracy. To that date, 18,937 body parts and 287 whole bodies had been found in the rubble, and 972 identifications had been made—which meant that there was no trace yet of 1,852 victims. Only two of the sixty-five people (not including the hijackers) aboard flight 175 were identified, which is no doubt an index of the incinerating heat that accompanied their deaths. By contrast, 182 of the firemen, who wore protective gear, have been identified, out of the total of 343 dead. But almost all of the remains were burned or mangled beyond recognition. The identities of only ten victims were confirmed by visual identification alone. All the rest were done through dental records, fingerprints, and, above all, by DNA testing.

Families faced heartbreaking choices that sometimes even the most well-designed bureaucratic procedures could only make worse. Do you bury a part of a body and hold a funeral, or do you wait in the hopes that more of the body will be found? What if you have a funeral without a body and then the medical examiner calls to tell you months later that a body was found? Do you have another funeral, or just a burial or a cremation? If only part of a body is found, do you bury it in a full-sized coffin or in some smaller container? And, if you have buried what was initially found of a body and more is found later, do you disinter the original remains and rebury them with the newly found parts? And if your loved one is found mangled almost beyond recognition, or if you are only burying parts of a body, do you view the remains? Painful as it sounds, many counselors recommended that the remains be viewed on the grounds that it might help in accepting the tragedy that had occurred, in providing what is commonly called closure.

Beata Boyarski, twenty-five, whose thirty-four-year-old brother Gennady Boyarski's body was found in the rubble, called the medical examiner in an effort to be sure that the body had not been misidentified. In her grief she entertained the suspicion that the city might just be trying to get rid of bodies without worrying excessively about who they belonged to.

"Tell me like it is," she said to the medical examiner, whom she managed to get on the phone. The body was horribly mangled, the medical examiner told her, and only about three-quarters of it had been found, along with a wedding ring and a wallet. The identification was made from a driver's license and the cause of death was given as "blunt impact," which provided Ms. Boyarski with no information about how Gennady, who left behind a wife and a seven-year-old son, had died and where exactly and at what time. When Ms. Boyarski said that the family wanted DNA testing done just to be sure of the identification, she was told that that might take several months, so she went ahead with a burial, only to be told when it was already too late that the DNA testing could be done right away after all. If further remains were found, she said, "We would, I guess, bring him back up and include it."

The family of Shimmy Biegeleisen, who failed to leave his 97th floor office in the south tower before flight 175 crashed into it, found themselves in the immediate aftermath of September 11 dealing with the complex laws governing the situation wherein a husband and father has died but there is no body. In the Jewish way of mourning, there can be no funeral without the body, and, in many situations, the family cannot properly even observe the standard weeklong mourning ritual, known as sitting shiva, when they sit on low benches and friends and family come to visit. The situation is particularly agonizing for the wife of a dead husband, because she is deemed to be an *agunah*, a woman who is still bound to a husband, even though the husband is absent. The laws stem from olden days when a man might disappear on a trip to some faraway place and there was no way of knowing what happened to him. There are women in *agunah* who have spent the rest of their lives waiting in the hope that he would return.

"To Miriam it was very hard," Regina Biegeleisen, Shimmy's mother, said. "To have to wait."

Fortunately, though, several of the people who spoke to Shimmy when he was in the tower, and who heard his cry of "Oh God" in the last seconds of his life, testified before a rabbinical tribune, and the rabbis declared that there was no possibility that Biegeleisen was alive. Miriam and her five children were able to sit shiva, and to complete the process between the holidays of Rosh Hashanah and Yom Kippur. Many people came, including, one day, an entire busload of colleagues from Fiduciary Trust.

"By declaring it finished at that point, we were able to have an uninterrupted week," Mrs. Biegeleisen said. "It was something that was important to his children, to me, and to his family."

Right after that Shimmy's parents gave DNA samples, and the family waited, hoping that Shimmy's body would be recovered, since only then could a funeral and burial take place. In October, two thousand mourners heard several rabbis and friends of the Biegeleisens eulogize Shimmy at a memorial service held in the auditorium of the school his daughters attended. And then, the family waited over the months—October and November, December and January and February and March, without getting the news they were hoping for.

"One of the men he was in the office with was found at the beginning of October," Miriam Biegeleisen said, "so I kept saying, 'Why was he found and why not my husband?' It didn't make any sense to me. So at that point, I called up the medical examiner's office, and somebody suggested I bring two of my children, so we would have a backup with the DNA."

Miriam went with her fifteen-year-old daughter, Adeena, and Mordechai, nineteen, her oldest son, to give additional samples, and she remembers thanking God that the children didn't inquire too closely about the refrigerator trucks parked outside and what was inside them.

Then in April, on the second day of Passover, two policemen arrived to say that Shimmy's body had been found. The funeral was held in Borough Park and Shimmy Biegeleisen was laid to rest at the Beit Dovid, the House of David, Cemetery in Elmont, Long Island, where his grandfather and his great-grandfather are buried. Because it was in the month of Nisan in the Hebrew calendar, when no lengthy funeral orations are supposed to be given, only a few words were spoken by the head of the Belzer community in Borough Park. Then Mordechai said the words of the psalm that Shimmy had recited over the phone in the last minutes of his life. It is the psalm that is recited in the synagogue service when the Torah is replaced in the Ark of the Covenant, and Mordechai felt it was appropriate. His father was, he felt, going back where he came from. It is the Twenty-fourth Psalm of David, and it ends:

> Who is the King of glory?
> The Lord of hosts,
> He is the King of glory.

Susan Rescorla watched on television as the second tower crumbled into dust and she ran out of her house and into the street, and there she saw one of her neighbors, a woman whose husband was at a meeting on the 100th floor, do the same thing. It seems to have been a terror reflex, the impulse to get away from the television screen with its images of horror.

"From that moment on, for the whole day, and for the next week, we held vigil," she said later. Despite her hopes, Rick didn't come home that night, and he didn't call, and she was, of course, fearful that the worst had happened, even as she wanted to cling to some hope that it hadn't. "We did everything to find him," she said of herself and her two daughters. "Unfortunately, because of the chaotic situation there was a lot of misinformation. Hospitals were saying that people were on a list when they weren't. We got one report that somebody had seen him, but it must have been somebody who saw him inside the building. For one second we thought maybe he had gotten out, but he hadn't. We hoped that maybe he was walking around someplace in a daze, and then, at the end of a week, we understood there was no hope."

A month after September 11, the annual meeting of the Ia Drang veterans took place, with General Moore, about to be played by the actor Mel Gibson in the movie version of *We Were Soldiers Once,* in attendance. The whole group watched Robert Edwards's eight-minute documentary film, in which Rescorla predicted that terrorism rather than conventional war would be the next major national security threat facing the country. Joe Galloway, coauthor of *We Were Soldiers Once,* was there.

"You were looking at your friend who is now gone, and listening to him talking about everything that has happened to him, predicting what was going to happen to the U.S. before it happened," Galloway said. "The whole time we were watching the video, it was so emotional, so shocking. In a way it was a way of saying good-bye to him."

When it became clear that Yeneneh Betru, a standby passenger on flight 77, had indeed gotten on the largely empty flight, his sister, Ruth, couldn't get over her brother's bad luck. "It was as if he won the lottery for his own death," she said later, recalling the grief of Yeneneh's mother at the loss of her oldest born.

"I knew my parents, who were then in Ethiopia, would worry when they heard the news about the plane hijackings," Yeneneh's brother Aron said. At first, he said, he spoke to them on the phone and tried to reassure them that everything was all right, but they insisted on getting the full story, on checking every one of their four children, all of them in America.

"At that time I got the confirmation that Yeneneh was on the same plane," Aron said. "And I was crying in my car. . . . My mom went down the list inquiring about her children beginning with me. I told her that we were all OK," Aron said, recalling his desperate effort to postpone the moment when he would have to tell the truth, as if by not saying it, he could prevent it from being true. "When she got to the last name, I just couldn't say anything. And at that point, she started screaming on the phone. And that is how she knew her first child was dead."

Yeneneh's mother has had an especially hard time over the loss of her oldest son, and in the living room of the family home in Los Angeles, where once there were graduation photos of all four children, each of them wearing cap and gown, now there were eight photos of Yeneneh, put up after his death. In Ethiopia, more than a thousand people came to his funeral, held in Addis Ababa on November 12, including the country's high priest, who performed the last rights. In December, the *Addis Tribune*, an English-language paper, ran a full-page feature on Yeneneh and on the dialysis project that had taken much of his time for three years.

Now the family, led by Aron, has arranged with a Swedish medical technology company, Gambro, to donate four new dialysis machines in return for a contract by which the new Ethiopian center will purchase its supplies from that company. Funds are being raised for a new water filtration system, required for the new machines. The World Foundation for Renal Care has agreed to train the nurses in dialysis. Yeneneh had planned to name the new center after his grandmother, but now it will be called the Dr. Yeneneh Betru Hemodialysis Unit, and that seems entirely appropriate given that Yeneneh, through the center, will be saving lives even after his own was lost.

The ceremonies for John Ogonowski showed how many lives he had touched. The Department of Agriculture international farming assistance program under which he had helped Cambodian immigrant farmers was renamed the John Ogonowski Farmer-to-Farmer program in special legislation signed by President Bush. About twenty-five hundred people came to the memorial mass for "John Deere Johnny" at the St. Francis Church in Dracut that looked over farm fields there. There were four hundred uniformed airline workers, many of whom never knew about his other lives, as a New England farmer and an environmentalist and a man who donated some of his own land so new arrivals to the United States could get started in agriculture. Some people, like John Panarelli, another airline pilot, drove from as far away as Georgia. Massachusetts senators Edward Kennedy and John Kerry and Congressman

Marty Meehan were there too, along with a dozen of his middle daughter Caroline's school soccer team, and about thirty members of the Cambodian community of Lowell, Massachusetts, including some of those who had farmed vegetables on Ogonowski's land.

"Imagine that," his brother Jim said in his eulogy, "John helping victims of another terror."

"It doesn't get easier," Theresa Ogonowski, John's bereaved mother, said during the memorial service. "I just saw John tonight on TV and felt like he is coming home, but I know he is not. This will never have an end."[2]

Peggy Ogonowski meanwhile has been saving the hundreds, the thousands, of letters and gifts that have arrived in the mail at White Gate Farm—American flags, quilts, a stained-glasss panel depicting a bald eagle, an alabaster eagle statue with wings arched in a swoop and talons extended, and numerous medals, cards, plaques, and letters. American Airlines, which published a color pamphlet honoring all of the crew of flight 11, gave her and her three daughters a model of a 767 jet mounted on slender pedestals that each has put in her room.

But as Peggy has gratefully accepted the gifts, which have accumulated on end tables, in frames on walls, in baskets and on the tops of dresser drawers, she has been asking herself how she wants to live the rest of her life.

"I don't want it to be a museum," she said of the house that John built on the farm where they lived.

But she plans to stay, city girl that she is. She held the wooden urn of World Trade Center ashes that was given to her by the City of New York, and she allowed that, again while grateful for the gesture, it doesn't mean a lot to her, but the house does.

"I realize that I'm not the first woman who has lost a husband," she said. As the spring of 2002 brought warmer weather, she has thought about putting a larger window into her bedroom to improve the view of the roadless eastern tract of her property. She wants to spend more time reading in the Adirondack chairs on the lawn. On the west side of the house, it was time to take down the storm-window paneling and to put up the screens on the three-season porch, which is shaded from the summer sun by apple trees. She thinks it's time to have somebody tighten up the panels of the slate roof.

"Life is still good, even though we've lost him," she said. "We don't have to leave this house and we don't have any plans to."

On April 19, 2002, the FBI allowed the relatives of people killed on flight 93 into a large conference room in Princeton, New Jersey, so they could hear the plane's cockpit voice recorder. For months the federal government had denied the families' requests to do that, on the grounds that, first, the tape was confused and jumbled and didn't hold any answers to the plane's crash in Pennsylvania, and, second, that the tape would be used in evidence in the upcoming trial of Zacarias Moussaoui, and was therefore protected by judicial secrecy. But the families persisted, and they were invited to hear the tape, though they first had to sign a waiver promising not to sue the government in any matter connected to it. About a hundred people, according to one estimate, sat in the conference room. They listened to the tape on headsets installed at each seat, and they watched a written transcript on a large screen in front of them.

The family members' comments on the tape confirmed earlier press reports about them. Shouts of "Get them, get them" could be heard, and so could somebody saying in Arabic, "They're trying to get in." An unidentified woman could be heard saying, "Oh God, Oh God." But the basic questions—Did the passengers actually get into the cockpit? Did the struggle with the hijackers cause the plane to crash, or did the hijackers crash, or blow up, the plane intentionally?—were not resolved. And there were no answers about what role any given person played.

"I didn't hear anything that indicated what my son had done," Jerry Guadagno, the father of Richard Guadagno, said later. "There was really nothing there. I guess the big question mark still remains, and it always will."

Lyz Glick went to the tape playing also, and she is convinced that it does prove the success of the passengers in breaking into the cabin. What else would all that shouting and commotion mean?, she wonders.

"But when it came to the last two minutes, which is just the sound of the wind in the cockpit, I stopped listening," she said. "I started shaking. I'm glad I listened to it, but I knew how much I could listen."

At least, she feels, she knows what happened to Jeremy, and she was connected to him in his final minutes, and she knows that, in its way, that was a rare privilege among the survivors of the victims of September 11.

"In a way it does make things a little easier," she said. "So many people don't know what happened, but I do know. I had the phone calls. I heard the black box."

During those same weeks, after the tragedy and after she too had given up hope that her husband might still be alive, Migdalia Ramos, left now to care by herself for her two children, asked herself over and over a single terrible question: her husband, Harry Ramos, had died, she believed, because he refused to abandon a man he didn't know and whom he had just met in a stairway of the north tower. Why, Mrs. Ramos wanted to know, did Harry put this stranger ahead of herself and their two girls?

He didn't, of course, not really, and Mrs. Ramos understood that he didn't one day at the end of September when she went with a group of relatives and in-laws and their children to empty an apartment where her recently deceased mother had lived. The apartment was on the 7th floor, and while the Ramos group was carting out boxes and furniture, a fire alarm sounded and Migdalia saw smoke billowing out of a hallway. First she ran down the stairs and then, when she found out that the fire department had not yet arrived, she thought of her mother's elderly, nearly blind neighbor, and she realized that she was still upstairs and couldn't get out by herself.

Migdalia ran upstairs and found the fire in the kitchen of an apartment upstairs where a woman her mother's age was struggling to breathe through a scarf over her nose and mouth. Migdalia put out the fire, which she found in a toaster oven. Afterward, she remembered that when she was running up the stairs, she actually said to herself: "Harry, what am I doing?"

"The feelings I was having, it crossed my mind that he had had those same feelings," she said later. "The fear. The anxiety. The heart palpitating. The adrenaline rushing."

Mrs. Ramos's sister-in-law suggested that maybe Harry himself was trying to tell her why he had stayed behind to help the stranger named Victor.

"I did the same thing Harry did," Migdalia said later. "It took me to how he would be feeling. I realized that Harry did what he did because that was Harry's nature."

A while before that, Migdalia had gotten a call late one night from

Rebecca Wald. Mrs. Wald said that she had read about Harry Ramos and she was sure that the man he had tried to help in the north tower was her husband, Victor Wald. Rebecca told Migdalia that she had two little girls; the Ramoses had two little boys. One of the Wald girls was named Alex and so was one of the Ramoses' sons. The two women then met at a gathering of May Davis employees, hosted by the company's cofounder, Owen May, at his home in New Jersey, and over the weeks they stayed in touch.

In the meantime, Harry was honored for his selflessness and courage. A scholarship in California, a golf tournament in Puerto Rico, and a bowling league in Newark were all named for him, and the Puerto Rican Day Parade in New Jersey was dedicated to his memory. While all that was happening, Rebecca Wald called to say that her husband's body had been found. She would have a burial and a funeral, which she did. Victor's remains were interred on November 23 on what would have been his fiftieth birthday.

For a while Migdalia Ramos hoped that, since Harry and Victor must have died side by side, the discovery of one meant that the discovery of the other would come as well.

"It would be closure to a certain extent," she said. "When I go to my mother's grave site, I pray for her, and I can talk to her. I can't do that for Harry."

Migdalia has not had an easy time of it. Henry Ramos, her brother-in-law, went to see her every day for a couple of hours to help her through. She wasn't forgotten. She was invited to run a leg of the Olympic torch procession during the winter, and she did, holding it aloft from Queens to Manhattan. And while she now knows what went on in Harry's mind, she still wonders about his decision to help Victor, which cost him his life. She's thought about the moment on September 11, at 8:49, when Harry called her. He told her that something awful had happened but not to panic, he had to go. Barely awake, sleep-deprived from infant care and from the weeks when she had had to care for her mother, Migdalia was so groggy that she didn't answer. She does remember that just before he hung up, she could hear him shouting and other people screaming in the background. She never talked to him again, and that phone conversation has been one of those events that come in life that you wish you could somehow pull back and do over. What, she has wondered, if she had screamed at Harry to get out of the building as fast as he could?

Would it have made a difference? Probably not, because Harry didn't know that the tower was in danger of collapsing, and, anyway, he was constitutionally unable to turn away from a person in distress right there in front of him. And Victor was calling for his help.

As of April 2002, eight months after September 11, Harry's body had not been found.

Meanwhile, Rebecca Wald was considering her husband Victor's fascination with mystical interpretations of things in Judaism. She's remembered a vision she had a few weeks before September 11. One night, she awoke to find something hovering in the air above her, a man, part flesh, part skeleton, with a cloak the color of the gold beads on the Mikasa pear in her coffee table centerpiece. She knew it meant something and she now believes that it was a premonition of Victor's death.

Victor died on the 36th floor of the south tower, and the number 36, in the kabbalistic numerology known as the gematriya, is the equivalent of a double "chai," the Hebrew word for life, and it also corresponds to the number of the passage in Exodus when Moses said good-bye to the children of Israel, who were going to the Promised Land while he stayed behind. She wonders if, in his way, Victor didn't plan this kind of death, with its Mosaic correspondences, knowing that it would be a way of being erased, honorably, from the world.

Like many people, Brian Clark went to a lot of funerals after September 11. He went to the funeral of Bobbie Coll, whom he last saw walking up the stairs, the wrong direction, helping the heavy woman who had told them they couldn't go down. He went to the funeral of Jose Marreno, the man who he saw on the 68th floor and who walked back upstairs to help a colleague. In the week right after the disaster, he spent a lot of time answering the phone calls of people who were still hoping that their missing relatives might yet be alive. They asked him if he had seen them, and if he had spoken to them, and whether he thought they might have made it out safely.

"I couldn't help them, but I would tell them that they had to remain hopeful," he said. "I didn't want to dash their hopes but you had to be realistic as well."

Very few, if any, people whose relatives were missing in the hours after the attack turned up alive in hospitals later. After a week or so, like Susan Rescorla, most relatives realized that there was no hope.

Clark himself got a new job at Euro Brokers. He became president of the Euro Brokers Relief Fund, Inc., whose purpose is to raise money to help the families of the sixty-one Euro Brokers employees who died. About eight months after September 11, he had raised about $3 million. More than $1 million came in from a Charity Day that the company announced, a day on which 100 percent of the revenues—revenues, not profits—went into the fund, a total of about $1.2 million. Other money came from donations, including donations from both Euro Brokers customers and competitors.

"It's sort of an endless process," Clark said. "There are children who will have needs going into the future, medical insurance needs, education needs, whatever they are."

While friends and relatives of the victims mourned and faced the future, the cleanup at Ground Zero continued, and the authorities set up a viewing stand on the corner of Fulton Street and Broadway where people could go to look at the scene. You had to get a ticket at the South Street Seaport and you walked up a ramp—the ancient, sycamore-shaded graveyard of St. Paul's Church was on the right—to the platform itself, where you had the right to a half hour on the stand itself before a man in a blue jacket with the inscription "NYPD Community Affairs" politely urged you to leave.

By April, the mountain of debris had essentially disappeared, carted away truckload by truckload and sifted for human remains. Standing on the viewing stand, which looked east to west, you could see the foundations of the towers, surrounded on one side by the largely unscathed World Financial Center buildings across West Street, and several other skyscrapers still draped in netting. It no longer looked like a disaster site; it looked like a construction site, with all those rows of sheds you see in such places on the street level alongside an immense excavated rectangle.

Near the entrance ramp, visitors by the thousands had left small mementos—fire department hats from across the country, T-shirts, banners, pictures of victims, prayers scrawled on squares of cloth or on the plywood sheets that served as partitions for the viewing stand. Most of all, people just wrote their names, tens of thousands of them, and the places they had come from, or they left a little message: "Arkansas prays for you," or "The Smiths are so soorry," with sorry spelled incorrectly, or "God Bless All of You," or "Aspire and Persevere." There were some obscenities as well, directed mostly at Osama bin Laden. There was what looked a bit like corporate sponsorship: "Southwest Airlines Loves NYC."

On the exit ramp was a large plaque, hung on a plywood partition, with the names of many of the victims, those who had died on flights 11 and 175 and those who had died in the north and south towers inscribed alphabetically. The framed plaque was festooned with flags, with roses, rosary beads, and pictures of victims. Nearby was a poster saying, "Imagine—a Department of Peace." The spire of St. John's Church, converted into a hospitality room reserved for rescue workers, soared above. On the plaque, which ran for perhaps thirty feet, was an inscription, the final sentence of the letter that Abraham Lincoln wrote to Mrs. Bixby of Massachusetts who lost her five sons, all she had, on the battlefields of the Civil War. Lincoln's letter was written for a very different circumstance, and yet, in its lean elegance, it seemed entirely suitable to soothe the afflicted spirits of those whose loved ones were taken from them on September 11:

"I pray that our heavenly Father may assuage the anguish of your bereavement, and leave you only with the cherished memory of the loved and lost, and the solemn pride that must be yours to have laid so costly a sacrifice upon the altar of freedom."

NOTES

CHAPTER ONE: *"We Saw People Jumping"*

1. *Washington Post*, September 24, 2001.
2. *Wall Street Journal*, September 14, 2001.
3. Ibid.

CHAPTER TWO: *Peshawar: The Office of Services*

1. See, for example, Karen Alexander, "Was It Inevitable? Islam Through History," in *How Did This Happen? Terrorism and the New War*, James F. Hoge, Jr., and Gideon Rose, eds., (New York: Public Affairs, 2001), pp. 53–70.
2. Ibid.
3. Citations drawn from Azzam Publications website.
4. Steven Emerson, *American Jihad: The Terrorists Living Among Us* (New York: Free Press, 2002), pp. 130–31.

CHAPTER THREE: *"We're Due for Something"*

1. *Washington Post*, October 28, 2001.
2. Ibid.
3. Ibid.
4. *Los Angeles Times*, January 27, 2002.
5. Ibid.

CHAPTER FOUR: *The Young Man from Saudi Arabia*

1. Mary Anne Weaver, "The Real bin Laden," *The New Yorker*, January 24, 2000.
2. *The Observer,* October 28, 2001.
3. Ibid.
4. Gilles Kepel, *Jihad: The Trail of Political Islam* (Cambridge: Harvard University Press, 2002), pp. 106–30.
5. Steven Emerson, *op. cit.*, pp. 6–7.
6. Jamal Kashoggi, *Arab News*, October 16, 2001.
7. *Frontline* broadcast.

CHAPTER FIVE: *Glick and Jarrah: An Open Life and a Closed One*

1. *Pittsburgh Post-Gazette*, October 28, 2001.
2. *Los Angeles Times,* September 23, 2001.
3. Ibid.
4. *Washington Post*, September 25, 2001.
5. Antony Black, *The History of Islamic Political Thought* (New York: Routledge, 2001).
6. Abbas Amanat, "Empowered Through Violence," in Strobe Talbot and Nayan Chanda, eds., *The Age of Terror: America and the World After September 11* (New York: Basic Books, 2002), p. 28.
7. *U.S. v Usama bin Laden et al.,* court transcript, February 6, 2001.

CHAPTER SIX: *Terrorism Arrives in America*

1. Laurie Mylroie, *The War Against America: Saddam Hussein and the World Trade Center Attacks* (New York: Regan Books, 2001), p. 90.
2. Mary Anne Weaver, "Blowback," *The Atlantic Monthly*, May 1996.
3. Steven Emerson, *op. cit.*, p. 134.
4. Mylroie, *op. cit.*, pp. 44–65.

CHAPTER EIGHT: *"In Time of War There Is No Death"*

1. *U.S. v Usama bin Laden et al.*, testimony of Jamal Ahmed al-Fadl, court transcript, February 6, 2001.
2. Ibid.
3. Ibid.
4. Ibid.
5. The letter in el-Hage's computer made available by *Frontline* at www.pbs.org/frontline.

6. *Wall Street Journal*, December 3, 2001.
7. *The Observer*, October 28, 2001.
8. *Washington Post*, December 8, 2001.
9. Citations from bin Laden from *"Osama bin Laden v. the U.S.*: Edicts and Statements," available at www.pbs.org/frontline.
10. 'Owhali's account drawn from the testimony of Stephen Gaudin in *U.S. v Usama bin Laden et al.,* trial transcript, August 7, 2001.
11. This group, which was also unknown to Western intelligence, surfaced again in 2002 when messages sent to Arabic newspapers in London said it was responsible for the bombing in April that year of a synagogue on the island of Djerba in Tunisia.

CHAPTER NINE: *Yeneneh Betru: Medicine for the Neediest*

1. *Los Angeles Times*, September 17, 2001.

CHAPTER TEN: *The Cell in Hamburg*

1. *Los Angeles Times*, January 27, 2002.
2. Ibid.
3. Ibid.
4. Ibid.
5. *Wall Street Journal*, October 16, 2001.

CHAPTER TWELVE: *While America Slept*

1. The letter from el-Hage's computer from *Frontline*, op. cit.
2. *Washington Post*, December 19, 2001.

CHAPTER FOURTEEN: *The Commandos in America*

1. *Los Angeles Times*, September 27, 2001.
2. Ibid.
3. *Washington Post*, September 30, 2001.
4. Edward Jay Epstein, "Atta and the BIS," www.edwardjayepstein.com.
5. *Washington Post*, September 30, 2001.
6. *Wall Street Journal*, April 4, 2002.

CHAPTER FIFTEEN: *Peter J. Ganci: Born to Fight Fires*

1. *St. Petersburg Times,* September 21, 2001.

CHAPTER SIXTEEN: *The Terrorists Stay One Step Ahead*

1. *Las Vegas Review-Journal,* September 21, 2001.

2. *Los Angeles Times,* March 20, 2002.

3. *Washington Post,* September 30, 2001.4rcrJanuary 27, 2002.

4. *Boston Globe,* September 25, 2001.

CHAPTER SEVENTEEN: *Like a Knife into a Gift-Wrapped Box*

1. *Sunday Times* (London), September 9, 2001.

2. *Boston Herald,* September 13, 2001.

CHAPTER EIGHTEEN: *"Protect the White House at All Cost"*

1. *Associated Press,* September 12, 2001.

2. *Washington Post,* September 12, 2001.

3. *TK*

4. *Newsweek,* December 3, 2001.

5. *Boston Globe,* November 23, 2001.

6. www.edwardjayepstein.com.

7. *Newsweek, op. cit.*

CHAPTER NINETEEN: *"We Had a Lot of Dying and Fire Up There"*

1. *Wall Street Journal,* September 14, 2001.

2. *USA Today,* December 19, 2001.

3. *Wall Street Journal,* October 23, 2001.

4. *Boston Herald,* November 13, 2001.

5. *Larry King Live,* September 12, 2001.

6. *Wall Street Journal,* November 12, 2001.

7. *Boston Globe,* September 13, 2001.

8. Vincent Dunn, www.vincentdunn.com.

9. *Wall Street Journal,* October 11, 2001.

CHAPTER TWENTY: *The Towers Came Down*

1. James Stewart, "The Real Heroes Are Dead," *The New Yorker*, February 11, 2002.

2. *Dateline* television broadcast, March 20, 2002.

3. *Wall Street Journal,* October 28, 2001.

CHAPTER TWENTY-TWO: *Aftermath*

1. *Asahi Shimbun*, March 11, 2002.

2. *The Sun,* Lowell, Mass., January 23, 2002.

ACKNOWLEDGMENTS

No author writes a book of nonfiction without help, but this book depended on the work of others far more than most. Certainly it could not have been written without the extraordinary reporting that has appeared in the *New York Times* since September 11, and, indeed, before that date. Dozens of reporters and foreign correspondents have written articles that I drew on in putting this narrative of September 11 together, and it would be impossible to list them all. But I do want to mention several of those whose work has been indispensable.

Jonathan Landman, Ann Cronin, and others on the *Times* Metro Desk have been enthusiastic in their support from the beginning. James Dwyer's reporting on the New York City Fire Department, and his many stories on the events of September 11 itself, have been amply absorbed into this book, and I have come to a deep appreciation of his brilliance both as a newsman and as a colleague. Among the others who covered September 11 in New York and whose work has been important in the writing of this book are: Kevin Flynn, Eric Lipton, James Glanz, Nina Bernstein, Matthew L. Wald, N. R. Kleinfeld, Mary Williams Walsh, Mireya Navarro, Jane Gross, and Amy Waldman.

Reporters in the *Times*'s Washington Bureau, in particular David Johnston, Don Van Natta, Kate Zernicke, James Risen, Benjamin Weiser, Philip Shenon, Neil A. Lewis, and David Sanger wrote stories on the investigation into the plot. Judith Miller and Steven Engelberg contributed to that reporting, and they also did investigations of Osama bin Laden and Al Qaeda that preceded September 11 by many months; much of the material in this book on the background to anti-American terrorism is based on their work. Several of the *Times*'s correspondents reporting from abroad contributed immeasurably, among them: David Rohde, C. J. Chivers, Raymond Bonner, Steven Erlanger, Chris Hedges, Douglas Frantz, John Tagliabue, Douglas Jehl, Susan Sachs, Patrick Tyler, Donald G. McNeil, Jr., and Neal MacFarquhar.

I hope I haven't forgotten anybody; my apologies if I have.

I want also to acknowledge several others. Kaya Laterman, my research assistant, was cheerful and indefatigable in her pursuit of answers to the infinite questions I asked, and she did much of the interviewing that went into the portraits of victims included in this book. Seth Solomonow helped enormously, pointing the way to useful sources and helping with interviews. David Sobel, the editorial director of the Times Books imprint at Henry Holt, has made numerous very useful suggestions and has been gracious and steadfast throughout. Without the inspiration and support of Mitchel Levitas, the head of the Times Books Development Office, this project would never have gotten started, much less finished.

Where the information in this book comes from reporting in the *Times*, or from the additional reporting of myself, Kaya Laterman, and Seth Solomonow, no source information is provided. There are many important instances where I have drawn on the fine reporting that has appeared in books, magazines, and newspapers other than the *Times*, and those instances are indicated in endnotes.

As always, those who helped deserve only gratitude. Any mistakes of fact or judgment in this book are solely my responsibility.

INDEX

ABOUT THE AUTHOR

In twenty years with *The New York Times,* Richard Bernstein has served as bureau chief at the United Nations and in Paris, as national cultural reporter, and currently as a daily book critic. Before that, he was the Beijing bureau chief for *Time* magazine. He has written five books, including *The Coming Conflict with China* (with Ross H. Munro) and, most recently, *Ultimate Journey: Retracing the Path of an Ancient Buddhist Monk Who Crossed Asia in Search of Enlightenment.* He lives in New York City.